War Reporters Under Threat

T0288146

War Reporters Under Threat

The United States and Media Freedom

Chris Paterson

PlutoPress
www.plutobooks.com

First published 2014 by Pluto Press
345 Archway Road, London N6 5AA

www.plutobooks.com

Distributed in the United States of America exclusively by
Palgrave Macmillan, a division of St. Martin's Press LLC,
175 Fifth Avenue, New York, NY 10010

British Library Cataloguing in Publication Data
A catalogue record for this book is available from the British Library

ISBN 978 0 7453 3418 9 Hardback
ISBN 978 0 7453 3417 2 Paperback
ISBN 978 1 7837 1032 4 PDF eBook
ISBN 978 1 7837 1034 8 Kindle eBook
ISBN 978 1 7837 1033 1 EPUB eBook

Library of Congress Cataloging in Publication Data applied for

This book is printed on paper suitable for recycling and made from
fully managed and sustained forest sources. Logging, pulping and
manufacturing processes are expected to conform to the environmental
standards of the country of origin.

10   9   8   7   6   5   4   3   2   1

Typeset by Stanford DTP Services, Northampton, England
Text design by Melanie Patrick
Simultaneously printed digitally by CPI Antony Rowe, Chippenham, UK
and Edwards Bros in the United States of America

Who overcomes By force, hath overcome but half his foe.

John Milton, *Paradise Lost*

Contents

Preface

As a teacher of journalism in the United States in the early 2000s, I found it troubling that the values espoused in textbooks and which seemed so integral to our teaching were so readily and fully abandoned in the post-9/11 age. The idea of an unfettered and independent press as a cornerstone of US democracy and an aspect of the US system of governance that other nations might emulate had always been worth treating with a dose of scepticism, constrained as it was by a market logic which has no inherent interest in participatory governance, but even sceptics like myself could acknowledge the value of encouraging aspiring journalists to pursue the *ideal* of a watchdog press, unwaveringly protected by law in its pursuit of truth, even truths which those with power would prefer to remain in the shadows.

I found, increasingly, that this idea bore little resemblance to the post-9/11 world, where the leading sources of news in the US played patriotic music, covered the television screen in flags, and lashed out at journalists daring to tell another story; where the brother of a journalist killed by the US Army had to give up his career to tour the US in a fruitless search for accountability; and where one of the international news agencies which had hosted me in my research had appeared to become a routine target of the US military. The ideals of free expression and the reality of post-9/11 international journalism were becoming increasingly polarised, and with little fanfare the US had become one of the most significant threats to the media. Remarkably, this is an issue that much of the analysis of this decade of conflict has let pass with little comment. After a decade exploring these concerns and the US 'pre-emptive war' in Iraq, and amid escalating concern about secret US government actions aimed at the press and the public, I offer this exploration. US behaviour towards the media should alarm us all, for these issues are not limited to the parochial concerns of journalists, media educators, or even those in government who stand accused of betraying the principles of liberal democracy – they are a stark warning of the potential for an Orwellian future where human rights and public disclosure become intolerable inconveniences for *all* states.

The title of this book was a compromise in the context of a market filled with similarly titled studies of the complex media–military relationship, and any number of particular aspects of this. Those books, and an even larger number of scholarly articles and research reports, provide a thorough record of that troubled and complex relationship – and the broader dangers of a Fourth Estate which exists precariously and consistently under threat. This book, though, sets out to tell a story which many others have only hinted at. This is the story of a superpower drunk with power and willing, both through wilful ignorance and through design, to sacrifice media workers and media independence to military adventures fuelled by a potent mix of Machiavellian strategy and paranoid fantasy, driven with remarkable success by a neoconservative cabal which has come to profoundly infect and affect US society and US foreign policy alike.[1]

The whole of this book's title is key: that war reporters *are* under threat will not be news to those reporters or anyone else; indeed, it is why they often hold a lofty, even heroic, status in their organisations and wider society (a status some commercial media organisations milk for all it is worth, as with 'scud-studs' and 'hotzone' correspondents). But what *is* new is the very idea that a threat to journalists should be linked to the nation which has promoted as policy – more consistently than any other – the ideology of a free and unfettered media: this is *news*. And it is *news* that news media have actively chosen to ignore at their peril. As leading historians of the military–media relationship, such as Knightley, Taylor and Carruthers[2] have documented well, the US has grudgingly accepted cooperation with the media at times of conflict in various forms and in countless wars – but it has never, until just over a decade ago, become a leading threat to media workers. This is a work more of compilation than investigation: the stories this book tells are (mostly) publically and thoroughly documented.

And so the aim of this book is to position the US among those states – and non-state actors – with little *meaningful* concept of 'media freedom' (or a broader human rights agenda), and to encourage media workers everywhere to confront their own double standards and take greater courage in challenging and defending their profession from a nation which, along with some of its closest partners in the Middle East, says one thing and does another when it comes to respecting and protecting the media. Any hopes we hold for governments to be accountable to the rest of us may depend on their willingness to do so. This is a goal which is vital to preserving what remains of US legitimacy internationally, and to preserving the US's ability, including that of its military where necessary, to play a positive international role, as it has done before and potentially could do again.

One of the central themes of this book is that a conventional hierarchy of media producers contributes to easy acceptance of the concept that some media producers – because they are foreign to us, or small, or affiliated with a government, or because they take an editorial stance we don't agree with – are inherently less worthy, and perhaps even deserving of violence directed toward them. For this reason, this text goes beyond the standard stylistic convention of italicising established periodicals – such as major newspapers – and uses italics to designate all media producers, whether *Fox*, *WikiLeaks*, *Reuters*, the *New York Times*, or *Al Jazeera*, as a means of highlighting their legitimacy – and corresponding right to expression.

I hope this book will be useful to researchers and educators, in offering a take on war reporting that prior scholarship has downplayed. My greater hope, however, is for it to shine light on a problem which is already well known to many in the news media and to scholars of international journalism, and which has been a key concern of the professional organisations concerned with the safety of journalists for over a decade – but which has yet to resonate with the much larger, escalating debate about what kind of presence in the world the US, and its third of a billion citizens, wish to be.

This is the story of a curious and disturbing trend in international journalism; a trend few people want to talk about, despite its potential to permanently shut the door to independent witnesses of international conflict. We begin by examining the evolution of a culture of intolerance to the Fourth Estate among US power elites and – among media itself – a commercially driven acquiescence to that intolerance; in other words, an abandonment of the watchdog role of the press. Together, these trends have permitted an increasingly hostile environment for investigative reporting to flourish and become normalised.

1

A Hidden War on the Media

The purpose of this book is to examine and expose a deadly paradox which has become apparent since 9/11: that of an entrenched culture of acceptance and impunity[1] which permits states that are nominally democratically governed, human rights oriented, and bound by democratically established national and international legal conventions, to conceal violations of human rights and rules of war, and to kill, injure and arrest those journalists who are in a position to witness and report on those violations. Such states do so virtually without challenge, for only infrequently do the many defenders of the right to practice journalism freely and safely[2] look closely at the democracies with vibrant commercial press systems, the world's 'models' of press freedom.

This chapter suggests why this vital story about the storytellers remains substantially hidden from public discourse, and situates press coercion and intimidation by the US within the context of that government's 'strategic narrative'[3] of the Middle East conflict constructed for international and domestic consumption. We also consider how, in an age of 'virtuous war'[4] and 'worthy and unworthy victims',[5] attacks on journalists come to be easily dismissed as irrelevant within a broader, highly ambiguous, global struggle.

In the mid-2000s, for the first time, the US was ranked by the Committee to Protect Journalists (CPJ), one of the leading journalists' rights organisations (and the US one at that), as one of the worst threats to press freedom, having imprisoned more journalists in the preceding year than all but five other nations. Had the CPJ included a more complete list of temporary detentions of journalists and those who assist them, the US would probably have ranked first. In his important essay on the pattern of violence until late 2003, veteran UK television journalist Nik Gowing writes that the accumulated evidence, 'suggests at best a culture of military indifference and inefficiency to the business of explaining the deaths of media personnel. At worst it suggests a policy of endorsing and covering up firstly the targeting, then either the maiming or killing, of media personnel'.[6] Since Gowing wrote, the evidence has only grown stronger.

The tendency to violently restrain the free practice of journalism and the free circulation of information has long been observed – and quite thoroughly documented – both in relation to undemocratic and autocratic regimes, and among many nations which permit some degree of democratic participation but which are widely regarded by commentators in international media to be, in reality, undemocratic: contemporary Russia or Zimbabwe are cases in point.

While arguably less deadly, it is ultimately more insidious and alarming for there to be extrajudicial and violent persecution of media workers by nations who do not fit into those categories: by the world's 'advanced democracies' – especially when such persecution becomes *uncontested* and *routine*. In the wake of the 10th anniversary of the commencement of the illegal US invasion of Iraq[7] and some of the most egregious attacks on journalists and the media generally, it has become reasonable to declare a precedent to have been set, with the practice of removing journalists and media workers in often violent ways when they are deemed to stand in the way of the objectives of the US government and some of its closest allies in the Middle East. This is, of course, sharply at odds with the US ideals (and Constitutional mandates) of free speech and due process, and that is why it is vital to shine light on these dark trends.

At the time of writing, the US government has been directly responsible for the violent deaths of over 40 journalists and media workers in Serbia, Afghanistan and Iraq. It has been indirectly responsible for the deaths of many more media workers and responsible for the injury, long-term detention and, in some cases, torture of still more. For the media this is a new and poorly recognised problem: it is neither wholly the euphemistically and poorly termed 'friendly fire' which has killed journalists in the past, nor unequivocal hostility from a clearly defined enemy. We might best term it the *friendly threat*: the new threat of violence and extreme forms of coercion facing journalists covering war, astonishingly coming from the US government and some of its closest allies and partners. These are the very institutions which journalists once extensively depended upon for protection. While the US has allied itself with many governments expressing hostility to free journalistic expression, the alliances referred to here are with those nations collaborating with, and heavily supported by, the US, while publically espousing similar claims for an unfettered press, including Israel and the new governments of Iraq and Afghanistan in particular.

Civilian Casualties in Iraq and Afghanistan

Civilian losses in both Iraq and Afghanistan have been of genocidal proportions. They have been far greater than their relative insignificance in most US and European news coverage of both wars would suggest; neither US nor British media have made the number of civilian casualties in Iraq and Afghanistan a substantial part of their narrative since the beginning of the conflict.[8] Yet outside of those countries it has often been observed that this is the most obvious macro-level news story of the conflicts, due to the sheer scale of the imbalance it describes. Put in the starkest terms, in response to the murder by 19 people (of varying nationalities) of almost 3,000 people in the US in 2001 (about 2,600 of whom were US citizens), somewhere between 100,000 (by some US government and news media estimates) and 1,000,000 (by the highest independent scientifically based estimates) mostly impoverished civilians in Afghanistan and Iraq, without the remotest connection to that 2001 event, have been killed. None of the hijackers who carried out the 9/11 attack in the US were from Afghanistan or Iraq.

It is worth noting that, since the earliest days of the Iraq and Afghanistan wars, the extent of civilian casualties has been a point of considerable contention. The only point of agreement is that every count is a rough estimate: the nature of the conflicts seems to preclude either accuracy or universal agreement over such tallies. Both the invading forces and major international media organisations, generally, have provided smaller – although still massive – estimates of casualties,[9] while a number of independent and scientifically grounded research projects have provided far higher numbers. While many have sought to discredit them, the first scientifically valid and peer reviewed studies which moved away from media accounts of deaths and official figures were conducted by a group of epidemiologists and published in the medical journal the *Lancet*. The second of their two reports concluded that between 2003 and 2006 alone there had been 654,965 excess deaths in Iraq – that is, deaths which would not have been expected had there been no war – of which 601,027 were violent.[10] Other standard survey research methodologies have suggested that over one million civilian, non-combatant, Iraqis have been killed since the invasion of that country.[11]

Some have suggested that a US military policy of targeting civilians for destruction and intimidation on a massive scale, while steadfastly maintaining that innocent civilians have nothing to fear, is in essence 'state terrorism', although that is a concept few in the mainstream Western news media have been willing to accept; doing so would complicate the stories they tell and challenge traditional 'good versus evil' narratives. John Pilger recalled his own experience of coming to question US military doctrine when he observed first hand, during the Vietnam War, that 'murder and destruction replaced military tactics. Almost every man, woman, and child became the enemy'.[12]

There is an unambiguous association between the willingness of the US and its allies to cause and accept civilian deaths on an enormous scale and their willingness to consider journalists as expendable or even legitimate targets within the context of a so-called 'just war'. Both phenomena have occurred as, in recent conflicts, the US and its allies abandoned the traditional rules of engagement, based on international conventions, which were intended specifically to prevent such losses. Journalists make up a minute proportion of civilian casualties in recent conflicts, but their injury, detention and death tends to attract far more attention than those of 'ordinary' civilians (although whether they receive *enough* attention is a matter addressed in Chapter 4). Perhaps if the media – especially the US media and global media organisations – focused more on reporting the injury, detention and deaths of civilians generally (which are rarely considered *news*, due both to their frequency and to many within the Western media having internalised the belief that they are somehow *legitimate*) the result would be a short-term increase in hostility towards the media from combatant states, but a long-term acceptance by governments of genuine international accountability which could provide real protection for media workers themselves.

Attacks on Journalists and Media Installations

The chapters that follow examine attacks on journalists in and near areas of conflict, by means of research specifically conducted for this book and a review of the numerous reports on these issues by journalists, scholars and non-governmental organisations (NGOs). This project was initially based on a systematic compilation of data about journalist casualties from a wide variety of sources, ongoing since the US invasion of Iraq, along with research into legal issues, military doctrine and attitudes, and media industry responses. While there have been many books addressing war and journalism in the past decade or so, there is remarkably little systematic academic research into journalistic casualties involving the US and governments closely allied to it. Indeed, some of the most widely cited of the many recent books on media and war have not ventured beyond brief mention of these events or have focused on, and often given credence to, official explanations. Some prominent journalists have spoken about the US threat to journalists and moved on, and some have been vilified. This project seeks to weave together a range of accounts, suggesting that much has been left unsaid about the connections between these events and about the news media's response to them.

The deaths of over 40 media workers attributable to the US military since 1999 include 16 in Serbia in 1999, and the events of 9/11 seemed to reopen the door to such attacks. There have been many hundreds of serious attacks on journalists in the Middle East since the US invasion of Afghanistan in 2001 (involving death, injury, long-term detention, and sometimes torture), and over 200 people have been killed undertaking or supporting journalism about Iraq and Afghanistan, with about one-eighth of those directly attributable to the US military. According to an analyst for the CPJ, 'At least 150 journalists and 54 media support workers were killed in Iraq from the US-led invasion in March 2003 to the declared end of the war in December 2011', and 'the actions of U.S. forces, including checkpoint shootings and airstrikes, were responsible for the deaths of 16 journalists and six media workers [...] Post-invasion Iraqi forces were responsible for the deaths of two journalists'.[13] Reporters Sans Frontières concluded that more journalists were killed in Iraq in two years than during the 20 years of conflict in Vietnam,[14] and by 2005 the CPJ was writing that US military fire had become the second most common cause of death for journalists in Iraq. In just the first two years of the Iraq war, about one-quarter of the nearly 200 attacks on journalists reported at that time, about which there was reliable information from multiple sources, could be reasonably linked to US troops or the (US facilitated) Iraqi government, and these included several reports of journalists being abducted and tortured, and dozens of detentions of journalists by those militaries.

A list of media workers whose deaths can confidently be attributed to the US military in the post-9/11 period appears in Appendix 1. There are additional uninvestigated cases of possible US troop involvement, and others that involve Iraqi government forces working under US military authority, as well as the deaths of journalists voluntarily accompanying US forces (the latter two categories are not the focus here). It is also noteworthy that some local media workers killed by non-state combatants were working for organisations funded by the US government. Just under half of the journalists and media workers listed in Appendix 1 were affiliated with European media organisations, and the rest affiliated with local media or pan-Arab media groups. Two were affiliated with a US media company.

Taken in combination with attacks on media facilities by the US government, the media organisations which have suffered most from US actions since 1999 have been Serbia's public broadcaster, *Radio Television Serbia*; the *Al Jazeera* and *Al Arabiya* regional television news channels; and the historically British, but now Canadian-owned, international news agency, *Reuters*. The cases of *Reuters, Al Jazeera* and *Al Arabiya* are addressed more thoroughly in Chapters 3 and 4. The great majority of the total attacks on journalists were undoubtedly the work not of the US military, but of anonymous gunmen and kidnappers, generally presumed to be affiliated with the organised insurgent groups fighting US occupation or the US-installed governments in Afghanistan and Iraq, but also sometimes regarded just as criminal gangs without clear political motivation. But without investigation of the deaths – and there has often been little or none – responsibility for the killings of many journalists cannot be reliably attributed. There are sometimes public statements of responsibility, and sometimes not, but their authenticity is often in doubt. Former *Al Arabiya* executive editor Nabil Khatib explained in 2006 that many insurgent attacks on journalists in Iraq are specifically to compel media companies' compliance in airing their statements and demands – to gain access to the airwaves:

> From time to time we get messages indirectly saying, 'You can work safely in Iraq if you will just go along with us, and you will air whatever we supply you with'. Of course we refuse, because we don't want to be used by any party, whoever it is. So we pay the price.[15]

What has not been clearly established in the case of US involvement in attacks on journalists in Iraq and Afghanistan is the extent of any link between the journalists attacked and the nature of their reporting. It is known that some had been in the process of revealing facts or images that were potentially embarrassing to the US military when they, or people they were with, were attacked. Generally speaking, similar fates have not befallen reporters whose writing has mostly conveyed the official US version of events, who have chosen to 'embed' with US forces, or who have avoided reporting in areas of high civilian casualties.[16]

If we extend the timeframe for analysis back to 1999, when a pattern of US government disregard for journalists' safety began to become clear, we can observe that in the course of recent conflicts the US military has shelled, bombed, or fired missiles at at least twelve predominantly or completely civilian media installations, most of which were widely known to house journalists and/or other media workers.

Many of those killed were television photographers and their assistants who, like still photographers, earn their living by being close to the action. This is not the case for reporters. *Guardian* photographer Paul O'Driscoll told Tumber and Webster:

> In my experience I rarely meet [reporters] out in the field. [...] It's not in the nature of their business to be in the front. It's in their nature to string together a story from different sources, put together a story from different pieces of string. They can't afford [...] to be there, right beside you. Whereas a photographer needs to illustrate what's happening and tends to have to be where it's happening, that's the closest you can get.[17]

While there has been ample interest in the military–press relationship, and many detailed histories of that relationship have been written, there remains a crucial and mostly untold story that will shape war reporting for decades to come. This book tells the story of a deteriorating and increasingly violent relationship between the media and the US government. It describes a process whereby respect for principles of free information flow and the sanctity of the Fourth Estate have been overtaken by an overriding objective to control public perceptions at any cost, and a willingness to disregard or manipulate legal regimes which challenge that.

From 1999, media–state relations at times of war changed fundamentally. In 1999, NATO, under US direction, bombed a major civilian media organisation – the public broadcasting company of a large European country. They killed 16 media workers and, crucially, temporarily limited the ability of *CNN* – which (until warned by the Pentagon to leave) had been operating from that location – to provide Serbian perspectives on the Kosovo conflict to the US audience. In an odd parallel, as Thussu[18] described, the first violent act of the Chinese government in the lead up to the Tiananmen Square massacre of 1989 was to shut down *CNN*'s transmission from the square. The US government deemed Serbian television to be a legitimate target, and a great deal has been said and written in the intervening years about whether it was or was not.[19]

This story also begins when US Army officers used an 'internship' scheme to gain access to *CNN* operations, at almost the same time as the television news image flow from *CNN* and other international broadcasters out of Belgrade was disrupted when US missiles struck the state broadcasting facility. The attacks on facilities hosting international television broadcasters would be repeated in Afghanistan and Iraq.[20] That was the beginning of a pattern which has continued to the present day, and which has had horrific consequences for two groups of journalists in particular: international news agency journalists, and journalists from Arab media organisations.[21] This book is intended as a counter to a discourse concerning press–state relations which broadly describes such violence against media personnel as a phenomenon involving *only* totalitarian regimes and developing countries, and makes rare mention of the role of the US or other Western democracies in propagating or supporting such violence.[22]

So Are They Targeted or Not?

In an interview at the start of the war in Iraq with Irish public radio, which was widely quoted by critics of US information control in subsequent years, veteran *BBC* reporter Kate Adie couldn't disguise her concern for her colleagues who were in Iraq or on their way there to report on the start of hostilities. Drawing a contrast with the reporting she had been directly involved in during the first Gulf War, Adie said:

> what actually appals me is the difference between twelve years ago and now. I've seen a complete erosion of any kind of acknowledgment that reporters should be able to report as they witness. The Americans (and I've been talking to the Pentagon) take the attitude which is entirely hostile to the free spread of information. I was told by a senior officer in the Pentagon, that if uplinks – that is the television signals out of Baghdad, for example – were detected by any planes, electronic media,

mediums [sic] of the military above Baghdad, they'd be fired down on. Even if they were journalists [...] They would be 'targeted down,' said the officer [...] Shameless. He said, 'Well, they know this, they've been warned.' This is threatening freedom of information, before you even get to a war.[23]

At the time, the threat – from a US military officer Adie didn't identify – was similar to many being given to the press by the senior civilian press spokesperson for the Pentagon, Victoria Clarke,[24] but was noteworthy in specifying that journalists' transmitting equipment would be attacked by the US military. Nik Gowing described an exchange of letters between *Al Jazeera* and the Pentagon after a US missile destroyed *Al Jazeera*'s office in the Afghan capital in 2001. Clarke wrote to *Al Jazeera* long after it had been widely accepted that *Al Jazeera*'s bureau was, really, just a bureau, stating 'we will continue to target those facilities and locations that have military significance'. Gowing commented: 'That raises a very powerful, problematic area for us. Does that mean we as journalists, and our colleagues out in the field taking the risks, are seen by the Pentagon now as having "military significance"?'[25]

From soon after 9/11, warnings that seemed to suggest that the media could be targeted at will by US forces were reinforced by the highest levels of the US military. US Navy Rear Admiral Craig Quigley, the senior Pentagon media representative, told representatives of the *BBC*, *Al Jazeera*, and the CPJ that the targeting of *Al Jazeera*'s bureau in Kabul by US missiles (initially dismissed by the US as an unfortunate accident) was neither a mistake nor a problem and, according to Knightley's summary of the meeting, that the Pentagon was 'indifferent' to media activity in territory controlled by the enemy.[26] Furthermore, in most of the cases described in this book, the US has admitted – although in a few instances only after considerable pressure – deliberately attacking media installations, but consistently with the proviso that the attack was justified by affiliation to a foreign enemy, whether unfriendly state or non-state 'terrorists'.

Journalists have sought to remind the US government that their work necessarily involves interaction with all parties to conflicts, as *Al Jazeera* pointed out when its Afghanistan bureau was bombed (described in Chapter 3). When the UK sent its military to the South Atlantic in 1982 to reclaim islands seized by Argentina, the *BBC* in particular was harangued by politicians and right-wing media for speaking to Argentinean sources. The same happened when the *BBC* reported from Serbia while NATO attacked that country in the 1990s. We could speculate that under contemporary US doctrine the response would be to bomb the *BBC*, rather than to have a debate about the role of the media in times of war.

Throughout the post-9/11 period US government spokespeople, civilian and military, have consistently declared that 'we do not target journalists'. There is indeed evidence of the US military specifically teaching its personnel about the nature of journalistic activity in conflict areas and about journalists requiring the protections which international law affords to any civilian, and that civilians, generally, must be protected. And yet the US track record of protecting civilians is poor indeed, given the evidence presented above and the fact that incidents of attacks on civilian media workers continued to escalate following the attack on the Serbian public broadcaster in 1999. Violent attacks finally appeared to decrease after 2007, only to be replaced by increasingly repressive surveillance and judicial and extrajudicial efforts to control free expression, as will be explored in Chapter 2.

That we have entered uncharted territory in regard to press–state relations during times of war is not an original hypothesis of this author. Nik Gowing is a television journalist who is also a widely published media scholar in his own right: the quintessential 'hackademic' – one of a small group of, mostly London-based, journalists with a foot in the media and academia. Gowing has voiced and published similar arguments for over a decade.[27] The idea has also been raised, although often timidly, in a number of anthology chapters and articles dealing with war journalism, but has been given more prominence by a few scholars, including Foerstel's (2006) *Killing the Messenger* and Lisosky and Henrichsen's more recent (2011) examination of news safety.[28] As early as 2001, Gowing publicly raised concerns with leading executives in the television news industry that the US military seemed to be targeting media installations. He told the industry's annual Newsworld conference,[29] 'It seems to me there is some evidence to be put to the Pentagon about the targeting of news organisations ... It seems people uplinking journalistic material can be targeted legitimately'. He observed that 'al-Jazeera has been providing some material that has been very uncomfortable'[30] and raised the same thesis put forth in this book – that this effectively became an unstated US policy with the 1999 bombing of the Serbian public broadcaster. Journalist and historian Philip Knightley has also written extensively about US actions.[31]

One of the key incidents in this story was when Eason Jordan, a senior *CNN* news executive, lost his job for publically expressing concern about the involvement of US forces in the deaths of journalists, as will be examined further in Chapter 2.[32] The prominent Washington political commentator David Gergen (an aide and speechwriter to four presidents, Republican and Democrat, who started his career as a speechwriter for Richard Nixon) was hosting the panel where Jordan made those remarks and subsequently asserted in the popular, deeply conservative online blog authored by Michelle Malkin: 'I was startled. It's contrary to history, which is so far the other way. Our troops have gone out of their way to protect and rescue journalists'.[33] Gergen was one of several prominent figures in the US media who mobilised quickly and concertedly to blast Jordan's remarks as outrageous. Sadly, they were anything but – they were, in fact, a cautious understatement, which simply naïvely ignored what has been termed 'journalistic paradigm repair': that is, as the conduits of established ideologies, prominent mass media institutions systematically expel and denigrate journalists who are too public in their questioning of commonly held beliefs and values.[34]

A few months before, Jordan told an interviewer:

We're working two very, very big stories right now that have a couple of things in common. One is they're enormously costly, but more importantly or more worrying is that they're both exceptionally dangerous, because we've seen something in both places that I thank God happens very rarely, and that is that in both places journalists are not only being killed but they're being targeted. There are combatants in both of these conflicts who are trying to kill journalists, and that is unusual and a very nightmarish situation.[35]

Perhaps Gowing and Jordan, with Knightley and a few other prominent journalists, were doing something more than expressing their frustration at the deaths of journalists and colleagues. They were opening a door for policy-makers and scholars to begin a serious dialogue about these issues. Over a decade later, it is a door few have walked through. One of the most important and damning reports to date is a report authored by Gowing[36] for the International News Safety Institute (INSI), in the early months of that group's formation. Writing in late 2003, Gowing drew most of the same alarming conclusions set out in the present book; and if anything, in stronger terms. And yet the situation in Iraq has grown far worse since he wrote. The incidents he describes as highly damning of US actions have yet to be properly investigated. Furthermore, Gowing's own industry – his managers and colleagues at the *BBC*, *ITN*, the major news agencies and, more importantly, his colleagues in the US media – has sometimes been surprisingly restrained in its efforts to confront powerful governments that attack the media. Journalists and news managers have at their disposal an extraordinary power to shed light and bring pressure – the power of the press – but have so far mostly decided that the killing of their own is not news, or at least not headline news. Gowing argues that:

> the new insidious development is that because of the impact of our real time capability to bear witness immediately, we are being actively targeted by warriors, warlords, and forces of even the most highly developed governments who do not want us to see what they are doing.[37]

He and other commentators tend to blame the increasing threat to journalists' safety at least in part on new technologies, which permit journalists, especially those reporting for television, to get closer to the combat for longer periods than ever before; but analyses of journalists' safety have been making that argument for some time. As early as 1986, Kirby and Jackson were claiming that 'the new technology has increased at once the influence and the vulnerability of the journalist'.[38] However, the focus on technology could be seen as an unnecessary distraction from the analysis of violence against journalists and its effects.

The Objective and the 'Unobjective' Media

The easy dismissal, by the media itself, of the vast majority of attacks on media workers and media facilities is, superficially, hard to fathom. Wouldn't self-interest, if not collegiality, inspire extensive public exposure, along with every possible behind-the-scenes effort, to ensure that those who attack the 'witness' are held to account? What makes this dismissal possible is the way in which the most powerful and well-resourced media professionals can easily divide the other media outlets into two camps: 'objective' and 'unobjective'. For the sake of preserving its credibility, and therefore its commercial value, the mainstream commercial media routinely engages in 'paradigm repair'. Berkowitz explains that:

when journalists stray from correctly enacting their professional ideology in a way that is visible to both their peers and to society, ritual news work in the form of paradigm repair is begun to demonstrate that while individuals might have strayed, the institution itself has remained intact.[39]

Berkowitz quotes Bishop's analysis of cases of paradigm repair, in which '"objective" journalists responded by engaging in the ritual of building barriers that would divide objective and unobjective journalists, simultaneously reasserting the objectivity paradigm and redefining which journalists deserved membership within its interpretive community'.[40] While the process of news paradigm repair has kept criticism of the US military presence in the Middle East generally, and US actions towards journalists specifically, mostly free of critique in mainstream US (and most UK) media, it is that process of building barriers within the media industry that is especially salient.

Once these barriers are erected, the 'unobjective' become, quite simply, unworthy of defence. But who is 'objective' and who is not is all very fuzzy, and becomes more so with each passing year. Sometimes it is easy to dismiss a set of media workers as 'unobjective' and therefore treat their assassination lightly – the US bombing of Serbian public television or *Al Jazeera* are prominent examples. It becomes irrelevant that in each case these were professional colleagues – often trained in the same ways, and even by the same schools and organisations,[41] as European and US media organisations. It is the public perception in the West of those outlets being propagandistic (or 'unobjective') and mainstream US and European ones as not propagandistic (and therefore 'objective') that matters most. The possibility of a different kind of journalism – a non-US-centric journalism, even a pro-government or nationalist journalism – having equal weight with a Western, commercial journalism holds sway with few in the Western media.

An illustration of this dichotomy is the way the highly nationalistic and ethnocentric – often inflammatory – *Fox News* channel in the US is simultaneously held in disdain by many in US and UK news organisations and vehemently defended by them as part of the established, Western, 'objective' order. This contrasts with the propaganda organs that those other, foreign, organisations the US government bombed are perceived to be. In October 2009, the Obama administration tried to exclude *Fox News* from White House press pool briefings, on the grounds that *Fox*

News did not behave like a mainstream news organisation but 'almost as either the research arm or the communications arm of the Republican party'. However, following protests from the other networks in the pool (*ABC*, *CBS*, *CNN* and *NBC*), threatening that if *Fox News* were excluded they would not participate either, the White House was forced to allow *Fox News* to continue to participate.[42] The US media could not accept the government deciding who qualifies as legitimate news media; however, they have not similarly protested when the US government has decided on the legitimacy of non-US news organisations and bombed them.

The media's attack on its own core function was played out again, with the battlefield shifting from Iraq to the US itself, when *WikiLeaks* journalist Julian Assange and prominent international whistle-blowers Chelsea (formerly Bradley) Manning and Edward Snowden all came under intense fire from the mainstream US media for revealing information in the public interest which was not previously known to the public – that is, for doing *journalism*. Many US journalists and commentators for major journalistic organisations worked hard to demonise and discredit the story sources, rather than providing, expanding on, and analysing the story. As *New York Times* columnist David Carr pointed out, in something of a late rebuke to his colleagues in US journalism, these weren't unimportant stories:

> we have learned that in the name of tracking terrorists, the N.S.A. has been logging phone calls and e-mails for years, recorded the metadata of correspondence between Americans, and in some instances, dived right into the content of e-mails. The Wiki Leaks documents revealed that the United States turned a blind eye on the use of torture by its Iraqi allies, and that an airstrike was ordered to cover up the execution of civilians. Wiki Leaks also published a video showing a United States Army helicopter opening fire on a group of civilians, including two Reuters journalists.[43]

There was, of course, much more to both stories – a great deal of it still, at the time of this writing, being widely discussed outside of the US but only barely making an impact on the US news agenda. Carr cautions that:

> by dwelling on who precisely deserves to be called a journalist and legally protected as such, critics within the press are giving the current administration a justification for their focus on the ethics of disclosure rather than the morality of government behaviour [...] the journalists

and organizations who did that work find themselves under attack, not just from a government bent on keeping its secrets, but from friendly fire by fellow journalists. What are we thinking?[44]

Carr quotes *Guardian* editor Alan Rusbridger's caution that 'The governments are conflating journalism with terrorism and using national security to engage in mass surveillance. The implications just in terms of how journalism is practiced are enormous'.[45]

Patterns of unprecedented information control, propaganda dissemination and violence against journalists by the US military are well documented and unambiguous (even though they remain contentious and vociferously disputed by defenders of US foreign policy). Since the run-up to the Iraq invasion – the immediate post 9/11 phase – these patterns are commonly discussed within the international news industry, even as they remain substantially ignored within their news product and so, not surprisingly, also by the public and most scholarship. The implications of each are profound, but while propaganda in times of war is hardly novel, the literal violence towards journalists by the world's most powerful military is. As many scholars and media critics have observed, the second Gulf War (hereafter the Iraq War) has been a war very much connected to, and premised on, propaganda, and was, at its inception, dependent on false propaganda. (Propaganda – the systematic distribution of information with the intention of swaying public opinion – needn't necessary be false; nor is it necessarily true.)

The initial justifications provided to the British and US public were that Iraq possessed threatening 'weapons of mass destruction', and that Iraq was linked to the 2001 attacks in the US; both claims were widely known to be false when they were made, but a willing media and a well-orchestrated propaganda effort efficiently convinced enough of the public that they were valid.[46] While some made a similar claim for the first Gulf War, it is more reasonable to claim that the second conflict in Iraq is the first 'media age war', due to the fact that the rationale for war was wholly contrived and dependent on unquestioning dissemination by major media. In other modern conflicts there has been at least some military action or humanitarian crisis to serve as a premise (whether the genuine rationale or not) for intervention by one or more nations. This is not an original claim – Keeble explores the notion, for example, that a myth of war in 2003 was manufactured to disguise other objectives,[47] and various people involved in the upper reaches of the US government have come forward in the past decade to describe an ideological takeover of the US military and intelligence services in the early years of the younger Bush's presidency, with an agenda to pursue conflict in Iraq.[48]

The official determination to control reporting of military activities has a long history. Knightley quotes a US correspondent describing the relationship between the US military and the press during the Korean war 'as the military saying: "You can write what you like – but if we don't like it we'll shoot you"'.[49] Variations on the theme emerge consistently. When Ronald Reagan ordered a secretive US military invasion of the tiny Caribbean island of Grenada in 1983, journalists who had been corralled together on a Navy ship away from the action were light-heartedly asked by Vice Admiral Joseph Metcalf, the Granada Task Force Commander, 'do you want to get shot?' (if they tried to cover the invasion unilaterally).[50] However, with the invasion of Iraq the press–military relationship entered a new era. Knightley writes that, in the first months following the US invasion of Iraq,

> The figures in Iraq tell a terrible story ... if you consider how short the campaign was, Iraq will be notorious as the most dangerous war for journalists ever. This is bad enough. But – and here we tread on delicate ground – it is a fact that the largest single group of them appear to have been killed by the American military.[51]

Knightley suggested that:

> the traditional relationship between the military and the media – one of restrained hostility – has broken down, and that the US administration, in keeping with its new foreign policy, has decided that its attitude to war correspondents is the same as that set out by President Bush when declaring war on terrorists: 'You're either with us or you're against us.'[52]

From the US government documents revealed by *WikiLeaks* identifying investigative journalists as threats; to the warnings (described earlier) by the US government to journalists not to operate near or behind the battle lines they defined; to President George W. Bush's remark to Tony Blair about bombing *Al Jazeera* (detailed in Chapter 4); to revelations of the wiretapping of journalists in Iraq by a former US intelligence analyst (detailed in Chapter 3); the evidence of hostility from US authorities and a lack of regard for the free conduct of journalism is unambiguous. But it is also hypocritical, for the US government has aggressively enforced a 'free flow of information' doctrine around the world, both through massive investment in counter-propaganda (or, depending on one's perspective, propaganda) news services and the enforcement of economic sanctions against governments which openly seek to control media reporting. In the case of other governments, such as Israel, parallels will be noted in the contradiction between free press policies and military attacks on the press, but the hypocrisy critique is less relevant, since these are not countries which tie press protection to foreign policy, as the US often does. In 2010, for example, the White House ordered the US State Department to 'expand scrutiny of news media restriction and intimidation as part of its annual review of human rights in each country'.[53]

The following chapters are intended to explore the trends and scraps of evidence suggesting that there is more to US information policy than most of the public debate has addressed thus far and, more crucially, that there are good reasons to suspect links between US information policy and the desperately treacherous situation for journalists in Iraq, Afghanistan and other contemporary zones of conflict. But this book also seeks to move beyond a review of the evidence to at least undertake a preliminary examination of what legal protections are in place for journalists when powerful states target them, and why these appear to be so ineffective.

A number of casualties among media professionals (or those supporting them) that have been linked to the US military are partly attributable to an acceptance of the use of excessive force against passive individuals and groups deemed to be suspicious (rather than individuals actively engaged in attacking the US military). The book will review certain of these cases and examine the evidence for such links. Although most cases discussed here have been subject to prior investigations – often with conflicting conclusions – by local authorities, the US government, media organisations and press freedom groups, other cases are included where there is little evidence of prior investigation by these bodies. This culture of seeing enemies everywhere creates a new kind of unpredictable threat for journalists and a motivation to avoid the close observation of US military activity. The focus of this book, then, is the hypothesis of violent and direct coercion against journalists as a means of controlling the flow of information from conflicts in which the US is involved; such a possibility can only be considered within the context of the extraordinarily comprehensive information war that has been waged by Washington since well before the invasion of Iraq in 2003. A Pentagon culture of increasing press hostility following the Vietnam War gave way to increasing threats to journalists in the 1980s and 1990s, then to active investigation of journalistic processes by the US military in the late 1990s, before leading into the patterns of violent attacks on installations and individuals, as will be detailed in subsequent chapters. As Chapter 4 will report, it is not only governments but many in the media who have come to dispute the concept of a military *obligation* of press protection.[54] The next chapter tells the story of the US government's increasing appetite for information control, domestically and internationally, and an acquiescent and patriotic US press which helped to facilitate the dangerous dismissal of the press role in a democratic society – which in turn, ultimately, facilitated the pattern of violence against the media that Chapter 3 describes.

2

The Culture of Press Intolerance: Collaboration and Suppression

This chapter describes the creeping governmental interference with a tolerant, cooperative and, at times, eagerly collaborative news media, which set the stage and created a friendly climate for the increasingly violent and repressive governmental interactions with the media that have taken place since 1999.[1] The immediate aftermath of the 9/11 attacks in the US was described to the US public by a compliant media, seeking favourable media ownership policies from the Bush administration.[2] Media with a non-US base, however, had few incentives to report compliantly and occasionally questioned US military and 'coalition' actions. A coordinated and sophisticated repertory of coercion from the US government and nations supporting it – much of it already employed within the US – was used to silence or 'correct' such journalism.

Washington's new propagandists are fanatically public relations-minded (in the classic Edward Bernays sense of 'engineering of consent'), believing the manipulation of news to be proper and justified.[3] The new order has little regard for independent or non-compliant journalism, nor for explanations of global affairs that differ from those of the White House. Investigative journalist and author Ron Suskind, whose revelations regarding the planning of attacks on *Al Jazeera* by the US are described in Chapter 3, believes the changing US government relationship with the press is more than just the desire to control information combined with a devotion to public relations. He tracks it to the Reagan administration in the 1980s, when Michael Deaver and other Reagan aides learned to manipulate media in new ways, with an unwavering focus on the power of the image over the word: 'the images are more important than the words'. The Reagan administration became adept at creating daily visual events for the media that could leave the public feeling positive, even about administration polices that were against the public interest, and which diminished the role of the news media in determining the public agenda and shaping debate. From the year 2000, he explained, 'you had the Bush folks carrying forward some of these Reagan concepts with a much more tactical forcefulness'. Suskind said this was expressed to him by many in the Bush administration as 'we don't view the media as having a special role [...] the media is just another interest group', a development he views with alarm given that the Bill of Rights of the US Constitution allocates an unfettered watchdog role to the press. This led, according to Suskind, to a willingness to bypass the media and to often see the news media as an obstacle to the delivery of their message.[4]

The US governmental culture of treating journalists as enemies requiring either suppression or co-optation is evidenced in part through cosy, and costly, relationships with particular public relations consultants. In one of the more recent examples, in 2009 the US Department of Defense hired a public relations company with close links to the Pentagon and CIA, the Rendon Group, to 'profile' journalists who wrote about the 'War on Terror'. John Rendon had been in the background of US pro-military propaganda efforts for years, and boasts of being the person who gave Kuwaitis thousands of tiny US flags to wave for the cameras at the end of the first Gulf war.[5] According to *Reuters*, the firm 'provided profiles of journalists that rated their output as 'positive', 'neutral' or 'negative', but the US government claimed it didn't use the ratings to deny or manipulate news coverage; it did, however, cancel the contract with Rendon when criticism became intense. According to the US military's own newspaper, 'the profiles included suggestions on how to "neutralise" negative stories and generate favourable coverage'. Aiden White of the International Federation of Journalists (IFJ) told *Reuters*: 'It strips away any pretence that the Army is interested in helping journalists to work freely. It suggests they are more interested in propaganda than honest reporting'.[6]

Other methods of information control range from the orchestrated provision of offended and insulted US diplomats and executives to answer anti-US sentiment (mostly coordinated by the press offices of US embassies worldwide), to rhetorical attacks on offending media (e.g. the Hutton inquiry in the United Kingdom[7]), to more direct intimidation and coercion of journalists, along with their editors and senior managers. US diplomats worldwide have always been primed to challenge every media report which conflicts with Washington doctrine, but their long-standing efforts have not been enough. The US set up additional 'instant response' offices in Washington, London and Islamabad to complain to local media about unfavourable stories, offer interviews with US officials, and feed favourable stories and sources to local media.[8] It is not a new effort, as some post-9/11 commentators have suggested, but a new, heavily funded twist on the Cold War obsession of the US Information Service, working out of US embassies worldwide.

The Wrong Time for Questions

During NATO interventions in the Balkans, the US military – finding themselves and their actions continuously under scrutiny, not just from the traditionally friendly and manageable US media, but from a sometimes questioning, even sceptical, international media – came to rely on a three-pronged strategy of information control, which would come to serve them well in the Post-9/11 Wars. Prong one was to flood the news media with information under NATO/Pentagon control, leaving little space for competing perspectives or contradictory facts. Prong two was to build and exploit cosy relationships with leading US media outlets, who were always eager to please high-level government sources who might share scraps of insight with them, ahead of their competitors. And prong three was the use of violence to eliminate competing messages, as elaborated on in Chapter 3. NATO's commander during the Kosovo campaign casually told an interviewer how such close relationships with the news media aided him:

> it's important that a [bombing] campaign not be unilaterally and prematurely terminated. [This] was captured beautifully by CNN, who said, 'Despite negotiations, NATO continues to bomb.' I called one of my friends at CNN and said, 'It's a wrong line. It's because of the bombing that the negotiations are continuing, and that's why we're going to keep the bombing up until the negotiations are completed'.[9]

So pleased with the news media's positive telling of their story were the architects of the US military campaign that senior US diplomat Richard Holbrooke, who engineered much of the US policy in the Balkans, told a gathering of senior US journalists during the bombing campaign: 'The kind of coverage we're seeing from the *New York Times*, the *Washington*

Post, NBC, CBS, ABC, CNN and the news magazines lately on Kosovo has been extraordinary and exemplary'.[10]

After 9/11, not every US and British media outlet was charging unquestioningly towards war, but most were. Mooney[11] and others have documented how nearly every major US newspaper not only avoided critical, investigative news coverage of the shallow justifications for war with Iraq put forward by the US and UK governments in 2002 and the start of 2003, but that they used their editorial pages to argue the case for war. From the earliest days of the George W. Bush presidency, US journalists did little to question or challenge foreign policy. The Bush administration kept its intentions regarding Iraq close to its chest from well before the 9/11 hijackings, with the mainstream US news media showing little interest in prising out what was hidden. Bush's first treasury secretary, Paul O'Neil, revealed to Suskind in 2004 that an invasion of Iraq was initially discussed at a January 2001 National Security Council meeting, soon after Bush assumed office, following the disputed presidential election of 2000.[12] This was nine months before 9/11, the event that was widely portrayed as the trigger for the US invasion of Afghanistan and Iraq. It was fully two years before mainstream news outlets began to report the certainty of a US invasion of Iraq, even though the majority of US and UK mainstream news outlets gave a great deal of credibility to the position that invasion was necessary from early in 2002, while providing little critique of that perspective and practically no investigation seeking to independently corroborate the now discredited claims of Iraqi 'weapons of mass destruction'.

There have been various explanations as to why the US media so easily sacrificed the questioning role suggested by traditional conceptions of media and democracy. Peity and Foley hypothesise that a form of institutional 'group think' took over the editorial agenda. They argue that, through the 'unquestioning conformism and authoritarianism' and end-justifying-the-means embrace of violence expressed in such group thinking, political conservatives dominating the US news agenda 'are coming increasingly to resemble Bolsheviks'.[13] When this author was interviewed by a senior reporter from one of the major network affiliate San Francisco television stations in 2002, I turned the questions back on my interviewer. I asked how it could be, especially in San Francisco, one of the most left leaning of any of the large US cities, that media discussion of an impending war could be so blatantly one-sided, so completely lacking in scepticism about the efficacy, legality or morality of the US attacking a country that had not attacked it. Where were the professional journalists at this moment – the people in a democracy constitutionally responsible for facilitating debate on major issues? The interviewer registered the point of the question but dismissed as preposterous that such questioning could be broadcast in the existing political climate, suggesting that even arguing for such coverage in his newsroom at that moment would be professional suicide. This was happening in every US city, and reinforces Piety and Foley's parallel with a Soviet-style authoritarianism.[14]

Former senior *New York Times* journalist Stephen Kinzer, who has become a vocal critic of US interventionism, commented on the 'ignorance, mendacity and embedded egotism [...] which shaped most coverage of Iraq in the US press'.[15] One study found that of the

> 1,617 on-camera sources who appeared on the evening newscasts of six U.S. television networks during the three weeks beginning with the start of the war [...] nearly two-thirds of all sources, 64 per cent, were pro-war, while 71 per cent of U.S. guests favored the war. Anti-war voices were 10 per cent of all sources, but just 6 per cent of non-Iraqi sources and only 3 per cent of U.S. sources. Thus viewers were more than six times as likely to see a pro-war source as one who was anti-war; counting only U.S. guests, the ratio increases to 25 to 1.[16]

A number of US journalists paid a high price for questioning conventional wisdom about Iraq. Television journalist Ashleigh Banfield was a prominent case in point. Banfield rose quickly from being a junior *MSNBC* (the cable and online arm of *NBC*) reporter to a prominent international correspondent, following her live reporting as the World Trade Center fell around her. But, apparently because a number of her reports attempted to provide more information about Middle Eastern cultures and attitudes than many of her US television colleagues were typically providing, she became a target of ridicule in right-wing media – oddly including right-wing talk radio programmes owned by General Electric which, as the owner of *MSNBC*, was also her employer.

General Electric had just cancelled a programme in which it had invested heavily – an *MSNBC* talk show hosted by prominent veteran US broadcaster Phil Donahue, which was at the time their most popular cable programme. Donahue was vocal in his opposition to the US war in Iraq, and was providing one of very few national broadcast venues in the US where dissenting views about war were occasionally aired. General

Electric saw the strongly pro-war talk programmes on *Fox News* gaining higher viewer ratings and revenue than Donahue.[17] Donahue's programme was cancelled when an external consultant reported to *NBC* that Donahue was 'a tired, left-wing liberal out of touch with the current marketplace' who 'seems to delight in presenting guests who are anti-war, anti-Bush and sceptical of the administration's motives'. There was a danger, the report told *NBC*, that the programme could be 'a home for the liberal antiwar agenda at the same time that our competitors are waving the flag at every opportunity'. The progressive media watchdog organisation FAIR (Fairness and Accuracy in Reporting) reported that a leaked *MSNBC* management email proposed that the network should benefit from the 'anticipated larger audience who will tune in during a time of war' by reinventing its programming with pundits linked to war coverage. It concluded that 'It's unlikely that we can use Phil in this way, particularly given his public stance on the advisability of the war effort'.[18] Consumer advocate and one-time presidential candidate Ralph Nader reported that Donahue was told by network executives in the final months of his programme 'that he had to have more conservative or right-wing guests than liberals on the same hour show'.[19] *NBC* had also recently removed one of the most experienced US war reporters, Peter Arnett, from their coverage of the early days of the US invasion because *Fox News* criticised his providing an interview to Iraqi television, and thousands of protest emails were received. The emails were orchestrated by a right-wing website.[20] Such was the corporate context into which correspondent Banfield sought to introduce a measure of critical reflection.

Given her prominence as one of the more thoughtful US television reporters covering the Middle East, Banfield was invited to provide an address at Kansas State University in late April 2003, soon after the beginning of the US invasion of Iraq. Banfield, in remarks that would get her ostracised from her profession, told her university audience that within the mainstream Western journalist corps with which she associated in Afghanistan and Iraq, few questioned the extent to which the war was being sanitised for US consumption. She recalled that this only changed when fellow journalists died: 'It had a very brief respite from the sanitation when Terry Lloyd was killed [...] and when David Bloom was killed and when Michael Kelley was killed. We all sort of sat back for a moment and realized, "God, this is ugly. This is hitting us at home now. This is hitting the non-combatants."' Of course, hundreds (at least) of non-combatants had already been killed by US bombs and other military action, but little of that had been reported in the US media. Banfield's was one of the more critical and least self-satisfied public explanations of the media role in the ongoing war coming from any well-known US journalist at the time. She observed:

> There is a grand difference between journalism and coverage, and getting access does not mean you're getting the story, it just means you're getting one more arm or leg of the story. And that's what we got, and it was a glorious, wonderful picture that had a lot of people watching and a lot of advertisers excited about cable news. But it wasn't journalism [...] Cable is for entertainment, as it's turning out, but not news.[21]

Her main points – that embedded journalism provided only a partial and therefore distorted view of war, and that the scurry among media companies to be more right-wing and pro-war than one another was probably dangerous for US society – were both widely acknowledged truisms at the time, even within much of the news industry. But when right-wing bloggers lambasted her comments, *NBC* proclaimed itself to be 'deeply disappointed and troubled by her remarks'. They had an interest in being troubled by them. As this classic quote (one of the most succinct testimonies to the dangers of corporate concentration ever uttered) from General Electric's Chairman attested, the corporation felt they had a special stake in 9/11. After 9/11, General Electric chief Jeff Immelt remarked: 'my second day as chairman, a plane I lease, flying with engines I built, crashed into a building that I insure, and it was covered by a network that I own'.[22] In the years following 9/11, General Electric was the 8th largest US defence contractor.[23]

NBC (with oversight of journalism at *MSNBC*) was a minor holding of General Electric and occasionally proving a nuisance: General Electric had developed a track record of correcting potentially damaging news reporting by *NBC* journalists.[24] No record has emerged of an explicit calculation by *NBC* executives that self-reflection or critique by one of their journalists cost their parent corporation much, but past incidents of corporate interference in their newsroom will have taught *NBC* that lesson. *NBC* subsequently refused to let Banfield report or engage in any journalism and took away her office, while refusing for over a year and a half to release her from her contract (which might have permitted her to provide her slightly more intelligent and critical version of television journalism to another news outlet).[25] At the time of this writing, a decade on, Banfield has returned to a prominent on-air position with *MSNBC* rival, *CNN*.

The mainstream US media had become monolithic and almost incapable of questioning the state; in fact, with *Fox News* as the main news source for US television viewers and playing the role of a propagandistic state channel, the Soviet allusion was complete. But it is in some ways worse, of course, when such a broadcaster pretends to be something other than that because it is funded by advertising. Citizens of the Soviet bloc knew they saw what the state wanted them to see when they watched television, but in a commercial media system state propaganda is well hidden behind the illusion of independence from government.[26] With the election of Barack Obama, *Fox News* effectively transitioned from state channel to unofficial channel of the Republican party (allowing the company to derail Obama's limited progressive agenda, while promoting a status quo position in foreign and domestic policy). *Fox* remains a principal proponent of a militaristic and imperialistic US foreign policy, and tends to lead the populist (rather than intellectual) charge from the US right-wing against any critique of that mission.[27]

Tremendously wealthy US political conservatives, representing much of the US business elite, have invested heavily in shaping media content 'through the back door' – that is, out of sight of the public – for over 40 years. Through experiments in media ownership,[28] to massive lobbying efforts to affect media policy, to the steady provision of 'experts' to media channels that comment on and subsequently shape nearly every policy debate, through to the orchestration of campaigns of flak[29] to correct media output viewed as incompatible with their world view, such institutions have played a huge role in ensuring that the mainstream US media never get firmly behind progressive social policies, never support organised labour, consistently advocate for excessive defence spending, and trumpet the mantra of 'free speech' for all domestically and globally, while casually relegating significant social critique or investigation of business elites to the margins of the 'alternative press'.

As Peity and Foley note, such efforts to influence the public agenda are often rooted in foundations established by right-wing super-rich families in the 1970s: the Coors, the Kochs and several others. These gave rise to the Heritage Foundation, Cato Institute and American Enterprise Institute which, along with massive industry lobbying organisations like the US Chambers of Commerce, have poured hundreds of millions of dollars into influencing countless public debates, while simultaneously seeking to directly influence policy-makers through political donations (or threats to support the opposition).[30] They have also steadily sought to shift public thinking by consistently providing television-savvy pundits to media organisations. The ingredients of their success include never expressing scepticism regarding whatever were being touted as 'American values' at the time, and to shift every debate ever rightward.

In the US there has never been anything approaching a counter from the left to this hegemonic ideological powerhouse; there is simply no source of revenue for it in an almost fully commercial media system. However, since the late 2000s the *MSNBC* cable television network – the same network we saw earlier seeking to shift rightward – has cultivated a different audience niche from its competitors *Fox News* and *CNN* by broadcasting increasingly popular news analysis programmes with a somewhat more cerebral and broadly left/centrist approach to the analysis of politics and world affairs. One of the best known is that hosted by commentator Rachel Maddow – an alumnus of an earlier, ultimately unsuccessful, attempt to counter right-wing broadcasting in the US: the progressive *Air America* radio network.

But the culture of militarism and a perception of foreign threat in the post-9/11 years stretched far beyond the US news media. The Pentagon, for example, joined forces with influential Hollywood producers to create the 'militainment' genre – 'patriotic' reality TV series starring US troops,[31] the beginnings of a trend that moved the US towards the militarisation of its culture, with a dominant patriotic military theme becoming prevalent across numerous forms of popular culture, as De Derrian and others have sought to document. De Derrian makes the point that the militarisation of US society works hand in glove with the powerful mythology of clean, bloodless, virtual war, with 'precision' bombings and 'targeted' killings conducted from thousands of miles away by drone 'pilots' who go home at night to suburban family life.

This radical and troubling reshaping of the US culture I knew as a child was brought home to me when I took my own child to a popular marine-life tourist attraction, only to find the displays given over to patriotic tributes to the US military. I had only ever experienced such a spectacle of militarisation of public culture once before, in a visit to the Soviet Union before Glasnost swept many such Stalinist remnants away. Public celebrations of nationalism, patriotism and militarism provide a potent base for the marginalisation of dissent and critique, or reasoned analysis; for anyone who doesn't get swept up in nationalistic pride stands all the more apart from the crowd, appearing subversive and threatening.[32] The corporate culture industries operating in the US have been eager to feed this dangerous pattern because it has been profitable, and because, even for them, raising questions about it is perceived as risky.

But further fuelling this cultural shift has been the massive infusion of public funds into the public and private defence and security apparatus, with tentacles across all walks of life. The US spends nearly a quarter of its national budget on items variously related to defence and security, ensuring that the corporate US has little interest in challenging the militarisation of society. The US spends more on defence than the combined expenditure of the next 13 largest defence spending nations, despite surveys which indicate that most US citizens are eager to see such expenditure slashed.[33] Norman Solomon, who wrote a book and made a film about US pro-war propaganda, quotes Martin Luther King's reference to 'the madness of militarism', a group psychology accepting any degree of mass slaughter in the name of advancing US 'democracy'. It is a process, he suggests, 'reinforced through the media process of omission and commission', the alternatives to war which are never discussed, and the half truths presented by the mass media to support calls for war.[34]

The Culture of Fear

News media collaboration with the process of escalating provocation and violence, which ultimately led to the modern, asymmetrical warfare that has proven so deadly for those in the media and for hundreds of thousands of other civilians, all begins with the central tenet of the Western journalist's professional identity: the rejection of an analytic role in reporting the foreign policy positions of their own home governments (much less an oppositional one). As Dower demonstrated so clearly in his powerful investigation of US and Japanese propaganda and press imagery of the enemy in World War II, national press systems consistently and easily fall into the trap of patriotism and nationalism, and end up aligning themselves and their communicative power with the narrow interests of the most bellicose political leaders.[35] In so doing, news media naturalise the concept of violence as first resort, rather than last, and exaggerate a sense of global insecurity which then generates support for war.[36]

In research by this author, with Boaz,[37] it was found that neglect and stereotyping of a potential enemy – in this case the people of Iraq

– was substantially less pronounced among the media of predominately anti-war nations. The latter (specifically, leading weekly news magazines) advocated a less aggressive, more internationalist, and more diplomatic foreign policy approach than the US media. Non-coalition media generally wrote more about Iraqi suffering, and generally gave more voice to those affected by the war than those executing it.

This process of enemy construction uses every possible rhetorical device to present to the audience a dehumanised enemy, including portrayal of the perceived enemy using metaphors of animals, vermin and disease.[38] As Dower explained, it is a process that lets members of one society take satisfaction in killing those of another.[39] One ten-year veteran of the US Army who would later describe US government spying on media organisations before the start of the Iraq war (described in Chapter 3) told an interviewer:

> people took 9/11 and the fear of terrorism to such extremes. My warrant officer actually said in the build-up to Shock and Awe [the 2003 bombing of Baghdad] that this was basically final retribution for 9/11 and that we were going to bomb those barbarians back to Kingdom Come. And this is the kind of guidance that was coming from our highest, highest person in charge. And talk about the racism and dehumanization that is just rampant in our military, it affects everybody everywhere, not just on the ground in Iraq or Afghanistan, but even working in an office building in the United States of America. And people took this fear and the fear of the unknown, and believing the administration when they said that Iraq was tied to 9/11, they basically used that to justify doing a lot of things that we should not have been doing.[40]

The pattern of demonising and dehumanising a perceived enemy transitions into the easy acceptance of massive casualties among that enemy when war begins – those casualties don't matter as much, and don't need to be reported as much, as the casualties of 'our side'. As expressed by Herman and Chomsky, in war reporting there are 'worthy and unworthy victims'. The tendency of the dominant media organisations to seek to conform to a mainstream political agenda,[41] to comply with the official sources upon whom they are overly dependent (especially in the era of 'embedding'), and even, in the US, to actively censor negative comment about or portrayals of US military activity, demonstrate a process of war promotion that, whether deliberate or not, is well established.[42]

Senior *Los Angeles Times* correspondent Robert Scheer complained at a University of California seminar in March 2004 that 'This has been the most shameful era of American media. The media has been sucker-punched completely by this administration'.[43] The initial popular support for war with Iraq (which polls in the US indicated had dissipated by 2005) mystified the rest of the world, but could be understood in terms of the propaganda model of media,[44] whereby the mainstream US media filters out dissent through long-established patterns of framing and source selection, and portrays the international victims of US aggression as unworthy of sympathy. As Boaz and Paterson observe, the cynical manipulation of public sentiment to promote conflict has deep roots:

> both media and government gatekeepers understand that all that is necessary to keep a national public on board is to frame issues in particular ways: 'The people can always be brought to the bidding of the leaders. That is easy. All you have to do is tell them they are being attacked and denounce the pacifists for lack of patriotism and exposing the country to danger. It works the same way in any country.' Although the source of this quote is a former Nazi official, it becomes easy to see how democratic governments can and must employ the same technique when seeking support for their policy agenda.[45]

Der Derian referred to this process as a 'mimetic war of images', 'a battle of imitation and representation, in which the relationship of who we are and who they are is played out along a wide spectrum of familiarity and friendliness, indifference and tolerance, estrangement and hostility', adding 'it sanctions just about every kind of violence ... people go to war because of how they see, perceive, picture, imagine, and speak of others'.[46] John Pilger – one of the few vocal critics of the mainstream media to himself command a considerable global following – succinctly explains:

> Journalists don't sit down and think, 'I'm now going to speak for the establishment.' Of course not. But they internalize a whole set of assumptions, and one of the most potent assumptions is that the world should be seen in terms of its usefulness to the West, not humanity. This leads journalists to make a distinction between people who matter and people who don't matter. The people who died in the Twin Towers in that terrible crime mattered. The people who were bombed to death in dusty villages in Afghanistan didn't matter, even though it now seems

that their numbers were greater. The people who will die in Iraq don't matter. Iraq has been successfully demonized as if everybody who lives there is Saddam Hussein. In the build-up to this attack on Iraq, journalists have almost universally excluded the prospect of civilian deaths, the numbers of people who would die, because those people don't matter.[47]

Pilger put the question of why mainstream reporters so readily accepted the demonstrably illegitimate claims of the US and UK governments regarding the reasons for going to war with Iraq to the *BBC*'s senior journalist at the time, their Head of Newsgathering Fran Unsworth. Unsworth replied: 'but they were in the mouths of legitimate leaders therefore we had a duty to report them'. When Pilger challenged that the press also have a role to hold power to account, Unsworth replied: 'We aren't there to accuse of them of lying though'.[48] Of course, the one example that is consistently held up as evidence of an effective watchdog press in the US is the Watergate scandal, when a prominent newspaper did precisely that.

The US and British media, especially, collaborated with their respective governments – both directly and indirectly – to build a sense of public anxiety about the supposed 'terror threat' that was (and remains) far out of proportion to the actual threat. This process, in both countries, actively displaced public concern about real public risks such as automotive safety or communicable disease, which could be empirically shown to have substantial impacts, and which could be substantially mitigated if only public resources went towards them instead of towards war. Phillip Knightley observed in 2012 that 'Genuine risk assessments of the dangers of terrorism tend to be played down because they show that the chances of an ordinary citizen dying in a terrorist attack is about the same as dying from a fall in the bath'.[49] Indeed, the paranoia about 'terrorism' manufactured by government and the media enabled the rapid overhaul of the US airport passenger inspection system at the expense of basic civil rights and what had previously been a tolerable and fairly convenient mode of transport. According to recent research, so despised did US air transport become that many tens of thousands of people took to road transport as an alternative, resulting in an increase in traffic fatalities that, since the new procedures began, has probably matched or exceeded the total number of people killed by the 9/11 attacks themselves.[50]

Where independent research on Al Qaeda and the potential threat it posed existed, that research generally concluded than any threat had largely dissipated following 9/11 and that early US military action disrupted what little remained of its organising ability. As Al Qaeda expert Christina Hellmich observed: 'A simple fact often overlooked in the international community's assessment of Al Qaeda is that the ultimate power of terrorism lies in its ability to create a sense of fear far in excess of the actual threat posed'.[51] But the view of independent experts with research experience in the Middle East rarely entered the news discourse in the run-up to war or after hostilities began. In their study of British television coverage of the war, Lewis and Brookes found that 'those who might have shed light on events – whether NGOs, weapons inspectors, academics, or experts on and in the Arab world – [...] played very little part in the story told by television news'.[52] US television has been widely criticised for its dependence on retired generals as principle commentators on the war, and a near total absence of informed and critical voices.[53]

The veteran theorist of our mediatised society, David Altheide, observed that:

> Promoting fear has become second nature to U.S. government organizations like the FBI. Even their highly expanded surveillance of citizens has been accompanied by dramatic presentation and exaggeration of very rare threats with entertaining popular culture and mass media reports about terrorism threats. Pew opinion surveys show that terrorism continues to be one of the country's top 3 priorities – much higher than reducing crime, providing health insurance, or protecting the environment. American citizens' consciousness and speech about the 'terrorist threat' is a product of the propaganda of fear that has defined a plethora of U.S. news coverage for more than a decade.[54]

Hoskins and O'Loughlin, drawing from a concept developed by Masco,[55] suggest an ongoing state of 'pre-mediation of the catastrophic', suggesting 'the resulting condition is that of *hypersecurity*, as new contingencies of threats reflexively feed in to shape responses that exacerbate the very fears they propose to mitigate'.[56] Altheide suggests that the US government has become so habituated to feeding the narrative of fear that they have gone to extraordinary lengths and expense to create media spectacles that reinforce the popular concept of a terrorist threat. He points to examples including '19-year-old jihadist wannabe' Mohammed Mohamud in Portland, Oregon, who was lured by the FBI in 2011 to participate in a fake bomb plot which they orchestrated, despite the FBI's own admission that their suspect 'had neither the means nor opportunity to blow up anybody'. Excited by the provision of dramatic FBI surveillance video to broadcast, the news media paid little heed to the human and civil rights questions raised by FBI stings and approvingly reported these incidents as part of the thoroughly naturalised narrative of an ongoing threat.[57] Knightley has described similar activities carried out by the British intelligence services.[58]

After 9/11 different understandings of 'civil liberties' and 'freedom of expression' rapidly emerged, in the US and globally. We all soon found ourselves in a new age: where neighbours are encouraged to spy on neighbours; where everyone is a suspect; where mass surveillance of every citizen by one state's giant intelligence apparatus is accepted with relatively little public concern; where leading CIA figures establish divisions of local police departments to spy on Muslim citizens, and census data are used to target communities and recruit neighbourhood spies;[59] where judicial oversight of government surveillance of citizens has no impact;[60] where the loved ones of journalists who investigate the intelligence establishment are detained and harassed;[61] and where a routine of threatening and occasionally killing media workers is normalised.

We in Europe and the US still point disparagingly to North Korea, and – albeit more cautiously – to its giant northern neighbour, proclaiming that they do awful things such as these to their citizens, and that is precisely why we are innately superior to them. When we find that we are not so different after all, we shift uncomfortably and change the subject, or apply our practised cognitive dissonance to deny the evidence before our eyes, or vehemently attack the messenger who dared to bring us such news. As this chapter has recounted, many in the US media can do all three at once.

In this new world, everyone is potentially a 'terrorist', and the word is left with little meaning, if it ever had any to begin with. In 2002, lawmakers in the European Union attempted to impose a definition of 'terrorism' across the European Union, which would have included people taking part in anti-globalisation demonstrations involving elements of violence – as many well-publicised public protests inevitably do these days.[62] 'Terror' laws have been used in the UK and the US to detain and take electronic possessions from thousands of people at airports and border posts, with practically no evidence of danger to the public ever being uncovered or prevented as a result.[63]

As a Statewatch/IFJ report cautioned in regard to 'terrorist' watch lists issued by governments, 'Few question whether all those proscribed are simply "terrorists" rather than, in certain instances, part of a popular liberation struggle, or legitimate resistance to occupation or state repression. These very concepts are casualties of war on terrorism propaganda'.[64] Author James Bamford, who had done more than anyone to chronicle the excesses of the secretive US National Security Agency (NSA) prior to revelations provided in 2013 by whistle-blower Edward Snowdon, reported that by 2009 the agency's 'terrorist identities data-smart environment' watch list contained the names of about half a million people 'thought to pose a danger to the country'.[65]

As the detention of the non-journalist partner of reporter Glenn Greenwald (a journalist who writes about state security issues) – in 2013 in London under a terrorism law – suggests, expressing concern over these issues (reader beware), or *knowing someone* who does (reader's friend beware), brings us all into the growing 'terrorist' circle.[66] One needn't have been a human rights activist or historian of totalitarianism to have felt a chill when British Foreign Minster William Hague asserted in defence of David Miranda's detention at Heathrow airport: 'if you are a law-abiding citizen of this country going about your business and personal life, you have nothing to fear about the British state or intelligence agencies […] Indeed you will never be aware of all the things that these agencies are doing'.[67]

As film-maker Laura Poitras would later write of the detention of Greenwald's partner, Greenwald told her 'I actually cannot believe they are doing this'. She continued: 'I kept thinking I wish it were me. Having documented and reported on abuses of government power post 9/11, we both thought we'd reached a point where nothing would shock us. We were wrong – using pernicious terrorism laws to target the people we love and work with, this shocked us'.[68] And through a *ProPublica/New York Times/Guardian* investigation of documents revealed by whistle-blower Edward Snowden, the public discovered that the US has spent over 800 million dollars since 2011 breaking and undermining the commercial internet encryption protocols that are widely used to reassure global Internet users that their communications are safe. The investigation revealed how the NSA worked with internet companies to 'insert vulnerabilities in commercial encryption systems' known only to the NSA, but not to Internet users, who, the *Guardian* notes, are referred to by the NSA document as 'adversaries'.[69] In August 2013, using data supplied by

Snowden, the *Washington Post* revealed that 'that National Security Agency staff members in Washington overstepped their authority on spy programs thousands of times per year', and reported that the judge leading the secret 'Foreign Intelligence Surveillance court' – the only legal oversight of the vast US spying operation – said the court had little ability to provide oversight and relied on the government to report on impropriety.[70]

In a blog posting publicised by media commentator Jay Rosen, 'novelist and former CIA operative' Barry Eisler suggests that the application by the US and British governments of 'anti-terrorism' practices is more than just a rhetorical slip, or an innocent zest for protecting the public good. Eisler suggests that

> Part of the value in targeting the electronic communications of actual terrorists is that the terrorists are forced to use far slower means of plotting. The NSA has learned this lesson well, and is now applying it to journalists [...] To achieve the ability to monitor all human communication, broadly speaking the National Surveillance State must do two things: first, button up the primary means of human communication – today meaning the Internet, telephone, and snail mail;[71] second, clamp down on backup systems, meaning face-to-face communication, which is, after all, all that's left to the population when everything else has been bugged. Miranda's [*Guardian* journalist Greenwald's partner] detention was part of the second prong of attack. So, incidentally, was the destruction of *Guardian* computers [by British authorities in July 2013, only later revealed by the *Guardian*'s editor[72]] containing some of Snowden's leaks. The authorities knew there were copies, so destroying the information itself wasn't the point of the exercise. The point was to make the *Guardian* spend time and energy developing suboptimal backup options – that is, *to make journalism harder, slower, and less secure.*[73]

Collaboration with the Military

The collaboration of US media with US military aims stretched beyond the omission of reporting that would question or contradict official policies, as the following example illustrates. While the story of US government violence towards the media begins with the bombing of a civilian television channel in Serbia in April 1999, in the months immediately before and after that bombing both *National Public Radio* (*NPR*) and *CNN* in the US spent months showing the US Army's Psychological Operations unit (PSYOPS) precisely how international broadcast news gathering works.

PSYOPS developed incrementally through the 1990s as the manifestation of the US government's propensity for interventionism and its determination to control information.[74] An example of this evolving mentality was a strategy report published by the US Naval War College in 1996, entitled 'Military Operations in the *CNN* World: Using the Media as a Force Multiplier'. It suggested ways for commanders to 'leverage the vast resources of the fourth estate' for the purposes of 'communicating the [mission's] objective and end state, boosting friendly morale, executing more effective psychological operations, playing a major role in deception of the enemy and enhancing intelligence collection'.[75]

At a closed-door symposium held by the Pentagon in early February 2000, Rear Admiral Thomas Steffens of the US Special Operations Command explained that 'new ways were needed to deal with unrestricted information flow in the world's hot spots'. He suggested that the US military needed to be able to impose an 'informational cone of silence' over areas of military activity, and said that 'in addition to feeding disinformation to the media [...] the military had to gain control over the Internet and commercial satellites'. A colonel from the 4th PSYOPS Group, 'called for greater cooperation between the armed forces and media giants' and intriguingly offered the example of how 'Army PSYOPS personnel had worked for CNN for several weeks and helped in the production of some news stories for the network'.[76] Some well-funded and (it must be said) well-meaning US organisations had already eagerly pushed for a closer working relationship between the US military and media. The Freedom Forum argued in the mid-1990s – following much discussion of the breakdown of press–military relations during the first Gulf War – that not only should members of the media attend military training courses and seminars, but that 'local media leaders should invite military personnel to visit their facilities, participate in editorial boards' and 'put some combat commanders in newsrooms to see how we operate'.[77] That both the military and the media saw their respective interests and goals as so convergent and compatible could be taken both as symptomatic of a breakdown in the Fourth Estate concept – with media acting as the independent check on government – and the looming militarisation of US culture.

Without apparent concern for what appeared to be a conflict of interests, *CNN* and *NPR* agreed to requests from the Pentagon for several

PSYOPS sergeants to work within their organisations as 'interns'. The fact that internship programmes within the US media were established as collaborations with universities, for the sake of giving university students practical experience, didn't bother *CNN* and *NPR*. After working within the news production teams of the two major national radio news programmes in the US (*NPR*'s 'All Things Considered' and 'Morning Edition') for up to four months from late 1998, the Army's focus shifted to international television, and the 'interns' moved to *CNN*.

Journalists working in the satellite transmission department at *CNN Radio*, and *CNN*'s southeast bureau in Atlanta, Georgia, allowed the small group of psychological operations specialists from the US Army's Fort Bragg to spend weeks closely observing the day-to-day processes of news gathering in which they were engaged. Such was the extent of trust between *CNN* managers and the Pentagon that nobody at *CNN* with responsibility for making these arrangements speculated that the US military might come to use the information they were being provided with for military advantage.

One of the PSYOPS soldiers, who spent ten weeks observing *CNN* operations, told an interviewer: 'I saw how crews were deployed. I learned how they put stories together. The people I worked with there really took me in'.[78] US media commentator Max Robins was told by sources within *CNN* that *CNN*'s human resources department had passed the resumes of prospective interns to the heads of the departments where they were requesting to work, which contradicted *CNN*'s official position that this had been an understandable error in judgement by human relations staff who didn't understand journalism. Eason Jordan, *CNN*'s president of news gathering and international networks, would later assert that 'They had no impact on how we covered the news', adding, 'but those interns had no business being here'.[79] However, Jordan would also qualify that statement, telling me years later that 'I never objected to U.S. military members having legitimate short-term, hands-off internships at *CNN* as long as they were not involved in gathering or reporting the news'.[80]

While nobody from *CNN* has offered further detail of what was an embarrassing episode for them, what the Pentagon's PSYOPS specialists will have been able to observe in minute detail was precisely what this author observed as an academic researcher spending weeks within international television news organisations in the 1990s. They would have learned precisely how television news coverage of conflict zones takes place, and how broadcasters and broadcasting organisations – such as

CNN, Serbian television, the European Broadcasting Union and *Al Jazeera* – work closely with each other to facilitate image gathering, editing and transmission of television pictures. Certainly, with that new depth of understanding will have come a very comprehensive knowledge of how to disrupt a flow of television pictures should one wish to do so.

It later emerged that *CNN*'s Eason Jordan submitted prospective commentators on the Iraq War to the Pentagon for vetting before allowing *CNN* to hire them. He explained:

> I think it's important to have experts explain the war and describe the military hardware, describe the tactics, talk about the strategy behind the conflict. I went to the Pentagon myself several times before the war started and met with important people there and said, for instance, 'At CNN, here are the generals we're thinking of retaining to advise us on the air and off about the war' – and we got a big thumbs-up on all of them. That was important.[81]

Media critic and film-maker Norman Solomon commented: 'It was something to say to the American people on its own network, "See, we're team players. We may be the news media, but we're on the same side and the same page as the Pentagon." And that really runs directly counter to the idea of an independent press'.[82]

Since 2001, various instances of the US media altering coverage at the request of the US government have emerged (no refusals to comply are known, which is not to say they do not exist).[83] *CNN*, which still sets the US television agenda despite the widely held perception that it diminished journalistic standards to compete with its downmarket competitors, told their correspondents in 2002 that all story scripts must be approved by editors in Atlanta – an extraordinary step for a network that pioneered 'real-time' reporting and had, until that time, been broadly seen as having spurred better and more thorough international news coverage on US television.[84]

Well after the US invasion of Iraq, the *New York Times* engaged in a bout of self-flagellation for permitting its star journalist, Judith Miller, to hype the threat of Iraqi weapons that never existed, bolstering the case for war. The fact that her source, Ahmed Chalabi, was a CIA agent never bothered editors; but when it was revealed that he was also an Iranian agent, they distanced themselves. Miller was also reported, by the rival *Washington Post*, to be directing operations of US troops in Iraq hunting for the elusive weapons of mass destruction, suggesting the depth of the collaboration between major commercial media outlets and government, and standing in stark contrast with government's treatment of less cooperative media.[85] Allan and Zelizer relate the following quote from *New York Times* foreign correspondent John Burns, with regard to Iraq: 'We knew we were placing ourselves in the bull's eye of a war [...] And I don't think a journalist can sensibly claim to have an exception in a war zone. [By] the very nature of what's about to happen, there's a significant risk that you can be killed.'[86]

While this acknowledgement by a senior US journalist is important in its own right, it might also be regarded as moderately disingenuous, for it was not long before Burns made the statement that Miller had been not only reporting on a US military unit in Iraq (the Pentagon's highly successful invention of 'embedding'), but actively participating in their work.

There have been other, more prominent, ways in which the US media have been complicit in their own destruction (metaphorically and physically), through the vehicle of their collaboration with the governments that threaten and harm them. Of particular interest here are two recent phenomena shaping the reporting of Iraq: one widely commented upon and the other largely ignored. The first is the 'embedding' process, through which media outlets were intimidated into receiving limited but highly controlled access to the frontlines (and the sometimes compelling stories and images those yield). The second was the complicity of the press in preparing for the Iraq War in cooperation with the US military in 2002–2003, while keeping those preparations secret and publically reporting that peaceful outcomes were possible.

Propaganda researcher David Miller referred to 'embedding' as the greatest public relations success of the war.[87] Journalists who expressed doubts about the war were barred.[88] The system is detailed in Brookes et al.'s study of war reporting in Iraq,[89] and numerous other analyses of modern war reporting, and so will not be further examined here. Many experienced international journalists with the non-US media, along with many novices, opted to stay clear of US and British control.[90] In their exhaustive study of the process, Tumber and Palmer concluded that 'the looseness of the guidelines gives military commanders who are less sympathetic to journalists the discretion to remove unwanted reporters',[91] and journalists who expressed doubts about the war were never selected by the military to be embedded.[92] Being embedded, for all its failings, was generally safer than acting as a unilateral (reporting independently), although some journalists did die in the care of the US military as embeds and some journalists felt the wrath of the military units they accompanied. *New York Times* journalist Chris Ayres, quoted in Tumber and Webster, recounted a US Marine officer 'fizzing with barely controlled rage' after reading one of Ayres' reports.[93]

Major media outlets from around the world who did not accompany US troops, and especially the European public broadcasters, were denied access to Iraq in the early stages of combat and were ruthlessly frustrated in their reporting by the US military. European papers on the left, like the *Guardian*, were reported to be selectively denied access to the places and events to which other major media organisations were invited. Their foreign editor cited a visit to Europe by Donald Rumsfeld, or media visits to Abu Ghraib prison after the story of torture broke there, as examples.[94] The European Broadcasting Union made a rare complaint to the Pentagon about what they termed a 'caste system' among journalists, enforced by US troops (who, of course, had no internationally recognised legal authority in Iraq to begin with). US actions ranged from the refusal to allow journalists access to transmission facilities, to the arrest of journalists attempting to operate independently (a trend examined further in the second part of Chapter 3).[95]

But it is less often acknowledged publically that major news organisations broadly anticipated and prepared for a war in Iraq long before the US declared that it had an international mandate to launch its invasion. Internally many treated the war as inevitable and invested considerable sums in preparing for it, while presenting to their audiences reports suggesting that diplomatic efforts were underway and that war could be avoided. It could be argued that they reported a global anti-war movement on an unprecedented scale (for its scope was unprecedented), while cynically accepting its impending failure. Representatives of US media outlets participated in 'embedded journalist' training in the US, and collaborated in the construction of a major media facility in Qatar and in the planning of the technical aspects of embedding – such as provisions for live television coverage from embedded journalists – well in advance of the official decision by the US government to go to war.

There are broader arguments to be made regarding this aspect of the media's role. It may be argued that the ongoing attacks on the press by both state and non-state actors in Iraq are a consequence – perhaps even a predictable one – of a situation that the international media were complicit in creating. As described above, content studies have exposed the role of major US, and to a lesser extent British, media outlets in disseminating inaccurate information from governments seeking to justify war in Iraq.

Many writers have questioned whether the Iraq war could have taken place if the media had provided anything close to a balance of pro-war and anti-war views or verified inaccurate government claims.[96]

The public, globally, had reason to be surprised by the US invasion, but the pre-war collaboration with the military demonstrates the media expectation of war. Rantanen found that about half of the member news agencies of the European Alliance of News Agencies, whom she surveyed in 2004, started their planning for coverage of the Iraq war 'as early as the autumn of 2002',[97] four or more months before the US bombing began. Such advance planning is not at all unusual, but it raises a vital ethical question that has yet to be addressed in the growing literature on Iraq war journalism: if the media know that a war is likely (and given limited news coverage budgets they would not invest heavily in preparing for coverage without knowing this) do they have the obligation to report that knowledge? In the case of the Iraq War, there was an alarming tendency in the media to treat this as *insider knowledge*, relevant only to news gathering logistics, unworthy of public dissemination, while many in the media simultaneously disseminated intensely pro-war commentary.

US government intimidation and threats against the press would likely have been far less successful over the past few decades were it not for a powerful mechanism of support offered by commercial and non-commercial online and broadcast media. While outlets like right-wing talk radio and *Fox News* are the most internationally visible of these, it could well be that it is a small army of right-wing bloggers who have the greatest influence. The right-wing blogger and author Michelle Malkin for example, then on the payroll of Rupert Murdoch's News Corporation, led the charge against former *CNN* executive Eason Jordan when he stated publically that US troops had emerged as a threat to journalists. She similarly led the charge against news agency journalists when they failed to report on US actions in Iraq favourably or use the terminology of the Right. A senior executive of the *Associated Press* – a service that strives to remain behind the scenes – was reported by several blogs to have made a rare public comment in defence of the agency's reporting.[98]

In late January 2005, *CNN* senior executive Eason Jordan sat on a panel at the exclusive World Economic Forum in Davos, Switzerland and, in response to a point about news coverage of the Iraq war made by another panellist, noted that a number of journalists had been killed not just by 'insurgents' but by the US military. When his remarks were made public, in violation of the Forum's rules, US conservative bloggers flew into a rage, and when major conservative media like the *Wall Street Journal* backed their calls for Jordan's resignation, an arrangement was struck with *CNN* for him to leave. One of the few senior news executives who spoke out in support of Jordan while he was being dragged through the mud was the *BBC*'s Richard Sambrook, who was also on the panel at Davos. The blogger Jay Rosen – whose site *Pressthink* was widely consulted at the time over all manner of media issues – shrewdly wrote to Sambrook for his side of the Davos story. He replied to Rosen that:

> Eason's comments were a reaction to a statement that journalists killed in Iraq amounted to 'collateral damage'. His point was that many of these journalists (and indeed civilians) killed in Iraq were not accidental victims – as suggested by the terms 'collateral damage' – but had been 'targeted', for example by snipers [...] He clarified this comment to say he did not believe they were targeted *because* they were journalists, although there are others in the media community who do hold that view (personally, I don't).

Although he hasn't elaborated, Sambrook might have referred to some staff at the news agency *Reuters*, and almost certainly to staff – including some senior editors – at the broadcaster *Al Jazeera*. Both organisations had ample reason to believe they were being targeted, and journalist Ron Suskind's interviews ultimately provide collaboration that, at least in the case of *Al Jazeera*, they were (see Chapter 3). Sambrook went on to tell Rosen – and Rosen's large US audience – that:

> A second point he made, which in my view is extremely important, is that when journalists have been killed by the military in conflict it has been almost impossible to have an open inquiry or any accountability for the death on behalf of families, friends or employers. Very little information is released, we know investigations do take place but the results are not passed on. This culture of 'closing ranks' coupled with hostile comments about the media from senior politicians and others, has led some in the media community (not necessarily Eason or myself) to believe the military are careless as to whether journalists are killed or not and no longer respect the traditional right to report.[99]

For making that observation, Sambrook himself came under attack both on Rosen's blog and within the conservative blogosphere.[100]

Sambrook replied to some of the vitriolic posts about his letter to Rosen for a time and then gave up, so that he could get back to running the *BBC*'s news operation. His latter point to Rosen, though, was put with extreme caution given the depth of feeling at the time within the media industry. Sambrook was aware that many journalists around the world were furious and very alarmed at US actions, and that there was a developing groundswell within the industry to increase the pressure on the US and other governments for press protection and an end to the culture of impunity allowing attacks on the press without consequence.[101] Sambrook's later work with the INSI was an important part of those efforts, although there were many others. In the final chapters we address the extent to which such efforts have been effective. The concern within the industry was strongly expressed at the Newsworld gathering of senior television news managers in late 2003, where *CNN*'s senior news manager joined a senior *BBC* correspondent and others in expressing alarm about the apparent targeting of journalists by combatants, including those affiliated with the US military.

US reporters who deviated from a positive story about the US military sometimes faced harsh consequences in the context of the disturbingly close collaboration between the state and the commercial media sphere in the era of post-9/11 militarism. The Bush administration developed a process for using friends in the conservative online media to rhetorically attack journalists when there seemed little possibility of applying any legal sanction. Few criticisms went unanswered. The IFJ and Statewatch reported, for example, how 'The Bush administration uses insidious tactics to attempt to discredit journalists who file stories that appear critical of the White House'. They recount how, in July 2003, Jeffrey Kofman, a television reporter for the US network *ABC*,

> filed a story about the plummeting morale of the troops in Iraq on ABC's World News Tonight in which he interviewed soldiers questioning the credibility of the US Army. One soldier interviewed angrily suggested that Secretary of Defense Donald Rumsfeld should resign.

The IFJ report recounts that the next day a White House official contacted the popular website *The Drudge Report* seeking to discredit Kofman, 'telling Drudge that Kofman was not worthy of credibility in that he was gay and held Canadian citizenship'. The report goes on to say that in the US 'There were numerous cases of individual journalists and news staff victimised for expressing views that were at odds with the conventional wisdom of the political and military administration'.[102]

In 2004, when US television photographer Kevin Sites came under a barrage of criticism in the US for photographing a US soldier killing an injured insurgent fighter, a US newspaper reporter named Darrin Mortenson, with whom Sites had worked in Iraq, tried to come to his defence. Sites had written a public letter to the Marine unit he was embedded with, stating:

> So here, ultimately, is how it all plays out: when the Iraqi man in the mosque posed a threat, he was your enemy; when he was subdued he was your responsibility; when he was killed in front of my eyes and my camera, the story of his death became my responsibility.[103]

Mortenson had himself served in the US Army in Iraq before becoming a reporter. He wrote:

> the blame-the-messenger mentality, which is always a sign of weakness in a democracy, is contagious and miserable. [...] When the news is good, everyone hails those hardworking reporters who live in the dirt and danger to accompany the troops, as long as their reports make us feel good. But when the images make us uncomfortable or force us to ask questions, we blame the media.[104]

For his efforts, Mortenson himself became a target of abuse in the US media, to the point of even fearing for his own safety and that of his family. The US newspaper trade journal *Editor and Publisher* printed some of the abusive emails he received in order to highlight how intolerant of free expression, and the advocacy of free expression, the US public had become.[105] Intriguingly though, with revelations that the US military itself attempts to shape public debate by participating in Internet discussions (sometimes anonymously), there remains the possibility that some online threats against critics of the military, and some online pro-war comment generally, did not actually originate from the general public at all.[106]

Shaping the Foreign Mind

When reporting the military exploits of the US and its allies around the world, just a few representatives of major corporate media outlets have been consistently critical or questioning. One of the keenest critics of a Western press in bed with Western militaries is Robert Fisk of the London newspaper the *Independent*. He is quoted throughout this book precisely because he is the one reporter from a major Western newspaper who has consistently noticed, and written about, the misrepresentations, obfuscation and press intimidation of Western militaries and the occasional complicity of his media colleagues. Philip Knightley tells of how, when 'the great maverick reporter Robert Fisk' tried to evade military control to report on the first Gulf War independently, another correspondent told him to 'get out of here, you arsehole. You'll prevent the rest of us from working'.[107]

Philip Hammond reported that during the Kosovo conflict in 1999, 'when Robert Fisk's article in the *Independent* contradicted the outlandish claim that the Serbs had bombed Pristina themselves, one British television correspondent stood up at the briefing in Brussels and urged his fellow reporters not to ask NATO any awkward questions'.[108] Fisk's account of *CNN*'s reporting of the Kosovo war was especially damning. He reported, for instance, that

> In Belgrade [...] a CNN reporter astounded one of his English colleagues after NATO had bombed a narrow road bridge in the Yugoslav village of Varvarin, killing dozens of civilians, many of whom fell to their death in the River Morava. 'That'll teach them not to stand on bridges,' he roared. This was not the kind of language he used on air, of course, where CNN's report on the bridge killings was accompanied by the remark that there had been civilian casualties 'according to the Serb authorities' – all this when CNN's own crew had been there and filmed the decapitated corpse of the local priest.[109]

The extent of US (and to a lesser extent, allied) efforts to influence public perceptions set the stage for the less well documented 'soft coercion' which has increasingly become a staple of US foreign policy, especially at times of international conflict. I employ this paradoxical notion to suggest something different from 'soft power' in its contemporary guise, associated with public diplomacy and an attempt to influence public narratives to facilitate a country's strategic and economic interests globally. 'Soft coercion' involves a more aggressive application of pressure (through a variety of means) on media outlets to limit or discredit critical press coverage and increase positive press coverage – this, contrary to

Nye's original conception of soft power, is highly coercive.[110] The media has been (sometimes nearly simultaneously) urged towards particular sources from US and UK officials, 'frozen out' of the information flow by those same governments, and subject to massive campaigns of flak[111] in multipronged campaigns to influence news coverage. This is symptomatic of an established understanding of the media as an adversary, to be controlled by any and all means (scholarship remains divided on whether this is mostly rooted in the 'Vietnam Myth'[112] or in far earlier expectations of a compliant press in times of war). Given the acquiescent nature of almost all US media in the run-up to the invasion of Iraq, substantial soft coercion was focused on the media of other countries in this period. It is likely that that this strategy contributed to acceptance of the use of deadly force against the media, and even easier acceptance of deadly force against the non-compliant media.

Lewis and colleagues summarised the US approach based on their interviews with Pentagon staff and analysis of the news coverage, describing how the embedding programme was designed to generate so much 'news' from within the US government orbit that it would overwhelm any contrary messages:

> The sheer volume of frontline footage from embeds was designed to avoid a 'news vacuum' into which less favourable pieces of analysis or counter responses from the Iraqi regime might seep. On occasions when negative footage did appear – scenes of civilian casualties from marketplace bombings, or of coalition casualties or POWs, images taken by Iraqi TV and broadcast by al-Jazeera – a concerted effort was made to undermine it, either by displays of moral outrage that such scenes be transmitted or by protracted denials and then promises of full investigations.[113]

Indeed, in a study of news magazine coverage across five countries, this author, with Boaz,[114] found that two US administration officials (Secretary of Defense Rumsfeld and Secretary of State Powell) were referenced and cited much more frequently than even the heads of state of key countries, including those in Europe and the Middle East. We concluded that

> the US government was especially successful at setting the international agenda on Iraq by dominating the perspectives covered. Even when other media were critical of these perspectives, the overwhelming

amount of coverage given to the US administration's view lends it some (perhaps unjustified) legitimacy.[115]

Representatives of the Bush administration made a number of appearances in the Arab media in an attempt to tell their story to the Arab world and correct perceived biases.[116] US officials sometimes seemed to feel favourable coverage of their polices from the world's media was something they had every right and reason to expect. *Al Jazeera*'s Yosri Fouda, the reporter who elicited Al Qaeda's first interview about the 9/11 plot, would express the growing frustration among non-US journalists at the increasing barrage of manipulation: 'the President of the most powerful nation on earth said at one point, "You are either with us or against us." Hello. I'm a journalist. My job is all about being in the middle'.[117]

John Pilger commented that 'most of the lies were channelled straight to Downing Street from the 24-hour Office of Global Communication in the White House'.[118] Independently of White House efforts, the Pentagon established an 'Office of Strategic Influence' to manage and, if necessary, plant international propaganda.[119] It was affiliated with the Army's Psychological Operations Command, which had conducted the research on international television journalism inside *CNN* in 1999, as described earlier in this chapter.

Within months of 9/11 it was clear to the Bush administration that the US corporate media posed no threat to ambitious plans to clamp down on civil liberties at home and launch imperial wars abroad. The concern became the press of the nations that would bear the brunt of the invasions, and the press of 'friendly' nations whose support in the United Nations and in sharing the cost of the adventures was crucial. In the lead up to Iraq, France and Germany were written off as irrelevant 'old Europe',[120] perhaps because efforts to significantly influence their press coverage were proving unsuccessful.[121]

More routinely, US officials reacted quickly and forcefully to foreign media reports, as when Pilger was corrected by a Rumsfeld deputy for referring to dead Iraqi civilians who *could not exist*, given the accuracy of US weapons.[122] Journalists would be frozen out of the flow of information by the US and UK governments in response to coverage that was perceived as unfavourable.[123] *Guardian* editor David Hearst said that relations between the British papers – even those on the left – and US foot soldiers, as well as long-standing contacts in the US State Department and intelligence communities, had traditionally been good. The pressure, he said, came from the White House and the Pentagon. For example, *Guardian* correspondent Julian Borger received a sharp rebuke in a letter from a Pentagon official who took issue with his reporting on US links to Ahmed Chalabi.[124]

Since 9/11, news executives in the US and Britain have been called to informal meetings by both governments and asked to avoid coverage of the enemy. Few details of what has been discussed, or agreed, at these meetings have emerged, but perhaps the most public fallout of such meetings was the resignation in 2011 of *Al Jazeera*'s managing director Wadah Khanfar, following revelations in US diplomatic cables published by *WikiLeaks* that he had altered *Al Jazeera* reporting as a result of just such US pressure. Some of the most consistent and vicious rhetorical attacks by some Western media on other media outlets have been those aimed at *Al Jazeera*. Major US media outlets, including *CNN*, have been quick to echo and amplify frequent denunciations of *Al Jazeera* by US government officials.[125] Like *CNN*, *Al Jazeera* functions both as an international broadcaster and as a news agency, and it was through its business as a news agency – providing pictures and interviews to other broadcasters which they could not obtain themselves – that it stayed financially stable and built respect from and cooperation with other media around the world, including with the leading British and US broadcasters. Apparently *Al Jazeera* was considered the most important news source in the Middle East by President Bush himself. Bob Woodward reported that 'Bush and Andrew Card were watching CNN and *Al Jazeera* on March 2003 in the White House as commandos first went into Iraq, to find out if the media knew about it'.[126]

Rhetorical attacks from the US government on Arab broadcasters escalated steadily in the days immediately following the 9/11 attacks and for most of the subsequent decade, eventually becoming more constrained and less emotive around 2006. What remains unclear is whether this was due to a new appreciation of media plurality in the Middle East and the rights of journalists to voice a variety of opinions, or due to the perception in the US and allied governments that continued pressure on these broadcasters had sufficiently shifted their editorial approach to the point that it was no longer regarded as threatening to US interests. As put by journalist Samantha Shapiro in a *New York Times* profile of the *Al Arabiya* channel in 2005:

It is unclear if the Department of Defense has changed its view of Al Arabiya since Donald Rumsfeld called it 'violently anti-coalition'[127] a year ago. 'At this point in time, we do not want to offer our evaluation of the editorial content or direction of a particular news outlet' a Department of Defense spokesman, Lt. Col. Barry Venable, told me late last month. George Bush did choose to give Al Arabiya an interview after the Abu Ghraib prison scandal, and Al Arabiya's business manager, Shafaat Khan, said he was visited by a few American generals in the summer who wanted to establish friendly relations. They summed up their view of the Arab media by saying that as they understood it, 'Al Jazeera is very, very bad, and Al Arabiya is bad.'[128]

Throughout the war and before it, the US military monitored the Arab language channels intensively, keeping a close eye on where their reporters and photographers were, and what they were saying. A concern was that the Arab channels were covering aspects of US military activities that Western media were downplaying or ignoring, and that public outrage and consequent political pressure to curtail those activities could result. One previously secret US Coalition Provisional Authority (CPA) report revealed by *WikiLeaks* reported that:

> Arab satellite news channels were crucial to building political pressure to halt military operations. For example, CPA documented 34 stories on Al Jazeera that misreported or distorted battlefield events between 6 and 13 April. Between 14 and 20 April, Al Jazeera used the 'excessive force' theme 11 times and allowed various anti-Coalition factions to claim that U.S. forces were using cluster bombs against urban areas and kidnapping and torturing Iraqi children. Six negative reports by al-Arabiyah focused almost exclusively on the excessive force theme. Overall, the qualitative content of negative reports increasingly was shrill in tone, and both TV stations appeared willing to take even the most baseless claims as fact. During the first week of April, insurgents invited a reporter from Al Jazeera, Ahmed Mansour, and his film crew into Fallujah where they filmed scenes of dead babies from the hospital, presumably killed by Coalition air strikes. Comparisons were made to the Palestinian Intifada. Children were shown bespattered with blood; mothers were shown screaming and mourning.

This report urged superiors to reconsider the absence of Western media covering Fallujah (which it incorrectly attributed to the fear of attack from insurgents rather than the US military's ban on media, and which

ignored the few independent Western reporters who did go), and 'led
to further reinforcement of anti-Coalition propaganda'.[129] Importantly,
Al Jazeera's reports generally stood up as accurate when compared later
with eyewitness accounts taken by other reporters and the ultimate
casualty tallies.

Shapiro's research for the *New York Times* story uncovered 'a general
feeling around the *Al Arabiya* offices that since [Abdul Rahman] Al-Rashed
was named news director, the channel has become pro-American'. One
editor, asked repeatedly to cover more US military successes and fewer
civilian casualties, asked Shapiro:

> 'How can you "balance" civilian deaths?' [...] 'Maybe you could show
> dead soldiers, but the American government doesn't even want us to
> show them. When you talk about the agonies of civilians, there is no
> way to balance it – they are a different category of people. The Iraqi
> government says, "Please concentrate on positive aspects." Why should
> we concentrate on good things?'

An *Al Arabiya* assignment editor was reported by Shapiro to have
complained to the station's management that pushing the channel towards
being pro-US would put their staff in Iraq in even greater danger than they
already were (a point we return to in Chapter 4).[130]

Defending the Homeland From Journalism

There is an increasing anti-press mood among government officials at all
levels in the US – probably as a consequence of the 9/11 attacks and many
years of right-wing, security establishment-oriented governments – and
US politicians have found a rhetoric of security far more successful in
recent years than a rhetoric of civil liberties. In the name of that security,
various means of influencing the foreign press have been implemented
with little fanfare. Since the 1990s, reporters from other countries seeking
to report on the US or, in some cases, even to visit the US for personal
reasons, have come under suspicion and sometimes been subject to
detention, questioning, searches and seizures of their personal property
which are supposed to be barred by the Fourth Amendment to the US
Constitution.[131] In 2004, the US government decided for the first time
that foreign journalists visiting the US had to be specifically identified

and their movements in and out of the US monitored. The prohibition against 'represent(ing) the foreign information media during your visit' was inserted into new rules requiring all non-US citizens to obtain visas. Statewatch and the IFJ reported that:

> During 2004, a number of global press freedom groups, including the IFJ, protested to the United States authorities over pressure on journalists, citing unprecedented restrictions being imposed on journalists wishing to travel to the United States for their work. New visa rules imposed by the authorities require journalists to have a special visa and to undergo interviews at local embassies with US officials before being allowed to travel, imposing greater restrictions than those which apply to business travellers. Journalists were banned from using the visa-waiver programme which applies to most European countries.[132]

They reported that this led to the detention and deportation of 15 non-US journalists who came to the US with normal visas in 2004. The US Society of Journalists and Authors also protested that this visa policy was a violation of press freedom laws in the US, including the First Amendment.[133] British journalist and author Elena Lappin was one of the many non-US reporters forcibly detained at a US airport and deported within the first year of the programme. On 3 May 2004, Lappin travelled from London to Los Angeles on assignment for the *Guardian*, believing that as a British citizen she did not require a visa. She was wrong: as a journalist, even from a country that has a visa waiver agreement with the US, she should have applied for an 'I' (for information) visa. Because she had not, she

> was interrogated for four hours, body searched, fingerprinted, photographed, handcuffed and forced to spend the night in a cell in a detention facility in central Los Angeles, and another day as a detainee at the airport before flying back to London. [Her] humiliating and physically very uncomfortable detention lasted 26 hours.[134]

Lappin would later write in the *New York Times*: 'By requiring foreign journalists to obtain special visas, the US has aligned itself with the likes of Iran, North Korea and Cuba, places where reporters are treated as dangerous subversives and disseminators of uncomfortable truths'.[135] Following protests from press freedom organisations, the US Commissioner of Customs and Border Protection announced that, while the rule would remain, non-US journalists would only be detained and deported on their second attempt to practice their trade in the US without State Department authorisation.[136]

In June 2003, for example, the State Department cabled all its diplomatic and consular posts, urging them to pay attention to 'an increasing number' of journalists being denied entry. 'Aliens coming to practice journalism are not eligible on the visa waiver program or a business visa', it explained. 'Journalists who attempt to do so [...] are subject to removal'.[137] Lappin writes that 'ostensibly, this information is meant to apprise visa applicants of the rules of entry and spare them later distress. Still, the approach seems that of a police state with a repressive ideological agenda'. Lappin traces this to the McCarthy era:

> The I visa was initially conceived against the background of the highly controversial McCarran–Walter Act, enacted in 1952 at the peak of the McCarthy era. One of the bill's co-authors, Senator Pat McCarran, boasted that the act was an effective screen against subversives. [...] Brent Renison points out that the bill listed journalists as 'a new class of non-immigrants' and removed them from the visitor category. [...] As late as 1991, *The New York Times* reported that the State Department 'maintains a list of hundreds of thousands of aliens who are considered to have dangerous beliefs or intentions and ought to be kept out of the country.' The [2001] Patriot Act revived much of the McCarran–Walter Act. It placed antiterrorism measures in a peculiar conceptual proximity to laws supporting the control and removal of undesirable aliens, although with a new emphasis: journalists have become the new subversives, even when they have no agenda at all. [...] In the name of fighting terrorism, The Patriot Act has transformed a free, open, inimitably attractive democracy into something resembling an insular fortress of Kafkaesque absurdity.[138]

As in the US, authorities in the UK have created a dubious legal framework to escape long-established search and seizure prohibitions through the claim that officials at ports and airports follow a different set of rules. In the UK, Schedule 7 of the 2000 Prevention of Terrorism Act allows government officials to search and seize without any need to demonstrate reasonable grounds for suspicion to a court, or to the person targeted. The law was used to justify the nine-hour detention of the partner of *Guardian* journalist Glenn Greenwald at Heathrow airport in London in August

2013, and the seizure of all the electronics he carried. *Guardian* editor Alan Rusbridger lamented:

> You have a kind of vacuum which is not quite Britain, not quite not Britain, in which this act enables people to interrogate people for up to nine hours and seize all their belongings with no checks and balances and so that doesn't seem a very good way to treat people who are engaged in journalism.[139]

Unlike in the US, the use of the law in the UK is a matter of public record: in the UK, over 60,000 people were subject to such examinations during a one-year period beginning in 2012, and 24 people were arrested between 2011 and 2012 on terrorism-related charges.[140] But the situation is less clear in the US, and when one US Senator complained to the US Department of Homeland Security, they replied that:

> officers must verify the identity of persons seeking entry into the United States and determine the admissibility of aliens, as well as look for possible terrorists, terrorist weapons, controlled substances, and a wide variety of other prohibited and restricted items.

But in the most prominent detentions investigated by the American Civil Liberties Union, no questions were asked about trademark, terrorism, or illegal materials; instead, the questions focused entirely on what these US citizens were saying in public and the people with whom they choose to associate.[141]

Glenn Greenwald suggests that of the thousands of airport detentions and seizures of personal electronics, the case of Oscar- and Emmy-nominated, Peabody Award winning journalist Laura Poitras is 'perhaps the most extreme'. In one questioning session at a New York airport in 2010, Poitras, who is a US citizen, informed her Homeland Security questioner that she wished to invoke her journalistic privilege to refuse to answer questions about people she met with (the Supreme Court recognised right-of-source protection upon which US journalism is premised). She was told, according to Greenwald's account, that he 'finds it very suspicious that you're not willing to help your country by answering our questions'.[142] Poitras estimates she has been detained over 40 times while attempting to transit through US airports. She wrote:

It's a total violation [...] That's how it feels. They are interested in information that pertains to the work I am doing that's clearly private and privileged. It's an intimidating situation when people with guns meet you when you get off an airplane. [...] When did that universe begin, that people are put on a list and are never told and are stopped for six years? I have no idea why they did it. It's the complete suspension of due process. [...] I've been told nothing, I've been asked nothing, and I've done nothing. It's like Kafka. Nobody ever tells you what the accusation is.[143]

Non-journalist US citizens who have made efforts to support whistle-blowers have also been detained at airports and had their electronics seized.[144]

One organisation in the US attempting to defend the rights of journalists to practice their profession is one of the communications media's professional unions, the American Federation of Television and Radio Artists (AFTRA). According to their affiliate, the IFJ, AFTRA 'condemned the increasing use of legal pressure to intimidate journalists and to limit journalists' ability to gather information'. AFTRA cited two cases of journalists being arrested in the US, noting: 'Although neither case is linked directly to the war on terrorism, they represent an alarming trend, [...] whereby reporters are increasingly subject to threats of legal action or intimidation by police'.[145] In his sweeping 1989 study of anti-press violence in the US, Nerone identified a number of similar cases of heavy-handed repression or intimidation of the press, but stretching over a far broader period – suggesting the pattern of press intimidation in the US is escalating.[146]

News outlets outside the US – and outside any war zone – have also been attacked by the US government. In October 2004, the FBI collaborated with UK authorities to remove the hard drives from the computer servers of the *Indymedia* independent cooperative news organisation, temporarily disabling their reporting in the process. The FBI referenced a secret court order in the US, which wasn't provided to *Indymedia* or the company which owned the servers, and no explanation was offered of what legal grounds permitted the FBI to enforce a US court order in London.[147]

As violence towards journalists increased in the Middle East, US surveillance of journalists increased at home. It has recently been revealed that spying on US journalists has been far more significant than previously expected, with revelations in late 2013 that the NSA spied on prominent journalists, including Tom Wicker of the *New York Times* and Art Buchwald of the *Washington Post*.[148] CIA whistle-blower William Binney told *Nation* journalist Tim Shorrock that in 'using the NSA to spy on American citizens [...] the United States has created a police state with few parallels in history'. Binney said: 'It's better than anything that the KGB, the Stasi, or the Gestapo and SS ever had'. He compared the situation to the Weimar Republic, a brief period of liberal democracy that preceded the Nazi takeover of Germany. 'We're just waiting to turn the key', he said.[149]

This followed a revelation that shocked the US press. A government-wide culture of demonising and criminalising journalists and treating interactions with media as extrajudicial matters escalated to dramatic new heights within the US in the spring of 2013. As with the preponderance of attacks against *Reuters* in the Post-9/11 Wars, it was one of the two major international news agencies that fell victim. According to a report by the *Associated Press* (*AP*), in May 2013 they were informed that two months of records of 20 telephone lines had been secretly seized earlier that year by US government officials, including records of the home telephones and mobile phones of journalists. What astounded and alarmed the US media was that this seizure happened not in a war zone but at the *AP* offices in Connecticut, New York, and Washington, DC. The *AP* angrily deplored it as 'serious interference with *AP*'s Constitutional rights to gather and report the news'. The *AP* suspected the seizures were related to a story they had written about CIA activity in Yemen a year earlier, but the government never provided a reason, or evidence of any legal authority for the seizure. The *AP* responded that:

> these records potentially reveal communications with confidential sources across all of the news gathering activities undertaken by the AP during a two-month period, provide a road map to AP's news gathering operations, and disclose information about AP's activities and operations that the government has no conceivable right to know.[150]

The incident sparked calls from the Obama administration for a 'press shield' law to prevent such government action in the future, despite Obama's resistance to such a law only a few years earlier.[151]

The President's sudden defence of press freedom was viewed by many as disingenuous, as distrust of government intentions towards the press has reached new heights in the US as a result of the *AP* wiretapping, a spate of prosecutions of people suspected of leaking information, and revelations about mass surveillance. The *New York Times*' public editor Margaret Sullivan wrote that Barack Obama's presidency is

> turning out to be the administration of unprecedented secrecy and of unprecedented attacks on a free press [...] This isn't just about press rights. It's about the right of citizens to know what their government is doing. In an atmosphere of secrecy and punishment – despite the hollow promises of transparency – that's getting harder every day.[152]

In May 2013, the Reporters Committee for the Freedom of the Press, on behalf of nearly all the major US media companies and professional organisations, stated in a letter to US Attorney General Eric Holder:

> In the thirty years since the [US Justice] Department issued guidelines governing its subpoena practice as it relates to phone records from journalists, none of us can remember an instance where such an overreaching dragnet for news gathering materials was deployed by the Department, particularly without notice to the affected reporters or an opportunity to seek judicial review.[153]

Conclusion

As Skoco and Woodger concluded in their analysis of NATO and the US military's relationship with the media following the Kosovo conflict, for democracy to function:

> independence of the media from the government, military, and other institutions is a mandatory precondition, and prior acceptance of a natural right to military intervention more than highlights the media's low expectation of the potential of their role.[154]

But beyond that easy acceptance, as described in this chapter with regard to the invasions of Afghanistan and Iraq, it is probably also the case that astonishing levels of ignorance within the ranks of some US media made them easy targets for manipulation, being spoon-fed contrived information from the only sources with which they had relationships and knew how to deal: the US military and administration.

Al Jazeera journalist Yosri Fouda, who obtained the first confession from the two planners of the 9/11 attacks, provides a telling example. On the day he was contacted by a mysterious intermediary for Al Qaeda's leadership as a prerequisite to that interview, he was amused when a producer for what he calls (with generous discretion) 'a famous international news network' from the US rang him to ask a favour (*Al Jazeera* was, and still is, often courted by competing news organisations seeking to exploit the contacts and access they've established in the Middle East). She asked, he recalls, 'Would you happen to have a phone number for one of these Al-Qaeda people? [...] We need their reaction to some reports'. Initially not understanding that she was serious, he suggested she call directory enquiries. Fouda and co-author Fielding write that this producer represented for them a common stereotype of

> many of those in the Western media who were chronically ill-informed about the background of the 11 September attacks. As far as many of them were concerned, the whole thing was seamless – 11 September, Bin Laden, Islam, Arabs, Afghanistan, Middle East terrorism: they all ran together.[155]

As the IFJ put it in a 2005 report:

> Western media struggle to maintain even basic levels of profes-sionalism in a charged atmosphere of fear, violence and intolerant political rhetoric. In the US, constitutionally the home of the world's freest media, journalism has suffered, particularly as a result of self-imposed censorship.[156]

In Chapter 3 we review the pattern of violence towards the media which developed from 1999, taking root in the fertile soil provided by a fearful and militarised US culture, a compliant US media, and a US government leadership increasingly regarding the news media as a minor nuisance to be ignored or overcome by military means.

3

Patterns of Violence: The Media Installation and the Media Worker

Part 1: Escalation

The compliant nature of most of the US news media in the post-9/11 period, in combination with an entrenched acceptance in the US government that a non-compliant media was not to be tolerated in the new 'War on Terror' they were planning, proved a lethal mix that would come to underlie a new, deadly approach to the civilian information media. Attacks on the news media by the US and by its closest Middle Eastern allies (Israel, Saudi Arabia and the quasi-democratic US-backed regimes in Iraq and Afghanistan) take a variety of forms but have many shared characteristics:

- They have escalated sharply since the late 1990s, and were especially deadly for the media between about 2000 and 2005, as US and British troops poured into the region.
- They have almost universally been greeted with legal impunity for the attackers and minimal public debate (despite being the object of considerable behind-the-scenes diplomacy and legal activity by news media, which is the subject of Chapter 4).
- The perpetrators appear to share techniques in press intimidation and control among themselves.

The forms of aggression used against news media have ranged from extrajudicial monitoring of journalistic activity, through the detention and harassment of media workers, to the more visible armed attacks on individual journalists, their homes, and their workplaces. As suggested in Chapter 1, although appalling and unacceptable in itself, many in the media and public alike readily accept government mistreatment of journalists in Middle Eastern countries like Israel, Iraq, Saudi Arabia and Pakistan as *inevitable* and *expected*, given the occasionally apparent brutality of Middle Eastern politics and the proximity of myriad long-standing conflicts. What is more surprising and newsworthy, since it stands in such flagrant contradiction of public perception and the national ideology, is persistent US involvement in attacks on media workers.

This chapter describes the emergence of a pattern of attacks of various kinds that has developed since 1999, when the US led a multi-nation attack on Serbia that was in many ways a rehearsal for the military adventures in Iraq and Afghanistan a few years later. Most of the incidents recounted in this chapter are far more thoroughly described elsewhere, across a wide range of reports by NGOs, news media and academic studies; I cite many of those sources in the notes so that the reader can seek greater detail if desired.[1] Instead of recounting all the details and controversies of each case in this single chapter, I provide a year-to-year summary of the circumstances of each case, focusing on the US government role, and seeking to reveal the relevant circumstances of each case that were obscured in the immediate aftermath.

In broad terms, there have been two kinds of anti-media violence routinely perpetrated by the US military. The first is the pattern of military attacks on media facilities dating from 1999. These attacks have sometimes resulted in deaths and injuries, and sometimes not. In some cases the US government has acknowledged targeting these facilities, and in other cases claimed that unfortunate but excusable errors were made. The second kind of violence is that directed at individual journalists by parties to the current conflict in Iraq (and to a lesser degree, Afghanistan), in addition to a wide range of other attacks involving – according to the journalists involved and their media organisations – injury, detention without charge, harassment, the destruction of recordings and equipment and, in some cases, torture.

As noted in Chapter 1, there is a good deal of evidence – mostly from well-attended press conferences in early and mid-2003 (as the US bombed and then invaded Iraq) – that journalists have been told to expect to be shot at if they fail to comply with US military demands about where they go and what they do in areas where the US military is active, or planning to be active (especially in regard to the use of transmitting equipment, which is a necessary part of modern journalism). But there are telling contradictions in US statements to reporters about the risk they take.

There was a string of warnings, some veiled, some not, that journalists will be attacked if they report outside of prescribed parameters. The Pentagon public relations chief in the early days of the Iraq war (officially, Assistant Secretary of Defense for Public Affairs), Victoria Clarke, frequently told journalists at Washington press briefings that anyone not embedded with the US or British military would be 'putting themselves at extreme risk'. She asked the media organisations to 'exercise restraint, especially with journalists who are reporting *freely*'.[2] The italics in the previous quote are mine, to highlight this specific instruction from the senior media liaison of the US government, which clearly intends to curtail press freedom, a strikingly clear violation of the spirit, if not the letter, of the free press clause of the First Amendment of the US Constitution.[3]

Such warnings were not unique to the ongoing Post-9/11 Wars, as noted in Chapter 1. A similar pattern of veiled threats can be identified through the history of the war correspondent.[4] If there was any mistaking Clarke's intention, it was made perfectly clear when later military investigations into the deaths of the journalists in the Palestine hotel in Baghdad made reference to the repeated warnings to journalists by US officials that Baghdad was not a 'safe' place to be. Those earlier references to risk were, in effect, used to excuse the killing of three journalists on 8 April 2003 (described in more detail later in this chapter).

The story of the US government's threat to media workers began in earnest in 1999, but its roots can be traced to several factors. These are:

- The persistence of the 'Vietnam syndrome', the discredited but nonetheless enduring myth that critical news media coverage of the latter stages of the Vietnam war resulted in US defeat by eroding public support for an otherwise winnable campaign.
- The evolving belief – in the decades after Vietnam – in the Pentagon and among US politicians that the ongoing projection of US military power was necessary and useful, but best undertaken away from public and congressional scrutiny. In the post-Vietnam period, US covert warfare has taken place almost continuously around the world, most of it with the barest acknowledgement within US media and little congressional debate.
- The emerging interest within the US military since the 1980s in 'information warfare'. This increasing desire to control what people think about – near the battlefield and far from it – became an obsession of the Pentagon and the US Congress in the 1990s and the

recipient of considerable funding, aspects of which were described in Chapter 2.

• The demonstration, beginning as early as the 1980s, that the US public and US news media which address them show little concern about government attempts to control the press, and little sympathy for press victims of such efforts, whether those efforts are violent or not.

Since the start of the pattern identified here – 1999 – the US military (and in some cases, its private contractor surrogates) has killed approximately 48 media workers (including those supporting news reporting operations in some way). In many – perhaps most – of these cases, there are ample indications that US military commanders and/or the soldiers involved were aware that the people they were aiming at were journalists or other media workers. Their names, where available, are listed in Appendix 1 with a brief summary of the circumstances of their deaths.[5] Few other countries have accumulated such a record of killing journalists in recent decades but, because many of these attacks have been reported as accidents of war (what former *CNN* news chief Eason Jordan would later call 'de facto cases of mistaken identity'[6]), press freedom groups and many in the news industry do not generally regard the US as ranking among the most severe threats to journalists.[7] This chapter will not recount the details of the various attacks on journalists; as noted earlier, these are well documented by the major journalists' rights groups and media reports.[8] But some particularly significant examples are worth reviewing, as these demonstrate an evolving pattern that is tantamount to the normalisation of state violence against the press by the US.

In the mid-1990s, the US military, in conjunction with NATO, began a policy of using violence to ensure control of the 'information space'. After the 1994 genocide in Rwanda – substantially orchestrated by the incendiary broadcasts of one Rwandan radio station – and amid lingering questions about whether US President Bill Clinton could have used US military power in some way to mitigate that tragedy, US interest in controlling the flow of information increased substantially, although this interest had been building steadily throughout the post-Vietnam period. It is difficult to pin down a precise moment at which an interest in influencing communications (through public affairs efforts, the dissemination of propaganda, efforts to restrict and influence news coverage) shifted to a willingness to use deadly force to disrupt and destroy 'unfriendly' communications, but a particularly crucial turning point was when the US military began to routinely target the transmitting towers of radio and television stations when intervening in the Yugoslav civil war in 1997. They were easy targets and their destruction could briefly deprive military and political leaders of a platform.

Importantly, at this moment, the seizure or destruction of civilian media facilities – the transmitting towers – became a matter of *policy*, despite the prohibition of attacks on civilian facilities and infrastructure under international law. Price et al. report in one example: 'U.S. troops seized a television broadcast tower in Udrigovo, a northeastern town, under the pretence that they were trying to prevent possible clashes between Plavsic's supporters and Karadzic's supporters'.[9] In these instances, US military planners could claim (and indeed, probably felt they had) a significant degree of international legitimacy for the destruction or seizure of civilian media facilities in wartime – because they acted under the NATO umbrella and had a degree of United Nations support.

April 1999

For several years, an increasingly violent campaign had been waged in the Serbian province of Kosovo to free it of Serbian control. The staunchly militaristic and nationalistic Serbian government of Slobodan Milosevic determined in 1999 to put an end to the Kosovar resistance and the threat it posed to Serbs living in Kosovo, and moved its army into the province. Amid reports of brutality towards Kosovan civilians and forced expulsion, hundreds of thousands fled their homes, producing harrowing scenes on television screens around the world. US President Bill Clinton (whom some have accused of being eager to divert attention from scandals in Washington) and Western European heads of state agreed to deploy the collective forces of NATO, under Pentagon control, to attempt to protect civilians and drive the Serbian military back. The bombing of Serbia began on 24 March 1999, following Serbia's inevitable refusal of a NATO-proposed treaty, which would have led to Kosovan independence and allowed NATO troops into Serbia.

In its frequent reports to the press, NATO was accused of exaggerating and misleading, and showing more interest in propaganda than the welfare of the population they had come to protect.[10] Broadcasters were fed a steady stream of grainy black-and-white images from the cameras mounted on NATO jets and missiles, appearing to show a precision strike every time. Serbian state television, which had access to areas of conflict on Serbian territory, often presented a contradictory story, showing visual evidence of the 'collateral damage' of killed and injured civilians, including repeated bombings of columns of refugees, destroyed civilian infrastructure especially in the Kosovan capital Pristina, and worse. *Independent* journalist Robert Fisk complained that most of the journalists attending NATO briefings in Brussels

> allowed themselves to be used as a mouthpiece for the military, sheep who bleated appropriately when Nato boasted of the bombing sorties over Serbia or who passed on Nato's regrets when it killed civilians. By the time American jets had destroyed an entire hospital at Surdulica, they gave up, failing to challenge [NATO spokesman Jamie] Shea even when he claimed – untruthfully – that the hospital was a barracks.[11]

With the only images contradicting many of the reports NATO was giving to the press originating with Serbian television, the US government and NATO leaders pressured the French-based satellite operator Eutelsat into halting transmissions from Serbian television into the international television news exchange systems. Reporters Sans Frontières condemned the exclusion of the Serbian broadcaster from the Eutelsat network.[12] It was a contradiction of the mandate of the European satellite consortium, which was to provide satellite services to all European public broadcaster members, regardless of politics or ideology. It had the direct effect of making it impossible for the Serbian broadcaster to provide images it had recorded in Serbia of the effects of NATO bombs to broadcasters in the rest of the world (who could have chosen whether or not to use them). NATO's secretary-general was reported to have personally telephoned the management of the TV 5 network in Spain to complain when that broadcaster used images from the Serbian broadcaster without providing a commentary which was sufficiently critical of them.[13]

On 9 April, a NATO officer, British Air Commodore David Wilby, announced to the media that the Serbian national broadcast media were 'an instrument of propaganda and repression [...] It is has filled the airwaves with hate and with lies over the years and especially now. It is therefore a legitimate target in this campaign'. NATO thereby set the stage for an unprecedented military attack on a major civilian broadcasting organisation, Serbian public broadcaster *Radio Television Serbia* (*RTS*). Wilby, and NATO spokesman Jamie Shea, demanded that 'equal time' be given in Serbian state broadcasting for 'Western news broadcasts', but, according to the *BBC*, Shea later 'distanced the organisation [NATO] from earlier comments that TV transmitters would also be targeted unless the authorities allowed uncensored western news broadcasts to be broadcast'.[14] A reporter from the US *Public Broadcasting Service* would later ask the US general in overall command of the NATO campaign, Wesley Clark: 'Clearly, there was a lot of stuff that was non-controversial. But if you had something controversial like the TV channels, how did it work', to which Clark replied:

> There were [...] types of targets that had a high political symbolism, which went beyond their actual military value – like the television system. We knew that Milosevic used TV as an instrument of command and control. He used it to control the population, to inflame the passions of ethnic cleansing, and so forth. Because freedom of the press is one of our values, the symbolic value of that to Western nations is enormous [...] So that decision [to bomb it] had a huge political component. And we had to work it through the nations, step by step. [...] We'd [find] out who was in favor, who was opposed, and why, and work to assure them as we moved forward on these specific types of targets.[15]

Clark's public acknowledgement in this interview that bombing the media might contradict a principle of 'freedom of the press' is a rare early indication of the US military acknowledging this dilemma, but treating it as a political problem to be overcome rather than a bar to the kinds of attacks on the media they had started to imagine.

NATO did proceed to bomb television and radio transmitters around Serbia throughout its intensive April bombing campaign. The US anti-war campaigning organisation the International Action Centre reported that 'between 24 March and 10 June 1999, US/NATO bombs destroyed more than ten private radio and television stations, and 36 TV transmitters'.[16] The Pink and Kosava commercial radio and television stations in Belgrade were bombed, apparently without civilian casualties.[17] Both had clear ties to the Serbian government, and their destruction had little impact on the images flowing to broadcasters from inside Serbia. Western media took little notice, and few questioned NATO's goal of destroying mass media operations within the Serbian state. During the period of the NATO attacks, the US military was constantly transmitting Pentagon-produced radio broadcasts into Serbia from airborne transmitters, which seemed not to be, in the view of the US government, 'propaganda', despite precisely meeting the definition of the word.

According to Human Rights Watch, following a meeting on 23 April, '[NATO] alliance leaders decided to intensify the air campaign by expanding the target set to include military-industrial infrastructure, news media, and other targets considered to be of a strategic nature'. However, Human Rights Watch was also told by sources in NATO that 'there was considerable disagreement between the United States and French governments regarding the legality and legitimacy of the target', referring specifically to the *RTS* headquarters building in Belgrade, Serbia's public broadcaster (the Serbian equivalent of the *BBC*). Human Rights Watch were told that *RTS* was originally due to be bombed on 12 April, but it wasn't, apparently due to French government concerns. This suggests that if the US was determined to bomb the building, despite French concerns, they had eleven days to ensure that civilians were evacuated from it. According to Human Rights Watch:

> When the initial warnings were given to Western media, the Yugoslav government also found out about the intended attack. When the target was finally hit in the middle of the night on April 23, according to RTS and Yugoslav government officials, authorities were no longer taking the threats seriously, given the time that had transpired since the initial warnings. As a consequence, sixteen RTS civilian technicians and workers were killed and sixteen were wounded.[18]

Years later families of some of those killed in the US bombing took the head of *RTS* Television to court for failing to evacuate the building, and the court, accepting their argument, sentenced him to 16 years in jail.[19] In a fascinating account of US government pressure on their European allies to bomb the Serbian television facilities, as well as US efforts to spare the lives of US journalists, *Washington Post* reporter Dana Priest would write:

> France also reluctantly agreed in mid-April to airstrikes on Belgrade's two main TV towers, one of which was atop the Socialist Party headquarters. The Pentagon warned Western reporters to stay out of those buildings. But as warplanes streaked toward the kill on April 12, the Pentagon got word that some (US) journalists were inside. Air Force Gen. Joseph Ralston [...] ordered the jets to turn around. By April 18, Clark was pushing to reschedule the strike, and Western journalists were warned again.

According to Priest, the Pentagon would continue to struggle with French dissent and even provided the French government with videotapes of 'nationalist propaganda' broadcast by *RTS*, eventually gaining French agreement.[20]

Human Rights Watch, in an exhaustive report published in the year 2000, 'confirmed ninety incidents in which civilians died as a result of NATO bombing' and that 'as few as 489 and as many as 528 Yugoslav civilians were killed' in those incidents. The Serb government claimed many more civilians were killed.[21] Because NATO chose to target a civilian media facility, at least 3 per cent of the civilians killed by the NATO campaign were media workers.

In the days preceding 23 April 1999, *CNN* and possibly other US broadcast companies were reported by Howard Kurtz of the *Washington Post* (and later an employee of *CNN*) to have moved their operations out of the *RTS* building, where they had been using the standard 'host broadcaster' arrangements historically used by visiting television news teams in any country to get their television news footage and 'stand-up' reports uplinked to a satellite and relayed to their own newsrooms around the world. The warnings 'from senior White House and Pentagon officials' told these US broadcasters 'that NATO would soon hit the facility'. *CNN* staff have not spoken about this alleged warning, or about the arrangements, but the head of *CNN*'s news operations at the time, Eason Jordan, downplayed any impact on *CNN*, telling me that '*CNN* reported from Belgrade for the duration of the conflict'.[22] But the impact on *CNN* was severe, and included the destruction of their own satellite uplink which they had temporary installed at *RTS*. This alone was a $400,000 loss,[23] sending a powerful message to a key US television news operation that there is a price to pay for reporting from behind enemy lines. In archived *CNN* reports from the time there is no mention of a NATO threat to bomb Serbia's civilian media; if *CNN*'s editors knew this, they apparently did not consider it newsworthy.

The deliberation in the bombing of *RTS* was clear. More alarmingly, the easy dismissal of *RTS* media workers as enemies to be killed was apparent, for this seems to be the one case of a US attack on a media installation where US media organisations were warned immediately prior to the attack.[24] According to Kurtz, '*CNN* and the U.S. broadcast networks, which had been feeding videotape from the building, abandoned it after receiving private warnings from senior White House and Pentagon officials that NATO would soon hit the facility.' Robert Fisk of the *Independent* would later write that *CNN* received two days' notice from the US government.[25] Indeed, *CNN* reporter Brent Sadler was well away from the city centre when the *RTS* attack happened, and could only report it by telephone to his Atlanta headquarters. He watched it on television, as a small commercial Serbian broadcaster reported that the *RTS* building was on fire. He told *CNN*'s audience by telephone from Belgrade that 'in the past several minutes, Television Serbia has gone off the air', providing NATO with the confirmation they required that their attack on Serbia's major broadcaster had been successful.[26]

While the attack will not have stopped *RTS* news teams from covering the war on the ground, the destruction of their headquarters and transmitters briefly prevented their stories from being broadcast within Serbia and prevented *RTS* from providing its pictures to the rest of the world's broadcasters via the European television news exchange system, Eurovision. *RTS* was a long-standing member of Eurovision, enabling it to feed its own news stories to other European broadcasters, to US networks who were associate members of Eurovision, and to the television news agencies *Associated Press Television News* (*APTN*) and *Reuters*, which would then have provided those pictures to broadcasters around the world.[27]

This is precisely the international television news distribution mechanism the US Army 'interns' would have been observing in operation at *CNN* in Atlanta at around the same time (see Chapter 2). Through that observation, and any further research they might have undertaken, the US military will have known that television stories being sent out of Belgrade via satellite would have normally been coming through one chokepoint – the play-out facilities (where videotapes shot in the field, sometimes roughly edited, sometimes not, are played for transmission via satellite to a news team's headquarters) and satellite dishes at the *RTS* building in Belgrade. A news agency or international broadcaster operating in an autocratic state without permission to use its own satellite uplink equipment typically has a single option, which is to depend on the good will of the local broadcaster to put aside their daily work, accept a videotape from the foreign broadcaster, and transmit the tape up to a satellite for the international broadcaster to use. While local broadcasters will sometimes do this for financial gain, and local governments will sometimes use this bottleneck as a way of monitoring and controlling what is transmitted about their country, on the ground there is typically a friendly and professional relationship between the visiting media workers and the local ones providing the help. In this case, the fact that *CNN* was permitted to bring their own satellite dish to *RTS* in Belgrade demonstrates an effective working relationship between the two broadcasters, despite widespread hostility towards *CNN* in Serbia (Serbian authorities would later seize much of *CNN*'s equipment). *CNN* generally relayed the Pentagon line that Serbian broadcasting was part of that country's military apparatus,[28] and there is no record of them acknowledging their own cooperation with *RTS* in the weeks prior to the attack and their private warnings to leave; nor has the US network, or other foreign companies working with *RTS* who received the Pentagon's warning, said whether they relayed warnings of the impending attack by the US to staff at *RTS*, or whether they chose not to.

But there is a more serious charge which was levelled at *CNN* by Robert Fisk, in a damning review of the media role in the Kosovo war written as the NATO action wound down in the summer of 1999. According to Fisk, 'Two days before Nato bombed the Serb television headquarters in Belgrade, *CNN* received a tip from its Atlanta headquarters that the building was to be destroyed. They were told to remove their facilities from the premises at once, which they did'. That much of the story had been revealed in other reports, although *CNN* never publically discussed it, but Fisk goes on to add that:

> A day later, Serbian information minister Aleksander Vucic received a faxed invitation from the Larry King Live show in the US, to appear on CNN. They wanted him on air at 2.30 in the morning of 23 April and asked him to arrive at Serb Television half an hour early for make-up. Vucic was late – which was just as well for him since Nato missiles slammed into the building at six minutes past two. The first one exploded in the makeup room where the young Serb assistant was burned to death. CNN calls this all a coincidence, saying that the Larry King show, put out by the entertainment division, did not know of the news department's instruction to its men to leave the Belgrade building.[29]

On the following day, 24 April, the second-largest facility of *RTS*, in the city of Novi Sad, was also bombed by NATO. All of the staff had evacuated when they learned of the attack on their colleagues in Belgrade the day before.[30] The Serbian government protested against 'the destruction of the RTS buildings in Belgrade, Novi Sad and Pristina, the brutal killing of journalists, the repeated destruction of radio-TV transmitters, the jamming of RTS signals'.[31]

In a NATO briefing for the media in Belgrade the day after the attack on *RTS*, NATO Public Information Officer Colonel Konrad Freytag stated:

> Last night NATO continued to disrupt the national command network and to degrade the Federal Republic of Yugoslavia's propaganda apparatus. Our forces struck at the regime leadership's ability to transmit their version of the news and to transmit their instructions to the troops in the field prosecuting their campaign of repression and destruction in Kosovo. The Belgrade Television and Radio Studio, the largest mass media institution in the Federal Republic of Yugoslavia, which orchestrated much of the regime's propaganda program, was struck. The building also housed a large multi-purpose communications satellite antenna dish ... Strikes against TV transmitters and broadcast facilities are part of our campaign to dismantle the FRY [Federal Republic of Yugoslavia] propaganda machinery which is a vital part of President Milosevic's control mechanism.[32]

Freytag's statement contained an intriguing warning that few in the media acknowledged at the time: that the US military (in this case, acting under the cloak of NATO legitimacy) was prepared to destroy media facilities and kill media workers specifically on the grounds that their 'version of the news' was not acceptable. This is the moment that the US became a leading threat to media workers and constituted an explicit rejection of NATO's legal obligations under the Geneva Conventions to protect civilians and civilian facilities. That *RTS* journalists and other media workers at the broadcaster were working under tight control of the Slobodan Milosevic regime is rarely disputed, and there is ample evidence that many of their broadcasts in the Milosevic years were distorted to be nationalistic and to stir ethnocentric and patriotic passions in their audience. Broadcasters around the world routinely provide a similar ideological framing of the 'news' they present, but never before had a distant country unilaterally determined to destroy the major media organisation of another country on the grounds that it reflected the views of those who fund or operate it.

Controversial NATO spokesman Shea had prepared a further defence of the attack on the broadcaster in case journalists asked him about it, which they did. He claimed:

> Radio Television Serbia probably bears as much responsibility, if not more, than the Serb forces themselves, for the chaos and mayhem

that we have witnessed in Yugoslavia since 1991. It has been largely responsible for inciting the nationalism, creating an environment of tolerance for barbarity that has allowed the forces then to go in and do their work, depressingly, sometimes, with the support or at least the ignorance of the Serb people themselves.

Shea adopts here, on behalf of NATO, an intriguing 'magic bullet' perspective on mass communications – one communications research had proven invalid and discarded decades earlier – assuming populations to be passive, even 'ignorant', victims of manipulation by whatever messages are beamed at them. A *United Press International* (*UPI*) reporter, questioning Shea the day after the *RTS* bombing, reminded him that NATO had retracted the warning to bomb *RTS* the day after it was issued. Shea replied:

> What happened earlier on at NATO is we made it clear that NATO was not striking the media because it was the media. I wanted to clear up a perception. We had nothing against the media. But RTS is not media. It's full of government employees who are paid to produce propaganda and lies. To call it 'media' is totally misleading. Its function is not to produce news and information, its function is to incite hatred and to distort reality – not to reflect reality, but to distort it. And therefore, we see that as a military target. It is the same thing as a military propaganda machine integrated into the armed forces. We would never target legitimate, free media. Let me make that point clear. But please – and I'm sure you're not doing this – do not confuse RTS with CNN Center in Atlanta, or BBC Millbank House, or La Maison de la Radio in Paris. They don't have anything in common.

When asked by journalists to explain the attack, another Pentagon spokesperson at the time, Kenneth Bacon, defended it by saying:

> Serb TV is as much a part of Milosevic's murder machine as his military is [...] It has stirred up nationalist passions in the country, it has misreported what's going on in a way that has, I think, made it extremely impossible [...] for the Serb people to grasp the full magnitude of the problem in Kosovo.[33]

And as with the explanation from NATO's Colonel Freytag, Shea made it clear that NATO was prepared unilaterally to judge whether or not media were 'legitimate', and attack with deadly force any that fell short of their standard. Shea would elaborate:

> Radio Television Serbia, despite the appearance, is an instrument of war. It's as much an integrated part of Milosevic's war machine as the MUP or the VJ (Interior Ministry Police and Army) or the paramilitaries or anything else. It may call itself a media, but it has nothing to do with journalism in the way that you or I would recognize that. In fact, the Democrats in Serbia a couple of years ago used to refer to it as RTS/TV Bastille, and they even organized demonstrations outside it and pelted it with eggs, and so on, and even tried to, as you recall, during the major demonstrations against Milosevic some time ago, tried to drown out its broadcast by banging pots and pans outside to drown out the evening news. But this television, even before Kosovo, was directly responsible back in 1991 for calling Croats 'Ustashis' and presenting an image that Serbs inside Croatia were about to be faced with massacres, and inciting the type of conditions that led directly to the destruction of Vukovar and the shelling of Dubrovnik. So this, therefore, for us is a military target, first and foremost, and a legitimate military target. Without RTS, the ethnic violence of Serbia would probably have not occurred, or would not have occurred in the same major way that it has.[34]

The US media quietly accepted the NATO argument and focused their attention on the technicalities of which NATO planes were flying and what the alliance planned to do next. Chrystyna Lapychak, the Eastern Europe director for the CPJ, presciently cautioned that the incident 'could permanently jeopardize journalists covering conflicts all over the world'.[35] In the aftermath of its most deadly and devastating attack on a media installation to date, the official US government justification could be summarised as the perception that the content of *RTS*'s news broadcasts was nationalistic and inaccurate. In the history of modern mass media, there are few incidents of media suppression as violent or ruthless, or so broadly targeted at anyone affiliated with a particular media organisation, whether journalist, technician, or office cleaner.

The US may have killed two more media workers in the Kosovo campaign two weeks later, when it bombed the Chinese Embassy in Belgrade, apparently, according to US authorities, as a result of using outdated maps in its targeting process. The Chinese media reported that two of the three people reported to have been killed were journalists, but information linking them to any media outlet was sparse.[36] Some Western reports, based on interviews with NATO officials, suggested they were intelligence officers. Reports emerged years later that the attack on the embassy was, in fact, deliberate, and either designed to kill Milosevic himself or destroy communication facilities alleged to be housed at China's embassy.[37]

October–November 2001
In early October 2001, less than a month after 9/11, the US government began an aerial bombardment of Afghanistan. In Kandahar, the country's second-largest city, *Al Jazeera* had established a bureau that it shared with local staff working for *CNN* at the time US bombs and missiles began to rain down on the city. On 19 October that shared media bureau was hit by one of the US aerial bombings. It was the first US military attack on a media installation since launching missiles at the Serbia public broadcaster two years earlier. After hearing from their Kandahar staff, a *CNN* reporter in Pakistan wrote: 'The CNN workplace was among the locations damaged during the continuing U.S.-led attacks. People there – including employees of CNN and the Arabic-language TV station Al Jazeera – were not injured, but the building was heavily damaged.'[38]

Apart from *CNN*'s brief mention, the news media took no notice of the attack on a media facility. Three weeks later, on 13 November 2001, the *BBC*'s World Service radio correspondent, William Reeve, had just reopened the Kabul office for the *BBC* when a US missile struck a building about 50 metres away, nearly killing Reeve and his cameraman.[39] Reeve was broadcasting globally on the *BBC* at the time, and so his presence in the *BBC*'s bureau would not have been a secret to US military planners. Four hours later, two US missiles struck the office and residential housing of *Al Jazeera* in Kabul, a short distance from the *BBC* bureau. The bombing of the Kabul *Al Jazeera* office happened a few hours before the takeover of Kabul by the US sponsored and directed 'Northern Alliance' forces.

Troops affiliated with the Northern Alliance found and assaulted *Al Jazeera*'s Kabul correspondent, Tayseer Allouni, who was later reported to be deeply traumatised upon his release.[40] A *Guardian* reporter wrote that at *Al Jazeera* 'two supposedly smart US bombs hit its office in Kabul and many suspect the attack was no accident. It happened at a strategic moment, just two hours before the Northern Alliance took over the city'.[41] *Al Jazeera* editor-in-chief Ibrahim Helal told Gowing that many of the major international television organisations operating in Kabul at the time used, or were about to use, the *Al Jazeera* office as a feed point (a location from which to send television stories via satellite to their newsrooms, as described above in the case of *RTS* in Belgrade in 1999).[42] These included *CNN*, *ARD*, *ZDF*, *ABC Australia* and *Reuters Television*. Helal said *CNN* was about to begin sharing the bureau with *Al Jazeera*. So the US strike occurred immediately before *CNN* gained a permanent presence and the ability – through *Al Jazeera*'s facilities – to easily provide the US audience with interviews with the (fleeing) Taliban government or images of the conduct of US troops, and their proxies, in Kabul, just as the bombing of *CNN*'s shared bureau in Kandahar had done three weeks earlier.

US Navy Admiral Craig Quigley, one of the key proponents of official US indifference towards journalists' safety,[43] told a Pentagon press conference two days after the Kabul bombing that it was not deliberate, and that 'a weapon went awry'.[44] He neither confirmed nor denied that the US military knew the locations of media installations in Kabul. But, at about the same time, a different arm of the US military provided a different story. Colonel Rich Thomas from the US Central Command told *CBS* that the *Al Jazeera* building was 'a known al Qaida [sic] facility in central Kabul [...] We had no indications this or any nearby facility was used by al-Jazeera. We had identified two locations in Kabul where al-Jazeera people worked, and this location wasn't among them'.[45] This contradicted both Quigley's assertion that the bombing was a mistake, and that those dropping the bombs took no notice of where media were located. Quigley would later tell the media that *Al Jazeera* in Kabul had been targeted because it had 'repeatedly been the location of significant Al-Qaeda activity'.[46] That activity, of course, consisted of interviews this news organisation was conducting with the main newsmakers in Afghanistan. As Gowing would later put it:

> The building that was used by *Al Jazeera* had been their office for twenty months. It had satellite dishes. American planes flying around and American human intelligence on the ground would have known precisely what was happening inside that building because they didn't hide the fact that they were a news organisation.[47]

And television correspondent Rageh Omaar was convinced the bombing of *Al Jazeera* in Kabul was deliberate, stating that *Al Jazeera* was warned by the US government and the bombing followed soon after.[48] Mohamed Jasem al-Ali, then *Al Jazeera*'s managing director, told the *Guardian*:

We had put cameras on the roof to cover the whole of Kabul when the Northern Alliance took over [...] Later, we sent a letter to the Pentagon asking why they bombed our office and we got a funny reply saying they didn't know al-Jazeera had an office in Kabul. For the whole war, they knew it was there. It was the only source of information except for the CIA.[49]

But we know from Pulitzer Prize winning US investigative journalist Ron Suskind's research that US intelligence officials and the US administration were very aware of *Al Jazeera*, and revelations by *WikiLeaks* would later verify this: according to the *New York Times*, US diplomatic cables revealed by *WikiLeaks* reported *Al Jazeera* managing director Wadah Khanfar telling US officials in 2005 that he had altered *Al Jazeera* reporting at their request. The cable reportedly stated that a US Embassy official in Doha 'handed Mr. Khanfar copies of critical reports by the United States Defense Intelligence Agency on three months of *Al Jazeera*'s coverage of the Iraq war'.[50] Khanfar's cooperation with the US was widely connected with his resignation from his post at *Al Jazeera* in 2011.

Suskind added a new dimension to the story of the *Al Jazeera* attack in his 2006 book, *The One Percent Doctrine*. Suskind, who had extraordinarily close access to senior Pentagon, CIA and White House officials, reported that after President George W. Bush and CIA director George Tenet failed to convince the Emir of Qatar, Sheikh Hamad bin Khalifa Al Thani, to intervene in the editorial policies of *Al Jazeera* in early October 2001, the CIA began to consider ways to silence the channel's reporting. Suskind writes that CIA Executive Director 'Buzzy' Krongard – the third highest ranking official in the agency – explained, with regard to *Al Jazeera*, 'it came down to a principle you'd hear again and again over the next few years about the Arab world. *Talk to them in a way they understand*' (italics in the original).[51] Suskind wrote that following the bombing of *Al Jazeera* in Kabul – and here his sources are unclear – 'Inside the CIA, and White House, there was satisfaction that a message had been sent to Al Jazeera'. Suskind, asked about the allegation on *CNN*, reiterated 'My sources are clear that that was done on purpose, precisely to send a message to *Al Jazeera*, and essentially a message was sent. ... There was great anger at *Al Jazeera* at this point. We [the US] were pulling our hair out. We thought they were a mouthpiece for bin Laden. And we acted'.[52]

In June 2002, the CIA and White House had reason to believe the attack on *Al Jazeera* had borne results. *Al Jazeera* journalist Yosri Fouda had been invited by senior Al Qaeda figures to interview them at a secret location;[53] they included Khalid Sheikh Mohammed, the individual identified as 'the principal architect of the 9/11 attacks' by the US government's 9/11 Commission report, and who, when later facing US torture at their Guantanamo Bay prison, would be reported to have confessed to organising just about every Al Qaeda-linked 'terrorist' activity in the previous decade. Al Qaeda sought to influence the manner in which the story of the one-year anniversary of 9/11 would be told in the international media. Fouda's intriguing account of the meeting can be found in his book *Masterminds of Terror*, written with British newspaper journalist Nick Fielding.[54]

According to Suskind, Fouda told his bosses at *Al Jazeera* about the Al Qaeda meeting for the first time in mid-June, and they referred it up the company's chain of command to *Al Jazeera*'s chairman, Sheikh Hamad bin Thamer Al Thani, the Emir's cousin. A few days later CIA Director George Tenet reported the full contents of Fouda's meeting with the *Al Jazeera* chairman to colleagues at the CIA, suggesting the Al Thani family understood that journalists at the Qatar-based television network would be treated as enemies of the US and attacked again if they failed to collaborate with the US.[55] Suskind asks rhetorically if Qatar's Emir was 'attempting to curry favour in spite of the fact that his station's office in Kabul was destroyed, or because of it? Did a show of force, in this case, produce a desired result?', and concludes 'Those who believe in the primacy of force said yes'.[56] Suskind says nobody in *Al Jazeera*'s management knew the Emir would provide Fouda's story to the CIA prior to its broadcast, if, as Suskind suggests, that is what happened.

The journalist Yosri Fouda had effectively become a CIA informant against his will, and turned from neutral journalist to spy without his knowledge or consent. However, when he co-authored his book with Fielding in 2003, Fouda believed that US intelligence had been kept in the dark until his interview was broadcast. He wrote 'until the interviews were published and Al-Jazeera Channel began running previews to Fouda's documentary, which was shown on 12 September 2002, US intelligence had little idea about the planning behind the 11 September attacks'.[57] Suskind would later explain that *Al Jazeera* was 'exercising traditional journalistic effort and sending that product out in way that is shaping hearts and minds throughout south Asia and the Gulf and the Middle East [...] and this was something the US government was unsettled by'.[58]

March 2003

By the start of 2003, the Bush administration was determined to invade Iraq, for reasons that remain obscure to this day. The public case for war – despite the lack of international support – was made to positive reviews from US and international commentators by the US Secretary of State, Colin Powell, in a speech to the United Nations Security Council on 5 February 2003. Powell would later call the largely discredited speech 'a blot on his record' that is 'painful now', and the aid who helped him prepare the speech would call it 'a hoax on the American people'.[59]

The first reporters to be killed as a result of the US invasion of Iraq were killed by US troops only a day into the war. At the outset of the invasion some international journalists decided to ignore the US warnings not to operate independently in Iraq. As US forces began to enter Iraq from Saudi Arabia in the south and from Turkey in the north, television correspondents who were not prepared to passively accept US government demands to 'embed' with the troops (as most of the US media did) sought ways to report the invasion safely, from within Iraq, but without official dependence on US forces. The *BBC*'s senior correspondent John Simpson sought to enter Iraq from the north, tagging along unofficially with US Special Forces until it seemed safe to move independently of them.

One of *ITN*'s most experienced correspondents, Terry Lloyd, entered Iraq on 22 March 2003 from the south, near Basra, along with French cameraman Fred Nérac, Belgian cameraman Daniel Demoustier and Lebanese interpreter Hussein Othman. Lloyd and his crew anticipated that marking their vehicles with the large, universally recognised, letters 'TV' would offer sufficient protection should they encounter fighting. The decision to proceed unilaterally into Iraq seems to have been driven by Lloyd, but had the reluctant agreement of his newsroom in London. Lloyd and his team encountered retreating Iraqi forces and turned their vehicles to head for the safety of advancing US tanks, when their vehicles were fired upon (whether US or Iraqi forces fired first remains unclear). Lloyd was wounded and placed by an Iraqi civilian in a makeshift civilian ambulance to be taken to an Iraqi hospital along with other wounded people. US troops then fired on that vehicle and shot Lloyd in the head, killing him. Fred Nérac and Hussein Othman were also killed in the incident, although Nérac's body has never been found. Daniel Demoustier survived.[60] Also at the start of the war, on 29 March and just before the more deadly attack which killed Lloyd, a four-person *Al Jazeera* crew in Basra was fired on by British tanks while they were filming Iraqi officials distributing food, and the IFJ and Reporters Sans Frontières reported that an *Al Jazeera* cameraman was detained by US troops for twelve hours.[61]

Investigators sent to Iraq by *ITN* spoke with US marines who admitted firing on Lloyd and his crew, and who also stated that no military investigators had spoken with them, despite a US military commitment to investigate.[62] The US soldiers recalled opening fire on cars marked 'TV'.[63] Journalist Barbara Jones was also attempting to report unilaterally inside Iraq at the start of the invasion and recalled how, 'on the third day of the war I came across this terrible situation where the *ITN* correspondent, Terry Lloyd, had been [...] caught in the crossfire and they'd shot the jerry cans on the top of his car and the whole thing had gone up in flames'.[64] One experienced former *BBC* journalist told me that 'Terry Lloyd got killed because he was in a place he shouldn't have been [...] you are going to have to make compromises. [The] *BBC* wouldn't have gone there'.[65] A colleague would later recount that Lloyd was determined to be on the frontlines of conflicts, and would say 'The only thing worse than being asked to cover a war is not being asked'.[66]

Ten years on from that killing, a sincere, compassionate US Marine veteran, Vince Hogan, sat in a Norfolk, Virginia coffee shop with the eldest daughter of Terry Lloyd in an encounter contrived for an *ITN* programme about Lloyd's death and her search for comfort. The soldier, who claimed to have ordered the machine gun blasts that killed Lloyd and his colleagues, told *ITN* reporter Mark Austin that of many 'engagements' in Iraq, this was the one that continued to haunt him. But he insisted 'I don't think anybody has any blame [...] it was a very unfortunate set of circumstances'.[67] Lloyd's death was the subject of an official investigation in the UK by a coroner's inquest, which would eventually record a verdict of 'unlawful killing'. But prosecution of Hogan and his tank crew was never likely, despite the fact that the purpose of such a verdict is to enable justice to progress, and prosecutions to take place; it is, according to the *BBC*, 'the strongest verdict a coroner can record', noting that it 'carries the same weight as that of a criminal court'.[68] A British military investigator told the hearing that the US military provided the British government with edited videotape taken by a camera operator working with the US tank crew (reports do not indicate if this was a military or civilian camera operator). The version provided by the US contained no footage of the shooting of Lloyd's team, instead only showing US troops looking at his wrecked vehicle after the incident. The *BBC* report on Lloyd's inquest raised the possibility that video footage of the incident may have been cut before being handed to the British authorities:

> The footage shown to the court was taken by a cameraman attached to the tank unit which is alleged to have fired on Mr Lloyd's convoy and it was given to the Royal Military Police by American authorities some months after the incident. A forensic video expert, who looked at a tape, estimated that 15 minutes of film may have been cut from the beginning. Major Kay Roberts, of the Royal Military Police, said she was told by the Americans the footage they handed over was 'everything that they had'.[69]

According to Austin, Hogan, who had not previously spoken publicly about the incident and who had refused, with US government support, to testify to the UK coroner's hearing, 'insisted he had no knowledge of any of his men firing on the makeshift ambulance that had come in to pick up Terry. No knowledge of the bullet that killed him'. The meeting, at least superficially and before *ITN*'s cameras, seemed to bring some comfort to Lloyd's daughter, comfort she'd been denied for a decade. She told Austin of Hogan, 'He was a good man, a nice man [...] and I think I know why he did what he did'.[70]

The US attack on Baghdad began in March 2003, with an intensive aerial bombardment. Hundreds of journalists from around the world hunkered down in two Baghdad hotels through each night as the missiles exploded around them. Human Rights Watch, in a later investigation, found that the US had attacked three media facilities: the Iraqi government's Ministry of Information, the *Baghdad Television* Studio and Broadcast Facility, and the Abu Ghraib Television Antennae Broadcast Facility. Human Rights Watch concluded, to the credit of the US military, that 'special care seems to have been taken to avoid civilian casualties when attacking the Ministry of Information, [while] the latter two facilities were completely destroyed. There were no recorded civilian casualties as a result of any of these attacks.'[71]

In an echo of the 1999 attack on the Serbian broadcaster, the Human Rights Watch investigators concluded that 'The U.S. targeting of the television broadcast capabilities of Iraq appears to have been aimed at denying Saddam Hussein and his government the ability to broadcast official statements on television', but added that 'The Iraqi authorities, like the Serbian authorities before them, maintained television broadcasts by using mobile assets and redundant broadcast capabilities'.[72] The (lack of) legality of such attacks is addressed in Chapter 5.

As had been the case in Belgrade, the attack on the public broadcaster in Baghdad appeared to be more than just the cautious elimination of a potential means of communication by the enemy, for the international news media had located cameras and satellite equipment there, much of which was destroyed in the US attack, probably including unmanned cameras left by *CNN* to provide live images of the US bombing.[73] Not imagining the further attacks on the media facilities to come just over a week later, the secretary-general of Reporters Sans Frontières warned that the US 'should not give the impression of routinely targeting media that oppose it'.[74]

At the end of March 2003 then, US bombs and missiles were destroying national broadcasting facilities in Baghdad, just as they had done four years earlier in Serbia immediately prior to the killing of many Serbian media workers.[75] About 500 foreign journalists and media staff had gathered in Baghdad at the start of the US bombing campaign, and about a thousand more were withdrawn by their companies just before the bombing began. According to senior *Reuters* journalist Samia Nakhoul, who was one of those who stayed in order to facilitate the very flow of news which allowed other media to leave, 'among those who left were US television networks [with] some of their staffers saying they had received explicit warning from the Pentagon that no target was off-limits'. The Pentagon provided no clear indications to the media at the time regarding what they considered to be a 'target', but the message to media workers following the bombing of media facilities in Serbia and Afghanistan should have been clear. The veteran *BBC* journalist Kate Adie told an interviewer that US forces threatened to launch missiles at any media institution transmitting information out of Baghdad.[76] On 19 March, *Reuters* managers decided that the hotel where their bureau was based, along with dozens of other journalists, was likely to be too close to the US bombs and moved everyone to the Palestine Hotel.

It would emerge years later that, during the run-up to the bombing and invasion, US Army intelligence analysts at Fort Gordon, Georgia, in the US, were listening to private satellite telephone conversations emanating from Iraq, regardless of whether the conversations were between civilians, and regardless – in contravention of US law – of whether either of the people being listened to were US citizens.[77] These included the conversations of 'humanitarian aid organizations, non-governmental organizations, who include the International Red Cross, Red Crescent, Doctors Without Borders, a whole host of humanitarian aid organizations [...] it also included journalists.' One of those analysts, Army Sergeant Adrienne Kinne, would later explain that despite knowing the law and protesting to superiors when she suspected it was being broken, she was ordered to continue to listen to the conversations involving US citizens 'just in case'.[78] It was at this time that Kinne recalls noting the presence of hundreds of journalists in the Palestine Hotel – she was listening to their conversations with their offices and families – and she recalled seeing the Palestine Hotel on a list of possible targets to be bombed.[79] She would tell US journalist Amy Goodman:

> One of the instances was the fact that we were listening to journalists who were staying in the Palestine Hotel. And I remember that, specifically because during the build up to Shock and Awe, which people in my unit were really disturbingly excited about, we were given a list of potential targets in Baghdad, and the Palestine Hotel was listed as a potential target. And I remember this specifically, because, putting one and one together, that there were journalists staying at the Palestine Hotel and this hotel was listed as a potential target, I went to my officer in charge, and I told him that there are journalists staying at this hotel who think they're safe, and yet we have this hotel listed as a potential target, and somehow the dots are not being connected here, and shouldn't we make an effort to make sure that the right people know the situation? And unfortunately, my officer in charge, similarly to any time I raised concerns about things that we were collecting or intelligence that we were reporting, basically told me that it was not my job to analyze. It was my job to collect and pass on information and that someone somewhere higher up the chain knew what they were doing. [...] the only reason now that I really remember that specific email is because I knew, having listened to journalists staying at the Palestine Hotel, talking with their families and loved ones and talking about whether or not they were safe and trying to reassure their family and co-workers and loved ones that they were safe, when I saw that hotel listed, I thought there was something that was going terribly wrong.[80]

According to news agencies, the Spanish Defence Ministry told Spanish journalists that the Palestine Hotel was designated as a military target two days before it was struck. When British Defence Secretary Jack Straw was asked by journalists about that report, he said it was 'extremely unlikely' that the Palestine was designated as a target in advance, but that he would look into it.[81]

April 2003

In April 2003, US forces rolled into Baghdad and soon gave journalists around the world reason to believe that they were under orders to systematically eliminate witnesses to their actions. That, of course, was not the case, and at least some of the tragic hostility towards journalists which took place in that month can clearly be attributed to US military negligence rather than deliberate aggression (which raises the question to be discussed in Chapter 5 of whether negligence absolves a government of responsibility). The extent to which there was an element of deliberate targeting in other attacks on journalists during this deadly month remains an open, nagging, question.

On the morning of 6 April, *Al Jazeera* prepared for a routine live report from the roof of their Baghdad bureau, to update the channel's viewers on the progress of the US troops beginning to enter the city. Robert Fisk claims to have warned *Al Jazeera* correspondent, Tareq Ayoub 'how easy a target his Baghdad office would make if the Americans wanted to destroy its coverage – seen across the Arab world – of civilian victims of the bombing',[82] but the *Al Jazeera* team felt some security in the knowledge that their headquarters had gone to great lengths to ensure the Pentagon knew the exact coordinates of their bureau, in order to ensure there would be no repeat of the attack in Kabul. Omar al-Issawi, *Al Jazeera*'s correspondent in Doha, Qatar, said the network gave the GPS location coordinates of its Baghdad bureau to the Pentagon two months earlier to protect itself against just such a scenario: 'The letter was addressed from our managing editor to Victoria Clarke at the Department of Defense', al-Issawi told Larry King.[83] The night before the attack, *Al Jazeera* spoke to US State Department official Nabeel Khoury in Doha, who promised that the bureau 'was safe and would not be targeted'.[84] As they began their satellite transmission on that morning, two US missiles struck them, killing their correspondent, Tariq Ayoub, and injuring their cameraman. Minutes later, another US missile struck the offices of another Arab satellite broadcaster, *Abu Dhabi Television*. Their staff had sought shelter away from the bureau and were not injured.[85] US tanks fired repeatedly and directly at cameras mounted on *Abu Dhabi Television*'s well marked building until they were destroyed.[86]

Just a few hours later, as many of the journalists who had set up their news gathering bases in Baghdad's Palestine Hotel gathered by its windows overlooking the Tigris River, a few US tanks rumbled along the opposite river bank and turned on to a bridge some distance from the hotel. As several television photographers recorded the scene, and others described it by telephone to their newsrooms back home, the first of the tanks aimed its gun towards the hotel, waited a few minutes, and then fired a shell into the hotel, devastating the *Reuters* news agency's Baghdad bureau and killing two television photographers, including *Reuters* cameraman Taras Protsyuk, who had survived the reporting of wars in Bosnia, Chechnya, Afghanistan and Kosovo. Many other journalists were seriously wounded, including three other *Reuters* staff. The killing of Protsyuk and Spanish cameraman José Couso, was described in detail by veteran journalists – dozens of whom were present – and has been the subject of a long-running effort by *Reuters* and the journalists' families to hold the US military to account.

The soldier who fired the shell would later tell the media 'We did not know that they had reporters in the Palestine Hotel. If we would have known that, we would not have fired a round over there. I don't even know if that information was given to the US Army. I do not know that. OK? If it was, it didn't get down to my level'. But US Secretary of State Colin Powell would later say, on a visit to Spain in May 2003, 'We knew about the hotel. We knew that it was a hotel where journalists were located, and others, and it is for that reason it was not attacked during any phase of the aerial campaign'.[87] As with every other incident involving journalists, the US military exonerated itself in a subsequent investigation, although they offered at least three differing accounts of what happened in the months following the incident, including frequent assertions that Iraqi soldiers were firing at US troops from the hotel.

Several non-military investigations have been conducted since, and each has condemned the military explanations as farcical.[88] Several have said that the main fault lay not with the tank crew who killed the journalists, but with the upper levels of command, who failed to pass on their knowledge that the hotel was a media centre. Despite early military claims to the contrary, none of the hundreds of professional journalists in the vicinity, nor local people interviewed by organisations investigating what happened that day, accepted that there was any threat to the US military anywhere in the vicinity of the media installations that were attacked. A French television reporter told *Interpress*: 'I was at the Palestine

Hotel at the moment of the attack, around one pm, Baghdad time, and my crew filmed everything ... Our film shows that the U.S. tank took its time at targeting the 14th floor of the hotel, where many journalists are hosted, at a moment of complete calm.'[89]

Spanish reporter Olga Rodriguez, present at the Hotel Palestine subsequently explained:

I talked with Spain by phone, and my boss said to me, 'The Pentagon has recognized that it was an American attack.' And I couldn't believe it, because I knew that they knew that that hotel, as everybody in the world knew, that hotel was the place in which were living 200 journalists from Europe, from America, and they were not far away. They didn't arrive ten minutes before the attack. They were there before, 36 hours before. They knew exactly where the Palestine Hotel was, even from the bridge. They could – you can go to the bridge in Baghdad, and you can see Palestine Hotel in English in the building.[90]

David Chater, of the UK's *Sky News*, reported to his audience at the time:

They knew exactly what this hotel is. They know the press corps is here. I don't know why they are trying to target journalists. There are awful scenes around me. There's a Reuters tent just a few yards away from me where people are in tears. It makes you realize how vulnerable you are. What are we supposed to do? How are we supposed to carry on if American shells are targeting Western journalists?[91]

Robert Fisk observed that the immediate US government response to the shelling of the Palestine Hotel came from US Army General Buford Blount of the US 3rd Infantry Division – the officer in overall command of the tanks that fired on the *Reuters* Baghdad bureau in the hotel. Blount claimed the tanks came under rocket and rifle fire from the hotel – a claim every civilian witness has denied and every investigation has shown to be false. Fisk was present between the tanks and the hotel and heard no shooting; he charged that 'For General Blount to suggest, as he clearly does, that the *Reuters* camera crew was in some way involved in shooting at Americans merely turns a meretricious statement into a libellous one'. But Fisk suggests something deeper and perhaps more sinister in Blount's explanation: that his 'explanation was the kind employed by the Israelis after they have killed the innocent'. Journalists hung white sheets from the hotel balcony the next day in the hope of deterring further attack.

We might ask if it is significant that it was one of just a few reporters who were risking their lives daily during the US bombardment of Baghdad to speak to the injured and understand who the victims actually were – as opposed to who the US military said they were – who was attacked in the shelling of the *Reuters* bureau at the Palestine Hotel. Samia Nakhoul had written eloquently and passionately of the horror she was witnessing daily before a US tank shell ended her reporting with serious injuries.[92] Her story about Ali Abbas Ismaeel, a young boy who lost his family and was crippled when the US bombed their home, was an especially powerful example; and it ended with a quote from a Baghdad doctor overwhelmed with the volume of civilian casualties: 'War should be against the military. America is killing civilians'. Her story was transmitted to the world's media by *Reuters* early on 8 April 2003. The following day Nakhoul was receiving requests by email from people asking how to help Ali. But she never got the chance to pass on those offers to the desperately injured boy (Ali would go on to receive far more media attention and accept UK citizenship). Nakhoul wrote later, reflecting on all she and her colleagues had survived covering wars in Congo, Afghanistan and the Balkans:

> Why had this happened now, I kept on repeating in my mind. We were not on the streets but in our office, in a hotel known to the world as the Baghdad headquarters of the international media. It was from there, morning and night, that journalists broadcast their accounts of the war to millions of homes around the globe.[93]

Even the US news agencies and broadcasters had publicly pointed to the hotel as the main base for journalists in Baghdad, as in this *UPI* story about a US citizen and others who had volunteered to go to Baghdad to deter the bombing of civilians: 'In the weeks before the war, the group lived two to a room at the Palestine Hotel, where journalists are housed'.[94] On the same day *CNN* reported on the US bombing of central Baghdad, noting it was just several hundred metres away from the Palestine Hotel where journalists were staying.[95] On 7 April, the day before the attack, Saddam Hussein's information minister Mohammed Saeed al-Sahhaf, who had been ridiculed for weeks in the Western press, put in a final appearance – coming for the first time to the Palestine Hotel to meet with journalists, claiming it was too dangerous for them to travel to the Information

Ministry, which by that time had been bombed and may have been in US hands.[96]

Following the killing of the three journalists in Baghdad, officials in the Pentagon, who refused to be named, provided the media with a set of questions to ask themselves, in an apparent effort to shift the blame for the attack to its victims. According to *UPI* – the only news agency I could find that would distribute the questions – the Pentagon, saying 'There are questions that news media organizations must answer as well' asked:

What were the reporters doing at that particular hotel in Baghdad in the first place? Were they invited or advised to be there by the Iraqi government?

If there was an Iraqi military presence in the building, were they aware of it or were they used as unwitting human shields?

Did they understand the risks of being in the Iraqi capital when they accepted the assignment?

Do they think their presence on the urban battlefield should garner more or less caution on the part of US military commanders than that of an average Iraqi civilian?

Should this incident be investigated as a higher or lower priority for the military because of the involvement of journalists?

Do journalists or should journalists expect a measure of protection on the battlefield from both sides in a conflict?[97]

Also at the start of April, a *BBC* employee was killed by US forces in Northern Iraq as he assisted a *BBC* television crew that was accompanying US troops. Kamaran Abdurazaq Muhamed was a young Kurdish translator who had been working for the *BBC* since March. He died when US planes bombed the convoy consisting of US Special Forces, Kurdish fighters supporting the US, and the *BBC*. The attack was attributed to poor communication between the various US forces.

2003 continued as a tragic year for *Reuters*. Before the story of torture by US soldiers at the Abu Ghraib prison in Baghdad became a major embarrassment for the US in 2004, it was occasionally the site of insurgent attacks. Following an attack in August, as one of *Reuters*' most experienced videographers, Mazen Dana, recorded images outside the prison (just after speaking with US troops) the gunner on a US tank aimed at him and fired, killing him. The incident is described further in Chapter 4.

2004

Several *Al Jazeera* and *Al Arabiya* television journalists have been killed by US forces in well-documented incidents. Given the massive amount of angry rhetoric from US officials, especially former Secretary of State Colin Powell and Defense Secretary Donald Rumsfeld, condemning the work of these networks as enemy propaganda, the attacks on their journalists and facilities are viewed with great suspicion by many in the media.[98]

In March 2004, three media workers from *Al Arabiya* were reported to have been killed by US troops near a US military checkpoint, while attempting to undertake their work. Two were journalists, while one was their driver. The US military would later claim it followed its own rules of engagement and had done nothing wrong.

By April 2004 things had gone so badly wrong for the US military in Iraq that a *USA Today* commissioned opinion poll found that 82 per cent of Baghdad residents saw US forces as occupiers as opposed to 'liberators'.[99] That statistic was referenced in a scathing commentary about the US presence in Iraq by veteran British television correspondent Julian Manyon. Manyon concluded his article by noting the death, as a result of US military action, of one of his sources for the story. He wrote: 'The views that I have expressed in the last few lines, though I subscribe to them wholeheartedly, are those of Dr Gailan Ramiz, the distinguished Iraqi political scientist. Unfortunately Dr Ramiz is no longer able to express them for himself, as he was recently killed.'

The killing of the 71-year-old professor, a prominent academic source for journalists and author of occasional commentaries for the Western press (including the *New York Times*),[100] suggests the incompleteness of the present analysis: while it may be possible to closely approximate the extent of US involvement in the deaths of professional journalists and some of those directly employed by them, it is ultimately their sources who matter as much, for there is no journalism without sources. Here is one prominent instance of a civilian, non-combatant source for numerous journalists who was killed due to US military action. The deaths of ten people alongside two *Reuters* journalists in 2007, documented by the 'Collateral Murder' video reproduced on the cover of this book, is perhaps another case. Any reading of the vast range of recollections of journalistic work in Iraq suggests there are many such cases, which, unlike the deaths of professional journalists, mostly pass with little accounting. Western journalists depended heavily and frequently on Ramiz, and so he was a rare exception.

Much has been written about the US military's attack on the Iraqi city of Fallujah in April 2004, and interpretations of what happened remain sharply polarised. For many in the US military and for right-wing commentators in the US, the battle was a challenging US victory that was both heroic and humane. For locals, and for the journalists who were able to tell their stories, it was anything but. The US military refused access to media representatives well before they launched their attack on the city.[101] One prominent embedded television photographer, Kevin Sites, was permitted to remain with the Marine unit to which he had been assigned, and accompany them into Fallujah. A few freelance journalists remained, while others wrote horrifying stories of what was happening there based on extensive interviews with refugees from the city. Such journalists included Rory McCarthy of the *Guardian*[102] and the Italian newspaper journalist Giuliana Sgrena, who would later be shot at by US forces (described later in this chapter). Various investigations, including those of Human Rights Watch and the International Committee of the Red Cross (ICRC), have confirmed violations of international law and human rights in the US attack.[103]

There are stories of journalists who did attempt to report from Fallujah during the attack finding themselves under attack from US forces. Some, including those from *Al Jazeera*, claim to have been deliberately and repeatedly targeted by the weapons of the US military. A local freelancer working for the US network *ABC* was fired on and killed by US troops as he stood with other journalists, and a local resident providing temporary accommodation to *Al Jazeera*'s team was also killed by US forces.[104]

Others were arrested while attempting to report, and later released far from where they needed to be to continue their reporting. One of those was Wael Essam, a young correspondent for the Saudi satellite television news service *Al Arabiya*. In a profile of the channel in the *New York Times* magazine, journalist Samantha Shapiro wrote of witnessing *Al Arabiya* staff learning of Essam's arrest, temporarily ending his reports from Fallujah. She writes that anxiety about the welfare of field staff was palpable in the *Al Arabiya* newsroom in late 2004; by that time the US military had killed three friends and colleagues of *Al Arabiya*'s journalists, and insurgents in Iraq had killed five and wounded many more.[105] A freelance journalist working for *Al Arabiya* in Fallujah at around the same time did not fare as well as Essam. The CPJ reported that reporter Abdel Kader Saadi, who was wearing a flak jacket identifying him as 'press', had been arrested by US troops and detained for at least a week after being ordered into a mosque by US troops.[106]

On 12 September 2004, US soldiers patrolling in the middle of Baghdad were fired upon, and more US forces in a Bradley armoured vehicle arrived to assist them. They were forced to abandon one of the vehicles as they left the area, and a crowd of Iraqis gathered around it, with some of them placing a banner associated with an insurgent group on the vehicle. As the crowd grew, television crews arrived. Soon after, two US military helicopters appeared overhead, one of which fired rockets and machine guns into the crowd. Thirteen people were killed, including *Al Arabiya* producer Mazen al-Tumeizi, whose death was captured on video as he reported from the scene. The grisly footage was shown frequently on his and other Arab networks, but had little exposure on Western television.[107]

On 1 November, US soldiers were fighting insurgents in the streets of Ramadi, Iraq. A lone freelance television photographer working for *Reuters Television*, Dhia Najim, had obtained pictures of the fighting. Najim was later found dead. The circumstances of his death remain controversial, but *Reuters* and independent press freedom organisations suggest he was shot in the back of the neck by a US sniper, while holding his camera. An unidentified spokesperson for the US Marines told the *New York Times* 'We did kill him [...] He was out with the bad guys. He was there with them, they attacked, and we fired back and hit him'.[108] *Reuters* disputed the US military account that he had been caught in fighting, since the footage on his camera showed the fighting had subsided when he was shot, and footage taken by another cameraman showed him being shot as he moved away from a sheltered position after fighting in the area had stopped.

2005

In August 2005 two *Reuters* journalists – a cameraman and a sound technician – were shot at by US troops after having gone to obtain pictures of a reported attack on a police convoy. In a report on the incident issued by the Pentagon years later, the military claimed the soldiers were right to fire at the journalists, since one of them had raised a small camera which troops assumed to be a weapon, and then they tried to drive slowly back upon realising they were in danger– as their *Reuters* safety training had taught them. Instead of disabling their car, the US soldiers shot the soundman in the head and injured his colleague. According to *Reuters* colleagues who arrived soon after to assist, the dead man's press identification cards – from *Reuters* and from the US military – were clearly visible, clipped to his shirt. A US officer told *Reuters*: 'They drove into fighting'. The badly injured cameraman was then arrested and held for a day before being allowed to receive treatment.[109] *Reuters* paid for an independent expert investigation into the shooting, which concluded 'the soldiers' use of force was neither proportionate nor justified'. The US military refused to reconsider its own conclusions that the soldiers had done wrong, and were unable to explain how a key piece of evidence, the video shot by the *Reuters* team, had disappeared in their custody.[110]

Many of the incidents involving killings or other attacks by US forces, including the missile attacks on media installations in Afghanistan, have happened soon after journalists communicated their precise location to the US military with the expectation of protection. This was again the case in one of the most high-profile incidents, in mid-2005. Italian newspaper journalist Giuliana Sgrena had been kidnapped and held by an unknown group for a month, soon after writing some of the most critical reports of US military actions to appear in any media. Her kidnapping silenced one of the leading critics of the US occupation. She was among the first, for example, to allege the US use of phosphorus shells in Fallujah, in violation of international bans on chemical weapons.

The Italian government negotiated her release, but while attempting to escort her to a waiting airplane at Baghdad airport, her car was fired upon at close range while approaching a US military roadblock on the airport road. The Italian government agent responsible for her release was killed, and she was seriously injured. The Italian government had been in communication with US military commanders in Baghdad before the incident, and did not accept US government explanations that the shooting was accidental, but they did not conclude that there had been a deliberate effort to assassinate Sgrena.[111]

2007

Two more *Reuters* news agency employees were killed in Iraq by the US military on 12 July 2007, and the details of the incident were hidden by the US military for several years. Video of the incident was among the first bits of information published by *WikiLeaks*, following the massive leak of US government information in 2010. The incident was well summarised by US media commentator Amy Goodman at a symposium in London:

This devastating video of an area of Baghdad called New Baghdad, where a group of men were showing around two Reuters journalists.

Well, one was a videographer, a young up-and-coming videographer named Namir Noor-Eldeen, and one was his driver, Saeed Chmagh. He was 40 years old. He was the father of four. And they were showing them around the area. The same Apache helicopter unit is hovering above. They open fire. The video is chilling. [...] The soldiers opened fire. You have the video of the target, and you have the audio of the sounds of the soldiers cursing, laughing – but not rogue, always going up the chain of command, asking for permission to open fire. In the first explosion, Namir Noor-Eldeen and the other men on the ground are killed. Saeed Chmagh, you can see him attempting to crawl away. And then a van pulls up from the neighborhood, and they're attempting to pick up the wounded. There are children in the van. And the Apache helicopter opens fire again, and Saeed Chmagh, others in the van are killed. Two little children are critically injured inside.[112]

In the ensuing debate about the 'Collateral Murder' revelations and the international condemnation of the US military which the careful packaging and publicity by *WikiLeaks* encouraged, there was little (if any) acknowledgement that the US press already knew about the incident and the callous, video-game mentality commentary of the Apache helicopter pilots who killed the *Reuters* journalists and ten other people near them, and had published a detailed account. The key difference, intriguingly, was that account presented the US military sympathetically to a sympathetic audience; the other simply used a neutral, journalistic language and the military video and audio itself (although with a clear mission to inspire international outrage). The first account was that of the US publisher Macmillan, which published a nearly complete transcript and narrative description of the helicopter gun camera video in *Washington Post* reporter David Finkel's acclaimed account of his period of embedded reporting with a US Army battalion in Baghdad in 2007.

Finkel watched the video and heard the audio, along with the soldiers in the battalion who responded on the ground after the Apache helicopter attack. His book was published in September 2009, and it was not until April 2010 that *WikiLeaks* unveiled the video, after working to decipher it and research its context.[113] This was presumed to have been a dramatic and strategic second release of information provided to *WikiLeaks* in 2010 from within the US military; the incident for which the young soldier Chelsea (formerly Bradley) Manning would eventually be arrested, tortured,[114] convicted and incarcerated for up to 35 years. Among the dozens of newspaper reviews of Finkel's book in the months after its release, there is no mention of his account of witnessing US troops killing civilian journalists.[115] For the US press, Finkel's gritty reporting of the challenging reality of life for US soldiers in Baghdad was *the* story.

The *Washington Post*, which had known the details of the killing of the *Reuters* journalists since the day it happened in 2007, curiously decided to report the story three years late under the headline 'U.S. gunfire kills two *Reuters* employees in Baghdad' only after the online publication of the Apache helicopter footage by *WikiLeaks* in 2010. It did so under Finkel's byline, and the story consisted only of an excerpt from Finkel's book.[116] While the *Post* was choosing not to report what it knew about this killing of journalists, managers at *Reuters*, which employed the two journalists, were struggling to obtain a copy of the military footage using the US Freedom of Information Act, but the Pentagon blocked those efforts.[117] *Reuters* journalists had to learn about the real horror of the deaths of their colleagues along with the rest of the world as they redistributed the video of their colleagues' murder, provided to them years later by *WikiLeaks*, not the Pentagon.

Part 2: Expansion of Anti-Press Violence

Journalist Deaths and the US: A Summation

The account in part 1 of this chapter describes some of the prominent cases of US military involvement in the deaths of journalists and destruction of media facilities, escalating gradually from an initial willingness to simply temporarily disable civilian broadcasting facilities suspected of inciting violence. But it could not address every known case. Appendix 1 provides a list of relevant cases, and is assembled from this author's compilation of reports on journalist casualties, a recent database completed by the IFJ, and lists compiled by the other major press freedom organisations that are generally based on their own extensive and independent investigations of each reported case. The following is a summary, which demonstrates why the US ranks among the leading predator nations with regard to the press and free expression in the last decade and half.

Approximately 48 journalists and media workers were killed by the US and US private contractors between 1999 and 2007. Approximately 24 of these were killed despite compelling evidence that the US military command structure was aware, prior to the attacks, that the places attacked housed civilian media workers; and/or multiple witnesses, confirmed that the media work was in plain view of those who killed them. Of twelve attacks on media facilities since 1999, responsible for 20 civilian deaths, in three of the prominent cases (*Al Jazeera* Kabul and Baghdad; Palestine Hotel) senior representatives of the US government have directly or indirectly acknowledged the attacks happened despite knowledge of the civilian media operations underway there.

In some, but not all, of the remaining cases, many media professionals and others have expressed the suspicion that these media workers were attacked because of their work, but the more credible explanation in almost every case is 'mistaken identity', although that terminology implies that US troops and allies in Iraq (such as private security firms and the Iraqi security forces) have consistently only fired their weapons at people who are proven, upon careful inspection, to be insurgents posing an immediate threat to them or to other civilians. But the record of violence in Iraq suggests that this common explanation is often overly generous, and that there has been a fundamental disregard for the right to life enjoyed by civilians under international humanitarian law; these media workers were innocent civilians whose lives were taken in the course of what many would regard as reckless military campaigns that have routinely failed to put the protection of innocent life ahead of military objectives (even if many individual soldiers have routinely done so). In his film *The War You Don't See*, Pilger reminds us that in World War I 10 per cent of casualties were civilian; in World War II 50 per cent were civilian; in Vietnam, the proportion of civilian casualties had risen to 70 per cent; and in the US war in Iraq 90 per cent of casualties were civilian.

Arrest and Torture

There is a widely held perception in the media, confirmed by limited evidence from the military itself, that among members of the US military (and more broadly, the militaries of Middle Eastern allies and partners Iraq, Afghanistan, Israel and Pakistan) a mindset persists whereby any person claiming to be conducting journalism should be viewed with suspicion and treated as an enemy. In both the private admissions of individual soldiers and in official statements, there is little evidence of recognition of the concept of the *neutral observer* or of a necessity for privileged and unfettered access to zones of warfare for news media. *BBC* journalist Nik Gowing told an audience: 'our experience is – and I have checked this with many of my colleagues before saying this publicly – that they [US soldiers] don't want us around even though we are there trying to bring you the images of what is happening in as accurate, balanced and as fair a way as possible.'[118]

The record of journalist casualties suggests that such suspicion, expressed on a scale ranging from distrust to extreme violence, has *escalated considerably* when the media worker in question appears to be from the Middle East or any number of Middle East-based media organisations. The suspicion *falls slightly* when the media worker collaborates with the military through acceptance into a programme of 'embedding'. In short, among US military forces involved in recent Middle East conflicts there appears to be a broad acceptance of a doctrine that:

- Ideally, there shall be no public reporting of military activity or witnessing of it;
- Where the acceptance of media witnesses is required, such witnesses should be controlled, coerced or exploited to the extent possible; and
- No witness can be neutral.

These beliefs are legacies of the Vietnam myth, ethnocentrism, ignorance about the normative social role of an independent press, and years of close collaboration with government by a monolithic and nationalistic US corporate media, as suggested in Chapter 2. There is no idealised age of respect of journalistic neutrality in wartime, just as there is no widespread track record among journalists of genuine neutrality, in the sense of dogged avoidance of a singular perspective in times of conflict (which inherently involves the clash of varying perspectives). The majority of conflict journalists have always reported from the perspectives of (a) their paymasters and (b) their audiences,[119] and tended to express widely varying concepts themselves of what neutrality means.

The belief that all journalism is *somebody's propaganda* – among some in the media itself and among governments and combatants of all stripes – has resulted in a substantial shift in how the battlefield journalist is perceived: from being separate from conflict to being always intrinsic to conflict, and to being, therefore, a legitimate rhetorical and actual target. Journalists cannot reclaim the mantle of objectivity, nor should they try, but they can, collectively, work to practice and defend 'neutrality', as the ability to have a perspective on the news while having a fully observational – witnessing – role and no actual involvement in the news. Many professional foreign journalists who have covered Iraq since 2003, and many in the Iraqi media itself, worked to practice just such a rigorously neutral form of information gathering, and many made dangerous enemies in doing so.[120] But the alternative – covering one side of a story exclusively for the purposes of promoting that side – turns the media worker into merely a publicist or propagandist, with no claim to either neutrality or journalism. Perhaps more crucially, this is ultimately a more dangerous strategy for all concerned, as it results in the loss of the only worthwhile defence: that of the neutral witness.

It is in the context of the broad acceptance of 'journalist' as propagandist at best, and enemy at worst, that extensive acceptance of, and impunity for, the widespread attacks of all kinds upon media workers becomes comprehensible. But an ideological hostility to journalists – and disregard for their non-combatant, witnessing role – is not enough to justify the various forms of surveillance, intimidation and violence that have been routinely employed against the media by democratic states. Those have required some quasi-legal justification, something that could fit the loosely interpreted and variously constructed 'rules of war'. For this, three tropes have circulated widely within the US military, despite little empirical evidence for any of them. These are: the myth of incitement, the myth of involvement, and the myth of the phoney journalist. I use the term myth in the sense of a false, widely held, collective belief, potentially with some distant, superficial origin in fact.

The myth of *incitement* reposes on the flawed premise that television (for the focus is almost entirely on television) portrayals of military actions are the cause of counter-actions by enemies: that television news *incites* people to fight. This belief has largely justified massive and costly efforts to restrict coverage of military actions by numerous governments, particularly the US, Israel and Iraq. The myth of *involvement* is in essence the denial of the possibility of neutrality, the idea that any media worker represents a side in the conflict, and that any media worker of Middle Eastern origin has sympathies with the enemies of the US (or similarly, among the Israeli military, that any journalist of Palestinian origin has sympathies with violent Palestinian resistance groups). In 2006 the *BBC*'s Richard Sambrook made the claim that 'Many US and Israeli troops believe Iraqi and Palestinian journalists are in league with the insurgents [...] Journalists and armed forces have made fatal assumptions, unfounded in fact or even practical expectation'.[121] The myth of the *phoney journalist* suggests that any apparent media worker must be treated as a potential enemy and threat because there is a possibility they might be an enemy combatant posing as a journalist.

While any of these three scenarios are possible, there is no evidence that any are likely, common, or could feasibly be common, within the logic of how the professional electronic media operate. But their widespread acceptance – with these beliefs both formally and informally promulgated within the governments in question – has served as ample internal justification for the consistent abuse and intimidation of media workers who have attempted to operate outside of the embedding systems which have afforded governments a degree of control over media output. An example of how such myths spread was a secret message circulating within the US military in Afghanistan in 2004, revealed in the 'Afghan War logs' published by *WikiLeaks*:

> Three well-trained terrorists (NFI) have been assigned by Osama Bin LADEN to conduct a suicidal attack against [Afghan President] KARZAI. According to the source, the three terrorists will pass Afghanistan border in ten days with counterfeit journalist passports, obtained from an Arab country, potentially PAKISTAN (NFI). They are planning to conduct the attack during a press conference or a meeting held by KARZAI. ... They will use their cameras or recorders as RCIED's or IED's [improvised explosive device] in this attack.[122]

Such reports will have served to confirm to foreign soldiers that anyone with a Middle Eastern appearance claiming to be a journalist, and carrying the professional equipment of a journalist, may indeed be an enemy combatant on the verge of committing an act of carnage. Plots for insurgents to pose as journalists may or may not have existed, but there appears to be only one such prominent case in the decade of conflict in Afghanistan, when a leader of the Northern Alliance, allied with the US, was allegedly assassinated by suicide bombers posing as journalists.

As serious as incidents of killings and the destruction of media facilities are, they are relatively rare in comparison to the extent of detentions and arrests of reporters by US forces and those with official authority operating with them in Iraq and Afghanistan. Two Iranian journalists, for example, were detained by the US military in Iraq for four months without charge.[123] Spanish authorities arrested leading *Al Jazeera* correspondent Tayseer Allouni, who was living in Spain to work on a doctoral degree,[124] and a Sudanese *Al Jazeera* cameraman, Sami Al-Hajj, was taken to Guantanamo

Bay by the US government after being arrested by the Pakistan government in 2001 while en route to Afghanistan on assignment for *Al Jazeera*. He was turned over to the US, reportedly beaten and tortured, but never charged with any offence, and was finally released without charge, explanation or apology, in 2008. He has the distinction of being the only journalist known to have been held by the US at Guantanamo Bay. Al-Hajj told his British lawyer that he was mostly asked questions about his employer, *Al Jazeera*, and that his interrogators seemed determined to establish a connection between *Al Jazeera* and Al Qaeda.[125] At one point, according to Al-Hajj's account of what happened to him at Guantanamo Bay, he was asked to return to *Al Jazeera* and act as a US spy. He was told his young child would be in jeopardy if he backed out of the arrangement.[126]

The *New York Times* only provided a detailed examination of the Al-Hajj case in its news pages well after he had been released without charge and had gone back to work for *Al Jazeera*, while he was still undergoing psychological treatment for the trauma he had suffered. The newspaper asked a Pentagon spokesman why he had been held for years and mostly asked about his employer, and were told 'all detainees were treated humanely while in custody', ignoring how thoroughly documented were Al-Hajj's years of torture (as defined under international law).

There are many less well-known incidents for which we have little detail. Robert Fisk wrote with alarm about an attack by US troops that he witnessed on a clearly marked press vehicle, driven by Arab journalists. There are many even less publicised stories, known only to the journalists involved in them and perhaps to a few colleagues, their companies – if they reported them and if they work for companies (as opposed to being freelance) – and sometimes to press freedom groups. As such, the extent of intimidation and interference with media workers by US troops in Iraq and Afghanistan remains extremely unclear. There are numerous reports suggesting it did, and does, routinely occur, but these accounts are not backed up with records or published investigations. The only evidence tends to be the testimony of the media workers involved or of other media workers who happened to be present and mention such incidents in their own publications or in later interviews. However, in 2006 *Reuters* wrote that 'as many as seven journalists for international media groups were held by the U.S. military in Iraq at one stage last year'.[127] The CPJ has written of routine arrests, involving 'journalists working for CBS News, AP, and Agence France-Presse, among others'.[128] Arrests in Iraq have been accompanied by brutal beatings of journalists by US soldiers on several occasions, and press freedom groups have catalogued an enormous number of non-lethal attacks on Arab journalists by US troops.[129] More characteristically, according to the CPJ, 'U.S. and Iraqi military forces routinely detain Iraqi journalists without charge or explanation, and some have been held for months'. As with some of the attacks on facilities and lethal attacks on journalists described above, certain media organisations seem to have been the focus of the US military more than others, especially journalists from *Al Jazeera* and from the television news agencies *Reuters Television* and *APTN*.

The *AP* reported that a Lebanese cameraman working for a German broadcaster said, after being attacked by US troops, 'They checked our identity badges and then let us go, saying they thought we were with *Al-Jazeera*'.[130] *BBC* reporter David Loyn wrote in the *British Journalism Review* following his experience in Iraq that

> A number of Iraqi cameramen have told me [...] they are routinely harassed and intimidated by American forces, who seize tapes and identity cards. American mistrust of local journalists has been very hazardous to some and a number have been arrested. An AP photographer, Bilal Hussein, has been held in American custody for more than a year for what is described as 'inappropriate contact with insurgents', and a stringer for another major news agency has had to leave his home in Ramadi to live in hiding after American forces stuck up 'Wanted' posters for him. In both cases, the journalists are believed by their employers to be innocent of the charges they face. The contact they had with insurgents was no more than they needed in order to carry out their jobs.[131]

One of the most famous Iraqi reporters of the war was Atwar Bahjat. While working for *Al Jazeera* in the early months of the war, a colleague recalled how 'when she was detained overnight by the US military and the soldiers crowded around to interrogate her, the men at *Aljazeera's* bureau became hysterical, but Atwar kept her cool'.[132] Iraqi journalist Omar Agha, writing for *Al Jazeera*, stated that 'Many of those who were later released without being charged, said they were detained simply because they were covering the other side of the story, the insurgency'.[133] In 2004 an Afghan reporter who worked for *Reuters* and the *BBC* was arrested by US troops as guns were trained on his family, and flown, blindfolded, to the main US base in Afghanistan, Bagram. His notebooks and production equipment were taken. He was released without explanation by the US government after the *BBC* made enquiries.[134]

The INSI reported weeks before the killing of a *Reuters* soundman by US troops in Baghdad, that another *Reuters* cameraman in the city of Ramadi 'was arrested by U.S. forces three weeks ago and is being held without charge in Abu Ghraib prison. U.S. military officials say he will face a judicial hearing as soon as Monday but have still given no access to the journalist or said what he is accused of.'

The cameraman, Ali al-Mashhadani, was held for five months before being released without explanation, only to be arrested again for twelve days, without explanation, a year later, while investigating reports of the killing of 15 civilians by US Marines. Mashhadani was arrested for a third time by the US military when he attempted to renew his press credentials in Baghdad in 2008. Also in 2008, an Iraqi cameraman working for *APTN* was arrested by US and Iraqi forces and detained for six months for 'imperative reasons of security'.[135] In some cases, detentions amounted to much more than brief detentions and questioning of media staff. In 2004, three *Reuters* journalists, with an employee of the US television network *NBC*, were abducted and tortured by US military personnel. Two *Al Jazeera* employees reported that they were tortured by US troops in 2003.[136]

There are other reports of harassment and detention of journalists by US troops where, given a lack of any plausible alterative explanation from the US government, the most credible explanation appears to be that journalists who investigated information that could portray the US occupation of Iraq negatively were being targeted. In 2006 the *Guardian* reported the arrest of one of their Iraqi journalists, who was working on a joint investigation for the *Guardian* and UK television's *Channel 4* about 'claims that tens of millions of dollars worth of Iraqi funds held by the Americans and British have been misused or misappropriated'. The film's director told the *Guardian*:

> The timing and nature of this raid is extremely disturbing. It is only a few days since we first approached the US authorities and told them Ali was doing this investigation, and asked them then to grant him an interview about our findings ... We need a convincing assurance from the American authorities that this terrifying experience was not harassment and a crude attempt to discourage Ali's investigation.

The reporter, Dr Ali Fadhil, had recently won an award from Iraq's Foreign Press Association as the young journalist of the year. He reported that, while shooting, US troops forced their way into the bedroom, where he was sleeping with his wife and two young children, and 'rolled me on to the floor and tied my hands. When I tried to ask them what they were looking for they just told me to shut up'. He was driven away with a hood over his head, questioned for a few hours and released. He wasn't charged with a crime or given an explanation, but videotapes that had been recorded for the *Channel 4* film were seized and never returned.[137]

The form of violence perpetrated by the US military that has most endangered journalists has also been one of the most dangerous for ordinary Iraqis. A considerable number of civilian cars have been attacked by US troops at roadside checkpoints, and seemingly always – according to press accounts – with the intent to kill the occupants, rather than just disable a potentially threatening car. Victims of US troops at checkpoints have included not just journalists, but allied forces of Bulgaria, Italy and the UK, workers from human rights groups, members of the Iraqi police, and many others. Compounding the problem is the concern of media organisations that a number of journalists have been killed by US troops at checkpoints while following announced procedures and despite clearly identifying themselves as journalists.[138]

One former US Army major with long experience in Afghanistan has made a number of press appearances, seeking to explain some of what has gone wrong in the US occupation of that country. Benjamin Tupper recounted his experience as one of a few US military trainers who accompanied Afghan troops on missions in the early years of cooperation between the Afghan and US militaries:

> Very few Americans – pretty much myself and one other American would be out on missions. And I saw how the Afghans approached these prickly moments when there's uncertainty, when it's a shoot/don't shoot moment. And, for the most part, they're laid back. [...]. They were more passive. They were more conservative in the use of force. And they reaped a lot of benefits from that, because, unfortunately, more times than not, when we react at that split second, we make the wrong decision. We may shoot the wrong vehicle. We may shoot the wrong person.[139]

It is precisely that 'shoot first and ask questions later' tendency among the US troops in Afghanistan, and more prominently Iraq, which has cost the lives of many media workers.

Israel and the Press: Mentor to the US?

Gowing observes that a close ally of the US had already compiled a deplorable history of attacks on journalists – especially television journalists – in the years preceding the Iraq war.[140] Reporters Sans Frontières and the CPJ, along with other human rights organisations and the many media organisations involved, have offered extensive documentation of attacks on journalists by the Israeli Defense Forces (IDF) since the mid to late 1990s and continuing through the present day, with at least 14 journalists reported to have been killed by Israeli forces since 1992, and over 200 attacks on journalists in just two years between 2000 and 2002.[141]

In many of the cases evidence that each was deliberately targeted – despite knowledge of their status as journalists – is strong. One of the best-known cases is that of the British documentary maker James Miller, and this was because Miller's family took the case to court in the UK. An independent investigation found Miller was shot deliberately and without warning while working with a production team and near another television crew in Gaza in 2003. In 2006, a British Coroner's Court concluded that 'this was an unlawful shooting with the intention of killing James Miller', but the Israeli government stood by an investigation of their own which they claimed cleared their soldiers of wrongdoing.[142] At least three other journalists were killed by the Israeli military in 2002 and 2003, with reports from numerous journalists saying the media were clearly being targeted.[143] Tim Lambon, an experienced combat cameraman who worked mostly for the UK's *Channel 4* and had long experience of covering Israel and the Palestinian territories, said of the Israeli military in 2004: 'They seem to have taken on a policy of targeting camera people and journalists'.[144]

As has been the case in Iraq, the photographers working for international news agencies – the people most directly responsible for bringing images of conflict to television screens around the world – have been one of the most affected groups. In a disturbing parallel to the deaths of *Reuters* photographers in Iraq, in 2008 *Reuters Television* photographer Fadel Shana was recording footage in the Gaza Strip when an Israeli tank fired at him from a mile away, killing him and eight other civilians, many of them children. The Israeli Army used a shell which burst over the victims, showing them with metal darts. Shana's flak jacket, marked 'Press', was not enough to protect him. After killing the cameraman, injuring his soundman, and killing the children nearby, the Israeli tank fired again to destroy the journalist's car. When the Israeli government again cleared its soldiers of any wrongdoing, as had been the case in the death of *Reuters* colleague, and fellow Palestinian, Mazen Dana in Iraq, the tank crew's claim that the professional television camera looked somewhat like a weapon was considered adequate justification for both men's killing. CPJ Director Joel Campagna responded: 'These findings mean that a journalist with a camera is at risk of coming under fire and there's not that much that can be done. That's unacceptable'.[145] Shana had been wounded two years earlier when the Israeli Air Force fired a missile at his *Reuters* vehicle.[146]

Canadian journalist Patricia Naylor made a documentary about the Israeli military's relationship with the press and record of violence towards them. She told an interviewer:

> The open anger toward us comes from many of the soldiers. It's no secret that the army doesn't like the media. They don't like the images of what they're doing being shown on television. But you know, lots of days, I would go to the West Bank and on the way down meet two dozen soldiers at the various checkpoints, and they'd be congenial. I think the larger problem in terms of these shootings seems to be the younger soldiers. They're 18 and they have guns and a lot of power. They feel they're under threat all day.[147]

Gideon Levy, a former deputy editor of the Israeli newspaper *Ha'aretz* said: 'Don't separate shooting journalists from shooting all the others, because it's the same rules of the game today. There is no difference between journalists and others. That's the policy of the army, not to investigate. There are very few restraints. Your life is in danger.'[148]

In Stephanie Gutmann's sympathetic, though usefully detailed, portrayal of Israeli press control efforts she writes of the effect of increasing concern from the Israeli government about shaping international opinion, describing the concern felt by the then Director of the Israeli government press office, Danny Seaman, that his government's anxiety about 'how things would look' was 'costing the lives of Israelis and endangering the state'. The press officer describes how he came to feel, upon observing the carnage of a bombed bus in Jerusalem, that the (then) accepted position that he perceived, of 'If we're nice to [the news media], maybe they'll be nice to us', was failing and (in Gutmann's words) 'it was time to get tough'.[149]

He told Gutmann 'one of my major purposes is to reduce the number of journalists coming here, to make it a less attractive place to come'.

This involved careful monitoring of the reporting of every international correspondent and denying government assistance – answering enquiries, setting up briefings, providing contacts – to those guilty of 'unprofessional behaviour'. Gutmann names several reporters, including those from the *Guardian* and the *Washington Post* whom Seaman decided to put on his 'shitlist' and boycott. Seaman claimed 'the editorial boards got the message and replaced their people', while parenthetically noting that the three media outlets she named 'vehemently deny Seaman had anything to do with [...] reassignment of the three correspondents'. In explaining persistent deportations of foreign journalists, Seaman said: 'It's the Interior Ministry, not me, that decides on deportations, but I certainly recommended it. Why should we be fair to them if they served as the enemy's mouthpiece? There's a limit to freedom of expression even in a democratic country.'[150]

Seaman's unilaterally determined 'limits' irked many international media companies for years, but his declarations of the need 'to get tough' and to make the reporting 'less attractive' closely resemble the position towards the media taken by the US military at the start of the Iraq war.

In Israel and the territories it occupies, shootings, arrests and intimidation of journalists has been almost routine since the 1990s (many journalists based there argue it is routine). In 1997, cameramen from *ABC*, *APTV* (which later became *APTN*), and *Reuters* were all shot with rubber bullets and wounded by the Israeli military in Israel as they sought to record images of protesters burning Israeli flags. *ABC* producer Deirdre Michalopoulos told Sara Leibovich-Dar of *Ha'aretz* that, while she and her crew were preparing to record images of the Israeli military in the occupied Palestinian city of Ramallah in 2000:

Two jeeps came toward us, then honked their horns and shot rubber bullets without any warning. I'd been in many war zones. I was in Afghanistan, Pakistan, Albania and Bosnia. I was in Israel in October 2000. Soldiers had never opened fire on me before. It's hard to work when you find that you've become a target. There was a moment when I was very frightened. I didn't know how far they would go. The worst part was that they didn't say anything. They didn't order us to leave. They just shot without warning.[151]

Gutmann quotes an IDF spokesman saying stun grenades were used to keep journalists 'from a closed military zone', but not rubber bullets.

Also in 2000, *BBC* correspondent Jeremy Bowen and a cameraman working with him narrowly escaped death as an Israeli Army tank shell killed his *BBC* colleague Abed Takkoush while their car was stopped, far from any military activity, on a road in southern Lebanon. When Italian photographer Raffaele Ciriello was killed by the Israeli Army in 2002 in Ramallah, Gowing explained that:

> He was killed when he pulled a small video camera out of his pocket in the same way that many of you do when you are in a place like that [...] pull a camera out of your pocket, cargo pants or backpack and think 'I want to take a snap of that'. You [thereby] become a member of the media. But in a situation like this you become vulnerable as well.

The International Press Institute said the shooting 'seemed to be part of a concerted strategy by the Israeli Army to control the press and the recent surge in armed hostilities in the region'.[152] Gowing also explained how a *BBC* cameraman, seeking to record images of a demonstration by peace activists, was shot at by Israeli soldiers well after he had identified himself to the soldiers.[153]

The Israeli invasion of the Palestinian city of Jenin in 2002 marked an escalation in press control, with the complete exclusion of journalists from areas of military operations. Seaman told Gutmann:

> We are concerned about our soldiers and we wanted them to concentrate on the mission at hand and not worry, 'Is that a terrorist? Is that not a terrorist? Is that a journalist?' Despite what the press say – 'Oh we're responsible for ourselves. We're big kids' – anytime they're in the area and they're shot, eventually – even if it comes out that it wasn't our fault – they still accuse us of doing it.[154]

One strategy used by Israel to make it difficult for news agencies and broadcasters to cover the Palestinian territories was to deny press credentials to many of the Palestinian journalists working there.[155] Some foreign media started to bring lawsuits due to the Israeli government – seemingly under Seaman's direction – consistently refusing press credentials for many of their Palestinian staff. A Palestinian *CBS* photographer, Khaled Zighari, was denied press credentials and accused by the Israeli government of having personal connections with a terrorist organisation beyond his work as a journalist; the refusal to grant him press credentials was upheld by the Israeli Supreme Court. But in 2003, *Al Jazeera*, *Reuters* and other media and aid groups argued to the Supreme Court 'for the right to give Israeli press accreditation to residents of the Palestinian territories'. The court would ultimately rule that the policy,

> as an across-the-board policy pertaining to a particular class, was contrary to the spirit of a free press. Denying [an accreditation] card to a resident of the territories makes it significantly harder for them to be journalists [...] making it harder for them to obtain this information (from the Israeli government) causes injury to freedom of expression and access to information.[156]

This ruling was temporary good news for Palestinian journalists, but is also interesting for its declaration by Israel's highest court that freedom of expression is the ultimate goal. Israel, then, manages to claim to *stand for free expression*, while seeking to closely control the practice of journalism, even to the extent of deploying violence against journalists.

One journalist with considerable experience of following US troops in Iraq, both as an independent and embedded reporter, is Nir Rosen. Fellow journalist Michael Massing wrote:

> in October 2003, Rosen spent two weeks embedded with a U.S. Army unit near the Syrian border. In sweeps through neighbourhoods, he said, the Americans used Israeli-style tactics – making mass arrests in the hope that one or two of those scooped up will have something useful for them. 'They'll hold them for ten hours in a truck without food or water,' he told me. 'And 90 percent of them are innocent.'[157]

But the similarities between the Israeli situation and US government practices in Iraq are considerable in other respects. Large numbers of journalists – the number now approaches 100[158] – have been wounded by gunfire from Israeli forces; there were far fewer cases of journalists being killed or wounded by Palestinians in the occupied territories, or in 'crossfire' incidents (a typical explanation given for journalist deaths and injuries involving the US military in Iraq); the journalists were consistently well identified and many had been in contact with the military before they were shot at; the journalists were generally some distance from any fighting that was taking place; there is little evidence of serious, transparent, investigation by the Israeli government; there is rarely any indication of Israeli soldiers being prosecuted under the terms of Israeli or international law; the Israeli government has generally been hostile to demands from mass media and the families of the victims for any investigation. Gowing concludes of Israeli actions:

> all the signals suggest that the IDF has little interest in gathering evidence or disciplining soldiers who assume the laws of war don't apply to them. Indeed the impression is that the IDF policy is to support them by not engaging in any disciplinary or investigative process, leaving the undeclared message that they have every right to target unarmed journalists and camera operators.[159]

These elements are also in place in the pattern of violence against the media by US forces in the Post-9/11 Wars, raising the possibility that there is not only an unofficial US policy behind the kinds of anti-press violence described here, but that it may be modelled closely on an unofficial Israeli policy.

A final piece of the story of the threat to the press in the Middle East from nations allied to the US, and expressing rhetorical support for free expression, is the poor track record of the new governments of Iraq and Afghanistan, both installed in elections organised under US occupation and substantially orchestrated by the US government. One US partner in the Middle East with a particularly poor record of press relations is the Afghan Army. *Al Jazeera* journalist Qais Azimy has been kidnapped by the Taliban and threatened repeatedly with death over two days, before being released, but has also been similarly treated by the Afghan Army, which was effectively established and trained by the US. He told fellow *Al Jazeera* journalist Rosie Garthwaite: 'In 2009 I was arrested by the Afghan Army. It felt like I was kidnapped. I had no contact with the outside world. I was blindfolded and they took me to a ditch, and I could hear gun noises, like they were going to kill me. They were pretending'.[160] And in Iraq, the state is simultaneously working with the media to establish mechanisms to provide for greater safety for journalists and – it has been claimed – using its own media channels to instigate attacks on journalists.[161]

This chapter has reviewed the disturbing turn to violence against the media by the leading global advocate of free expression, the US government, in concert with key Middle Eastern allies. We turn next to the question of what the media, and those advocating for it, have been able to do to mitigate such attacks and limit them in the future, and to the question of the legality or illegality of these attacks and the relative legal impunity of these state actors.

4

Media Response

The threat to media workers in conflict zones, posed by the US and other countries that traditionally advocate freedom of expression, has been typically met by the world's media not with public expressions of outrage, but with remarkable silence. While many larger media organisations have lobbied governments intensively behind the scenes, extensive public reporting and comment on the kinds of incidents described in Chapter 3 has been rare. There is a superficial logic which suggests that, as media organisations with the ability to reach thousands, millions or billions[1] with their words and images see their own personnel and sources, and those of other media organisations, repeatedly violently silenced, they would, and should, react by publicising those attacks as fully as possible, both for the sake of their own protection and for the sake of defending their ability to gather and disseminate information in the future. They would seem, at the very least, to have a compelling economic reason for doing so.

Even with their self-interest removed from the equation, by the standard news values of most large Western news organisations the killing of journalists should be highly newsworthy, for such stories involve elite nations, conflict, the unusual and unexpected, and are consequential in international relations. But, for a variety of reasons, such attention to journalist casualties occurs only rarely and minimally. There have been exceptions, suggesting it is not completely unacceptable for a Western news organisation to focus some of its reporting on its own people. An example was the well-publicised kidnapping of *BBC* correspondent Alan Johnston in Gaza in 2007, which became the focus of a concerted and very public campaign by the *BBC* to publicise his plight and pressure anyone with influence over his kidnappers. The *BBC* organised a half-hour global broadcast to publicise Johnston's kidnapping, which was aired simultaneously by *BBC World*, *BBC News 24*, and – remarkably – global competitors *Al Jazeera English* and *Sky News*, and the *BBC* also aired frequent news stories about the abduction. Johnston was released after four months. A similar campaign is being waged by the French media at the time of writing, in an effort to free French journalists kidnapped in Syria, who are among about 60 detained or missing.

There is no disputing the value of the *BBC*'s effort and how commendable such interorganisational cooperation was when one of their own was in peril, but the incident places in stark relief the silence of major Western media organisations in regard to the very many other attacks on journalists from both Western and Arab media organisations. And distressingly, when *Al Jazeera* conducted a campaign over many years to draw attention to the plight of one of its cameramen, who was detained and tortured by the US military[2] and held without charge for years, other media outlets showed scant interest.

The *New York Times*, for example, waited until 2009, well after Sami Al-Hajj was released from Guantanamo Bay, to write at any length about his case,[3] and at one point during their interview Al-Hajj had to rebuke the interviewer for using the US military euphemism 'enhanced integration techniques' to describe his years of torture. Al-Hajj told the journalist that in accepting such terminology 'we are giving the wrong impression [...] We as journalists are violating human rights because we are changing the perception of reality'.[4] While his newspaper and other US media were not making it a prominent news story, *New York Times* columnist Nicholas Kristof did use his online column to advocate examination of the Al-Hajj case, and observed in 2006 that when 'Sudan detained an American journalist, Paul Salopek, in August in Darfur, journalists and human rights groups reacted with outrage until he was freed a month later. We should be just as offended when it is our own government that is sinking to Sudanese standards of justice.'[5]

Similarly, when the national network *Telecinco* in Spain produced a compelling and meticulously researched documentary about the US military attack on Baghdad's Palestine Hotel, which killed one of their colleagues, the programme received only the most minimal international exposure, despite an English-language version being produced.[6]

That lack of attention to media casualties is not just the case in regard to the emerging and hypocritical threat from traditional advocates of press freedom, but also within the wider context of international news coverage. The long and bloody civil war in Algeria (1991–2002) suggested that when all parties to conflict seek to intimidate and target reporters – regardless of their ideology or origin – the story will disappear from the front pages of the world's press (in Algeria at least 70 journalists were killed). Events in Syria since 2011 suggest times are changing: access to widespread mobile phone, video and Internet technology – some of it augmented by external groups seeking to aid anti-regime activists in telling their story[7] – all now imply that the story of brutal and mostly asymmetrical war can be told by global media and kept, minimally, in the public eye, even though the immensely threatening and dangerous atmosphere keeps most professional reporters away. But such developments risk fuelling the idea that professional journalists do not need to be present to witness conflict.

In the case of the US-led invasions of Iraq and Afghanistan, and their aftermath, only a small portion of the total global news coverage has focused on the threat to civilians, and a far tinier portion of that upon the threat to journalists. Along with the *BBC*'s Nik Gowing, senior news executives from *CNN*, the *BBC*, and senior figures from *Reuters* have spoken about their concerns for some time, and leading British journalists such as the *Independent*'s Robert Fisk and Janine di Giovanni of the (London) *Times* have written about the pattern of violence against journalists that they have witnessed.

News executives often suggest they know of incidents which are not part of the public record – such as the more routine harassment of their media workers or seizures of equipment, which interfere with day-to-day news gathering – yet they tend to cautiously cite those which are well documented by press freedom groups. It is a protective strategy that risks ignoring other incidents, which those groups lack the means to investigate. Few media outlets, though, have made substantial efforts to publicise the attacks on their journalists as *news*. *Reuters* Iraq correspondent Andrew Marshall recalled, for example, that few US media organisations reported the arrest and torture of *Reuters* and *NBC* personnel by US forces in 2004, despite the considerable information he sent to them, and none sought to investigate the incident independently.[8]

Following the deadly set of attacks in March and April 2003 in which many media workers were killed by US government actions, veteran war correspondent Robert Fisk attempted to spark a debate about what was happening. The *Independent* published an analysis by Fisk under the provocative headline 'Is There Some Element in the US Military That Wants to Take Out Journalists?'. The article opens as follows:

First the Americans killed the correspondent of al-Jazeera yesterday and wounded his cameraman. Then, within four hours, they attacked the Reuters television bureau in Baghdad, killing one of its cameramen and a cameraman for Spain's Tele 5 channel and wounding four other members of the Reuters staff. Was it possible to believe this was an accident?[9]

A fairly small number of press stories over the past decade have described the various incidents that have occurred, but few have framed the story as part of a pattern, as Fisk and Gowing attempted to do early on. Each of the media organisations involved in the incidents described here have made strong protests, and seen their editors and senior executives write with demands for investigation to the press liaisons of the Pentagon and other parts of the US military, the White House and Congress – as have the CPJ, Reporters Sans Frontières and other press freedom advocacy groups – but these protests and demands for transparent investigation have had negligible effects.

Reports from the US military on press killings involving its forces have typically been released months or even years after the incidents took place, have mostly ignored reports of witnesses other than military personnel, and have typically concluded that troops acted 'within the rules of engagement'.[10] The lack of accountability from the US military continues to frustrate media organisations. *Al Arabiya* executive editor Nabil Khatib complained:

> of the 11 (of his staff) that were killed, three were killed by American troops and until now we never got any reports from anybody about this investigation, why it happened and how it happened. Five other people [...] were lost when insurgents bombed our office, and until now nobody in Iraq, the government or whoever, gave us any explanation or any results of any investigation of who might be the one who did it. I mean, there is no investigation. It's just going on and on with no special attention to fighting the phenomenon itself.[11]

The *BBC* was among several large organisations to seek explanations from the Pentagon directly and repeatedly, as did *Reuters*, *Al Jazeera* and *CNN*. For example, following the Kabul attack in 2001, the *BBC*'s Nik Gowing went to Washington on behalf of the *BBC* to find out why the *BBC*'s Kabul bureau had been almost completely destroyed, and its correspondent nearly killed.[12] Knightley, after speaking with media managers early in the Iraq war, observed that following Pentagon meetings by the *BBC*, *Al Jazeera* and the CPJ, 'all three organisations concluded that the Pentagon was determined to deter Western correspondents from reporting any war from the "enemy" side, would view such journalism in Iraq as activity of "military significance", and might well bomb the area'. The *BBC* did not publically express that view at the time even if they were convinced of it internally.[13]

Previously, a long-standing doctrine of 'deterrence by publicity' existed within international news media and the press protection NGOs that deal with journalists' safety.[14] It was presumed that public exposure of attacks on the press – by media and those NGOs representing their interests internationally – would always serve as a substantial (if not complete) deterrent to states that might engage in such violence. The Iraq war has proven that model to be mostly irrelevant. State actors in the Iraq conflict known to be responsible for attacks on journalists have shown contempt for complaints from commercial and public sector media – even when these have included the major media outlets of 'coalition' countries and the global human rights and free expression NGOs the US government has sometimes cited when condemning other nations' treatment of the press.

Al Jazeera and Reuters

Before moving to the general successes and failures of the international news industry in recognising and addressing the problem of anti-press violence from the US and its allies in the Middle East, the cases of two major media institutions, and major players in this story, deserve further examination. The regional television broadcaster *Al Jazeera* and the international news agency *Reuters* were (and remain) two of the most prominent conduits of information about conflict in the Middle East. Both have a considerable permanent presence across most countries in the region. Two *Al Jazeera* staff have been killed since 2003 by the US or its allies and at least four of its facilities have been attacked; at least six *Reuters* staff have been killed by the US, and more by its ally Israel.

While numerous books have been published about *Al Jazeera*, and it has been the subject of countless research projects as well as the 2003 documentary *Control Room*, Lisa Parks is one of just a few media scholars to publish a critical investigation of the attacks on the broadcaster, concluding that:

> US military attacks on commercial broadcasters such as Aljazeera
> constitute an unprecedented form of media violence, one that

represents a disregard for international journalists' integrity and safety, threatens the circulation of Arab viewpoints and voices, and symbolizes US officials' devaluation of democratic principles such as free speech and dissent.[15]

Parks hypothesised that the variety of US-originated attacks on *Al Jazeera* are interconnected, representing 'the US's patent attempts to quash difference in the mediasphere by destroying Aljazeera's facilities and resources, killing and detaining its employees, and interrupting the circulation of its signal'. She suggests that as a strategy in the promotion of US security, these attacks have been counterproductive, if we accept the premise that security is enhanced through cultures coming to better understand each other through unfettered channels of communication.

Al Jazeera had been bombed by the US in Kandahar and Kabul in 2001, and again in Baghdad, Basra and Fallujah in Iraq in 2003 and 2004, when one of their top reporters, Tareq Ayoub, was killed. The Iraqi and US militaries jointly raided their Baghdad bureau in 2004 and barred the company from reporting in the country.[16] News managers at Arab broadcasters probably limited their independent coverage of US operations following Ayoub's killing. According to *Al Arabiya*'s executive editor Nabil Khatib: 'Everybody now knows that Tareq Ayoub got shot by American fire, and in this case you only have no choice except to be embedded with American troops in order to follow a story where the American troops are involved.'[17]

International concern about US military treatment of *Al Jazeera* had reached new heights by 2005. A joint report by the IFJ and Statewatch remarked in 2005 that:

> The channel has been praised and vilified in equal measure. It has had its offices in Kabul and Baghdad destroyed by the US army. A reporter has been killed. Like Al-Arabiya, whose Baghdad offices were bombed by terrorists in 2004 killing five employees, and which also lost two staff members at the hands of US soldiers, it has paid a heavy price for its editorial independence.[18]

In fact, US Air Force or Navy aircraft were implicated in the *Al Jazeera* attacks, rather than the US Army (which was implicated in several other attacks on journalists). As this quote shows, the report makes a link between the US attacks and the editorial stance of the media organisation in question – suggesting that one led to the other. As the evidence examined in this book suggests though, that seemingly obvious leap cannot be made so easily. The US government and its supporters vehemently deny it, and few mainstream journalists dare to publicly suggest it.[19]

In November 2005, the British newspaper the *Daily Mirror* described a secret British government memorandum recounting a conversation between UK Prime Minister Tony Blair and US President George Bush at the time of the US military campaign to take control of the Iraqi city of Fallujah. It was reported to have documented that the US President advocated bombing the Qatar headquarters of *Al Jazeera*, and that British Prime Minister Blair dissuaded him. The British government did not deny the authenticity or accuracy of the memorandum; indeed, they indirectly confirmed its credibility and significance when they immediately, and without precedent, invoked the Official Secrets Act and warned other media against publishing the contents of the memo (although there is no indication that other media had access to it). A Labour member of parliament's researcher and a former Cabinet Office staffer were arrested in connection with the memo.[20]

Downing Street and the White House responded by deriding as bizarre the suggestion that the US would bomb a civilian media operation on the territory of its ally, Qatar. Many in the media accepted that the suggestion was beyond belief – that if Bush said it, it must have been a joke – and moved on. But the journalists, and facilities, of *Al Jazeera* had been attacked by the US military more than those of any other media organisation; and these attacks have been accompanied by a campaign of diplomatic pressure and intimidation against the Emir of Qatar, the main financial backer of the channel. After Blair left office, he was challenged about Bush's apparent plan on a visit to *Al Jazeera* in Doha. *Al Jazeera* journalist and CPJ board member Mohamed Krichen reported that: 'he met with a number of high ranking editorial managers and the bombing story came up in discussion. 'Thank you Mr. Blair for stopping this bombing,' I said to him with a smile. He smiled back and, as usual, responded with words that would neither confirm nor deny the incident.'[21]

Al Jazeera staff have also been harassed within the US. In 2001, their Washington correspondent was detained by 'police armed with M-16 rifles' at a Texas airport while trying to report on a summit meeting between the US and Russian presidents.[22] *Al Jazeera*'s business reporters were also denied access to the New York Stock Exchange and NASDAQ stock market.[23] When *Al Jazeera* hired former US Marine Josh Rushing to work as a reporter for their US bureau – a logical choice since Rushing had gained global notoriety as the US soldier with a critical consciousness in the 2004 documentary about *Al Jazeera*, *Control Room* – his reporting was routinely interfered with by US government officials. He told the University of Texas alumni magazine that when recording stories in the US, 'Customs officers would follow him and question every person he talked to'.[24] Right-wing bloggers published his address to encourage violence against his family, and *Fox News* broadcast his picture with the caption 'traitor' and had one of their popular hosts shout 'Do you love America?' at him repeatedly.

Attacks on *Al Jazeera* are also alleged to have gone beyond the rhetorical and physical, to the virtual. One of several hacking attacks on *Al Jazeera's* international websites was attributed to a patriotic young computer designer in California who may have taken US military attacks on *Al Jazeera* and threatening rhetoric about *Al Jazeera* by senior US politicians to mean he could hack their website – replacing their journalism with a US flag – without fear of prosecution. In the event, he received a sentence of community service and a fine of $2000.[25] It was revealed by *Spiegel*, as part of a collaboration with *WikiLeaks* in 2013, that the NSA had, as early as March 2006, been monitoring the secure internal communications of *Al Jazeera*, which it commented on as a 'notable success', with individuals whose communications were being monitored having 'high potential as sources of intelligence'.[26]

A sense of victimisation at the hands of the US military is deep in the professional culture of *Al Jazeera*, and serves to some extent as inspiration for their journalism. In his departing remarks to *Al Jazeera* staff upon stepping down in 2011, long-time managing director and director general Wadah Khanfar reflected on the human costs the channel has borne:

the Arab public are not naïve demagogues or irrational believers. They are intelligent, politically astute and have a level of empathy that the political elite lack. Our channel lives and dies by this audience and they will not forgive us if we deviate from the mission that we have lived for the past 15 years. This is perhaps the best guarantee that *Al Jazeera* will maintain its stellar record and lives up to its code of conduct. It is the mission for which Tareq Ayoub, and Rasheed Wali Ali Jaber gave their lives, the mission which Tayseer Alouni and Sami Al Hajj spent years illegally detained and for which many of you were harassed. Between our audience's expectation and your vigilance, I am confident that Al Jazeera will continue to report with integrity and courage.[27]

One of the characteristics of *Al Jazeera*'s war reporting which so antagonised Western governments was that they took a consistent editorial position to use images in presenting to their viewers the sometimes gruesome reality of the effects of violence on people. For decades, gory images of the aftermath of violent events have arrived in television newsrooms around the world and then been cut to address either perceptions of what local audiences could tolerate, or legal restrictions on what could be shown. Frequently, the most brutal and distressing images available were eliminated by editors at the news agencies distributing them, before even reaching the world's broadcasters (see Paterson, 2011, for further explanation).[28] The effects of modern weaponry on human beings, whether cruise missiles or IEDs, is horrifying, and television photographers arriving on the scene of such violence often strive to record exactly that horror, in the hope that creating a visual record might help to prevent it.[29] And they are often frustrated when Western broadcasters delicately extract the horror from the images they've provided due to perceptions of local sensitivities.

Al Jazeera's photographers were adept at being near the action in conflict zones across the Middle East and often captured such images. *Al Jazeera* made the decision to edit the footage available to it more lightly, and not avoid showing some of the most disturbing images. But many commentators, beyond just those representing the US government, noted a tendency in the early 2000s to sensationalise such images, using them at times as much for dramatic effect and promotion as for the illustration of news.[30]

The executive editor of competing regional broadcaster, *Al Arabiya*'s Nabil Khatib, complained of the damaging effects of many in the Arab media resorting to sensationalism:

> Sensationalism incites people to hatred. ... I have smelled the blood of hatred, and I cannot understand how someone in an air-conditioned newsroom feels that he has the right to manipulate people's emotions, to rile people up or to generalize about a group, when he sees the repercussions.[31]

If it was this tendency that bore part of the blame for inciting US military violence against *Al Jazeera*, perceptions of it were likely exaggerated when contrasted with the highly sanitised images of war being broadcast by British and US news channels. These channels had access to images of the aftermath of US bombings of civilian areas, for example, but generally chose not to show them or to show them with the most brutal images excised. Some of the more reflective news managers among them later regretted that decision, as these comments from the *BBC*'s Richard Sambrook demonstrate: 'As broadcasters we have responsibility for what goes into people's living rooms. You can do it without showing the most awful images, but I think in the 2003 Iraq war we oversanitised. It's a very difficult judgement to get right.'[32]

In the US, the sanitisation of images was more political, and was famously evidenced by a memo sent by *CNN* chairman Walter Isaacson in November 2001, ordering *CNN* staff 'to balance images of civilian devastation in Afghan cities with reminders that the Taliban harbors murderous terrorists', as put by the *Washington Post*'s Howard Kurtz.[33] Kellner observed that a report by embedded *CNN* reporter Walter Rogers, which showed a dead Iraqi, produced a furious reaction from *CNN* viewers 'demanding that they do not show any dead bodies, as if the US audience wanted to be in denial concerning the human cost of the war'.[34] No major US broadcaster was willing during the Iraq war to routinely and clearly show either the US dead, or the far greater numbers of Iraqi dead, largely through fear of the competitive disadvantage that doing so might yield, precisely as theorised by Herman and Chomsky in their 1988 description of the role of 'flak' – negative public feedback to a media outlet.[35] Flak has always been an important factor in determining the nature of the reporting of events in the Middle East. The *BBC* journalist Ben Brown told Tumber and Webster how cautious he feels he has to be in reporting, as a result of anticipating online reactions to his stories:

> with the Internet and everything you get ... a lot of email reaction to stories, especially if you're covering a story like Israel where both sides are incredibly vociferous ... [they] watch like a hawk everything, every word that every reporter says ... if you're somewhere like that, you're incredibly self-conscious about how you report it, and careful, just very careful. Because just one wrong bit of terminology and you can cause huge upset.[36]

Robert Fisk has charged that such censorship within Western broadcasters effectively amounts to complicity in hiding war crimes from the publics that are sponsoring them. In 2004, Fisk described a US helicopter gun video, showing the brutal killing of a wounded Iraqi who was trying to crawl away from the vehicle the helicopter had just destroyed. The audio with the video made it clear that the killing was ordered by the helicopter crew's commanders. Fisk wrote:

> British and most European television stations censored the tape off the air last night on the grounds that the pictures were too terrible to show. But deliberately shooting a wounded man is a war crime under the Geneva Conventions and this extraordinary film of US air crews in action over Iraq is likely to create yet another international outcry ... Only *Canal Plus* in France, ABC television in the United States and the *Canadian Broadcasting Corporation* have so far had the courage to show the shocking footage. UK military personnel in the Gulf region have confirmed that the tape is genuine.[37]

While *Al Jazeera* and *Al Arabiya* have born much of the harassment and violence directed towards media representatives by the US government, the two leading international news agencies have born a great deal of it as well. This is more surprising to people in the news industry, since both of these organisations – *Reuters* and *AP* – have been integral parts of the media industry, and the leading processers of international news, for over a century and a half. Journalists are broadly aware that there would be little international news without their efforts. The 160-year-old international news agency *Reuters* has, like *Al Jazeera*, been subject to a disproportionate amount of hostile rhetoric and violence from the US government and its vocal defenders among the US right-wing. *Reuters* is the news agency that has suffered the most attacks on its staff involving US forces, including the destruction of its Baghdad bureau in 2003 and the killing of six of its staff between 2003 and 2007 (and several more, if the actions of US ally Israel are included).

Attacks on the international news agencies by the US – whether the shootings and abductions of agency staff by the military or the angry rhetoric of right-wing bloggers – is, to the extent that any calculation lies behind it, certainly a form of 'friendly fire', for the Western news agencies are among the most reliable international purveyors of official US perspectives.[38] In the case of the lead-up to the Iraq war, Horvit examined the extent to which coverage by Western and non-Western news agencies differed. The Western news agencies were *AP*, *Agence France-Presse* and *Reuters*, the non-Western were *Xinhua*, *ITAR-TASS* and *Inter Press Service*. She found that 'Western sources accounted for 60 percent of the western news agencies' sources, while non-western sources averaged 36 per cent.

The reverse was essentially true for the non-Western news agencies'. The 'Western sources' she saw used were mostly US government officials. In other words, the story the principle sources of the media – the three leading news agencies – were supplying to the world's media was one framed substantially by the US government. Horvit concluded that:

> Given their dominance in the international news flow, the western news agencies might want to re-examine how well they convey the attitudes and beliefs of the non-western world to news consumers in the West, most of whom live in democratic societies based on the premise that information will lead to informed self-governance.[39]

But we might contextualise that conclusion with understandings of the production culture of the international news agencies, including research by this author. Decisions within commercial news agencies are not made for altruistic reasons, and senior news managers are eager to make that clear. Balance in international news flow is not high on their agenda. The story topics, story frames and nature of sources are all substantially dependent on the interests of the media clients who pay them the most: the major television channels and largest newspapers of the US and of the wealthiest European countries. News agency editors spend every day talking to journalists in those organisations about what they want and providing for that demand; the demands or even suggestions from smaller media in smaller countries, while not ignored, are not prioritised. Like any business, commercial news agencies spend their money (on the deployment of resources and the shaping of the product) in ways that are going to keep the biggest clients happy.[40] And so the global telling of the pre-Iraq war story from a US perspective, while significant, is not remarkable – it is simply structural: an artefact of the predominantly commercial and highly concentrated global news industry.

It is also not surprising that news agency television photographers have faced greater risk – and loss – than almost any other civilian media workers. News agency photographers – video and still – are legendary (one might say notorious) for their willingness to risk all to obtain the image no-one else has, and although news agency managers deny it, it seems to be a necessary qualification for the job.[41] Many of the television news photographers who have been considered the best conflict photographers of their generation have died violently doing their work. The core business of the television news agencies is to provide images of conflict that other media cannot obtain for themselves, or are unprepared to take the risk to obtain. Former *APTN* vice president Eric Braun told me that:

> a lot of the consumers of television news, particularly in the USA when they are watching any of the networks – CNN, NBC, Fox ... little do they realize that most of the most dangerous pictures are actually taken by the agency photographers, not by the people who work for the branded networks.[42]

Many of the news agency employees killed, injured or arrested in Iraq have been Iraqis hired by international news agencies to cover the breadth of the Iraq story more comprehensively and safely than news agency employees from outside Iraq might be able to. On every story, news agencies face a decision as to whether a local journalist will be more or less at risk than a foreign one. The role of local stringers and fixers for news agencies in providing much of the war footage the world sees is little acknowledged. Recent research by Murrel, Mitra and Venter in particular, and the earlier work of Pedelty,[43] has gone some way to rectifying that, but many of the standard texts on international journalism and war reporting still reinforce the misconception that photographers and star correspondents from the major Western media outlets are the people putting themselves at the greatest risk in order to witness violent events. The *BBC*'s world affairs editor John Simpson wrote in 2006:

> We do our own reporting, and, like every major television news organisation, we have access to the work of the two big agencies, Reuters and APTN. Their Iraqi cameramen, who are neither anonymous nor freelance, film just about everything that happens in Iraq; and we use their material in Iraq just as we use it everywhere else, because we know it is good and trustworthy.[44]

News agency journalists have sometimes complained that local employees are exploited, but with the increased focus on news safety during the past decade that problem may have diminished. Venter provided, for example, this admission from a seasoned television news agency photographer (in a rare bid to challenge existing practices) of 'how he would train non-journalists, such as soldiers, to use a video camera and to film the conflict on his behalf, in order to avoid putting himself in danger'. He chillingly explained:

I can actually recruit people on the ground to go out and do the things that I wouldn't do. Uninsured, non-professionals, unskilled, untrained who can go out there and get those images. That's one of my tactics to survive. If I have to go into a minefield, my fixer goes first. He dies before I do, for $100 a day.[45]

In the past decade, the news industry generally and news agencies in particular have made strides in recognising the vulnerability of the freelance and local journalists, translators and support staff they employ, and in providing them with improved protection and support. The Rory Peck Trust in the UK has been instrumental in promoting such change in the industry, a cause inspired by the 1993 death of Peck, a renowned freelance television photographer whose career was chronicled in David Loyn's epic book, *Frontline*.[46] But *Reuters* also continues to come under fire for putting freelancers at risk, a charge most recently levelled by their own former Baghdad bureau chief with regard to young Syrians providing pictures to *Reuters* from the civil war there.[47]

News agencies have been forced to devote a great deal of effort towards a defence of their long-standing role as wholesale providers of uncoloured (I avoid the loaded term 'unbiased') story information to the world's media outlets. The powerful symbiosis between the right-wing US media and right-wing bloggers created an intimidating flak mechanism that *Reuters* had already experienced after resisting the term 'terrorist' early in the Post-9/11 Wars.[48] In the weeks after the 2001 hijackings in the US, *Reuters* internally recommended to its writers to use caution in using the labels of 'terrorist' and 'terrorism' given their widespread and long-standing use around the world by governments seeking to demonise political enemies. *Reuters* took this position at some commercial risk, in contrast to most US media. *Reuters* explained the policy in a letter to US newspaper editors, which in turn sparked protest among conservative US and Canadian publications and blogs,[49] and might have created a perception in the US that *Reuters* wasn't 'on side'. In fact, *Reuters* wasn't a well-recognised entity to the US news audience, but it wasn't a leap of logic for some *Reuters* staff to imagine that the destruction of their Baghdad bureau by a US tank at the start of the Iraq war, and the deaths of many of their colleagues at the hands of US troops, was connected to their attempt to adhere to the position of journalistic neutrality, a commercial necessity for any international news agency.

As one of the two global news agencies and one of the three dominant providers of consistent news from Iraq for the world's media (with *AP* and *Al Jazeera*), *Reuters* might have been expected to be more successful than it ultimately was in preventing attacks on its staff and in holding the US government to account for them. *Reuters* as a company, along with many of their senior staff acting independently, had some successes in improving the situation for journalists in Iraq and have done much in the interests of journalists' safety generally, but we might speculate that their efforts were limited for three crucial reasons.

The first is that a news agency cannot risk exclusion from its main source, since its revenue stream depends on the flow of information from that source, and in this and a great many news agency stories the US government is the main story, and so the main source.[50] The second reason is that the general news service of the company is substantially supported by US media clients, and US media broadly supported the US government and so had little appetite for news portraying the US military or the US approach negatively. And third, many of the news managers most involved in dealing with these attacks left the company in the mid to late 2000s in the run-up to, and aftermath of, its takeover by the Canadian Thomson conglomerate and a general shift towards the prioritisation of business news (which had long been the main revenue source for *Reuters*).[51]

Reuters has repeatedly pressed its demands for investigation of the deaths and torture of its staff, despite US government intimidation and stonewalling, and despite few other major media organisations taking a strong public stance in either reporting or condemning the attacks. Following the deaths of six of their journalists, the torture of three others, and frequent harassment and detentions, *Reuters* has reason to be irate. The *BBC*'s Nik Gowing explained how the killing of one of *Reuters*' most experienced combat photographers and the torture of the *Reuters* employees reignited alarm through the news industry:

> *Reuters* has made public for the second time this week what happened to three of their Iraqi staff in the beginning of January. They [...] were threatened with sexual abuse, and were also offered sex by the American forces. They were held for at least three days and the Americans say there was no case to answer. We simply cannot believe that. It's a *Reuters* problem [and] also an industry problem for us.
>
> This after what happened outside the Abu Ghraib prison coincidentally on 17th of August [2003]. Mazen Dana, a *Reuters*

cameraman, a Palestinian who had been hit 60 times by the Israelis on the West Bank, was given permission to take these pictures next to this American roadblock. An American tank comes along. It's here [displaying video] in slow motion. The machine gunner doesn't like what he sees and kills Mazen Dana. The Americans will not admit responsibility for that.[52]

Reuters has made complaints to the highest levels of the Pentagon. Their global managing editor complained that US military conduct was spiralling 'out of control'.[53] The US military's only response to *Reuters*' requests for investigation following the abduction and torture of their journalists was a threatening demand that they drop their complaint.[54]

The Journalism Industry Responds

In late 2003, 30 news organisations collaborated to write to the US Assistant Secretary of Defense for Public Affairs to say they had 'documented numerous examples of US troops physically harassing journalists and, in some cases, confiscating or ruining equipment, digital camera disks, and videotapes'. The letter noted that US military rules stipulate that 'media products will not be confiscated or otherwise impounded'. A separate letter was sent by *AP* stating that US troops had been harassing and detaining journalists.[55] There was no immediate indication of any change in US military actions following these complaints.

Former *CNN* head Eason Jordan described an early effort by US broadcasters to work with the US military in Iraq to improve the safety of journalists. The 'Iraq News Safety Group' was an ad hoc group that included *ABC*, *CBS*, *NBC*, *Fox* and *CNN*. Other US-based news outlets and several non-US-based news outlets also participated at times. In addition to organising a routine of safety-focused conference calls between the foreign editors of US-based TV news organisations, along with calls and emails (on a weekly basis, and as needed in breaking news situations) between the bureau chiefs of Western news outlets in Baghdad, this initiative engaged directly with the US military.

Group representatives met with Pentagon leaders and US generals in Baghdad in an effort to ensure journalists in war zones remained safe. For example, after the US established the Green Zone in Baghdad, MNF-I[56] accredited journalists 'were forced to wait in long, unsecured queues with unaccredited civilians in the Red Zone for entry into the Green Zone'. Those queues were 'dangerous choke points that often came under insurgent gun and mortar fire'. Jordan convinced the US general responsible for Baghdad to establish a separate entry lane for accredited journalists to make a fast pass entry into the Green Zone, bypassing the long queue seeking Green Zone entry.[57] In 2004, amid constant and escalating concern from the media about the threatening nature of US military interactions with journalists, the Pentagon provided a dedicated 'hotline' telephone number to media organisations to alert senior US commanders of journalists in danger. The hotline was intended for 'life-threatening situations, detentions and other serious incidents involving journalists and other news team members covering Iraq'.[58]

As mentioned in earlier chapters, *CNN*'s Jordan also spoke out in 2004 at a Davos Economic Summit to raise concern about US involvement in the deaths of journalists. The result was not the launch of a Congressional investigation, or investigation by major media of the attacks in question, but was instead Jordan's quick resignation from *CNN* amid a firestorm of invective from right-wing media, politicians and bloggers – the 'flak' alluded to above.[59] In 2005, international journalists working in Iraq began to organise for the first time. Reporter Rory Carroll described how a group of 'angry and frustrated' correspondents met in early September 2005, and agreed to form a foreign correspondents' association and 'jointly lobby the US military and State Department'[60] for improved procedures in dealing with the media and serious investigations of attacks on the press. A month after describing that meeting in the *Guardian* and writing that 'American troops are out of control', Carroll was kidnapped by an unknown group, although he was one of the fortunate few to be quickly released.

Another high-level approach to the US government may have had more of an impact. In October of 2005, the CPJ enlisted the chairman of their board of directors, Paul Steiger – the managing editor of the influential *Wall Street Journal* newspaper – to personally contact senior Republican Senator John Warner. The call from Steiger, along with other communications from the CPJ and *Reuters*, prompted Warner to question Secretary of Defense Rumsfeld about detentions and shootings of journalists during a Congressional hearing. Rumsfeld committed to investigate these, and General George Casey, the top US military commander in Iraq, promised to meet with journalists in Iraq and address their concerns.[61]

Reuters was encouraged in March 2006, when the US military announced new policies to protect journalists in Iraq, including a commitment to treat detainees claiming to be journalists as 'unique' cases to be referred quickly up the chain of command, and a commitment to investigate allegations of abuse of detainees, including, according to *Reuters*, 'a beating in custody that left a *Reuters* cameraman unconscious'. Whether these procedures were the result of Warner's intervention is unclear. US Major General Jack Gardner also told *Reuters* that 'watching or filming combat or meeting insurgents were not in themselves grounds for arrest', despite that appearing to have been the basis for numerous arrests in the preceding years.[62]

While the media response to escalating revelations about the illegal surveillance of journalists has been similarly muted, there are increasing indications that this has provoked the ire of US journalists in ways that the US military violence against journalists in Iraq never did. Rupert Murdoch's *Fox News*, despite being one of several media victims of government snooping on the press in the US, has sought to politicise the issue and even to incite violent retribution against people who voted for the US President – blaming him personally for the surveillance: one *Fox News* radio journalist became so outraged while discussing Department of Justice targeting of journalists that she suggested listeners 'punch Obama voters in the face'.[63] Generally, the media industry has moved on to identifying practical solutions to the new challenges raised by revelations of surveillance by the US government. Writing for the Frontline Club's *Safety Blog*, Doug Brown advises the following:

> Use satellite phones with extreme caution, or not at all. Signals are easy to intercept and track down in real time due to their low prevalence in even the most technologically advanced regions. Most satellite phones also send the current GPS coordinates up to the satellite itself, and with the ease of interception these can then be used for near real time targeting.[64]

Press Freedom Organisations

The major response of the news industry thus far to the issues detailed in this book, and the broader escalation of attacks on the press internationally, has been the establishment in 2003 of the International News Safety Institute (INSI) to serve as a clearinghouse for information and to coordinate efforts to lobby governments. The establishment of

INSI was the result of the perception of managers of international news organisations that a more focused and proactive approach to escalating anti-press violence was needed.

The work of INSI has been significant, even if progress has been slow. Former *BBC* director of news Richard Sambrook wrote:

> Greater media-military understanding is seen as essential, though there is no certainty on how best to achieve this, especially when an army perceives the media or a particular news organisation as hostile. Again, we have been encouraged by the British Ministry of Defence's response to an INSI initiative ... For the first time it has written provisions for journalist safety into its 'Green Book' governing military-media relations in time of war. These include a pledge that British forces will never target journalists. Prompt and open inquiries where and whenever journalists are killed by military forces are a prerequisite.[65]

Outside of the news industry there have been long-standing efforts by a number of NGOs set up to defend freedom of expression and the rights of journalists. Although often funded by media companies, they have generally sought to stand apart from specific organisations, and NGOs such as Reporters Sans Frontières, the IFJ and the CPJ are at the front line of actions to help journalists in difficulty, including investigating attacks on the media. The leading international press freedom groups are listed in Appendix 2. The chronology of attacks on the media included in Appendix 1 is based largely on a recent investigation by the IFJ, which has been one of the most vocal critics of the US involvement in press attacks.

Even the CPJ – based in New York and funded mostly by major US media outlets, and directed by many editors and publishers of major US media – has recently become more sharply critical of the US government's interactions with the press. Their efforts have been useful, and much of their research into attacks on journalists is the most comprehensive available, but unlike the IFJ or other non-US organisations they have exhibited a historical reluctance to publicise attacks on the press by the US government or to lobby US media to do so. At the start of a recent protest letter to US Attorney General Holder, following the seizure of *AP*'s phone records in the US in 2013 (described in Chapter 2), the CPJ observed 'Dear Attorney General Holder and Deputy Attorney General Cole: CPJ's board of directors rarely has seen the need to raise its collective voice against US government actions that threaten newsgathering'.

Examples of the work of such organisations in documenting attacks on media include the 2003 report *Justice Denied on the Road to Baghdad: Safety of Journalists and the Killing of Media Staff During the Iraq War*, produced by the IFJ, and *Killing the Messenger: The Report of the Global Inquiry by the International News Safety Institute into the Protection of Journalists*, published by INSI in March 2007. The IFJ and other groups have also sought on occasion to draw attention to indirect US and Iraqi responsibility for the deaths of journalists in Iraq. In 2004 the Director of the IFJ specifically accused the US and Iraqi authorities of failing to protect local journalists in Iraq who were known to be targets of local fighters and who had requested protection. The IFJ called the failure 'unconscionable', adding 'it appears that by refusing to provide basic protection when requested, Iraqi and US security police are guilty of shocking neglect of their basic obligation to protect the lives of those directly under threat'. His comments followed the deaths of two local journalists following their kidnapping by insurgents. The murdered journalists worked for the former editor of a US-funded Baghdad newspaper, and this was believed to be the reason they were targeted.[66]

All of these efforts, in combination, have reduced the risks for journalists, even if they have made little progress in challenging the impunity of the US government and other states. But it could be argued that the US government has done much to *exacerbate* the divisions within professional media, which mitigate any effective collective response to anti-press violence while simultaneously increasing the danger to media workers. Whether through accident or design, they've accomplished both feats at once through the massive investment of US public funds in propaganda broadcasting, especially in Iraq. While some propaganda efforts are conducted by the US military and broadly recognised as such, the most ambitious and costly efforts mimic commercial news broadcasters, only with a tightly controlled pro-US agenda. The Washington-based Iraqi television broadcaster *al-Hurra* was funded by Congress in 2003 and went on the air in 2004, largely the brainchild of one wealthy US television executive, Norm Pattiz, who also sat on the oversight board of the other US government propaganda broadcasters, known as the Broadcast Board of Governors (successor to the US Information Agency).[67] The Statewatch and IFJ report quoted earlier wrote:

They claim to be editorially independent. But the explicit intention is to provide an alternative to broadcasters such as Al-Jazeera or Al-Arabiya and the station struggles for credibility when it luxuriates in funding from US Congress worth $62m for its first year. It is by far the largest single international media development project ever funded. Not surprisingly, *al-Hurra* provokes distrust and scepticism from Arab critics.[68]

Unsurprisingly, given the popular perception of *al-Hurra* journalists as the voice of the occupying power, a great many of them have been attacked in Iraq by insurgent groups, yet interestingly there are few reports of US troops attacking or harassing *al-Hurra* journalists working in Iraq.

In paying journalists to play an explicitly propagandistic role in Iraq, the US government ramped up public distrust and antagonism towards the media and dragged more civilian media workers into the conflict. Furthermore, by establishing rival media camps, efforts encouraging domestic and international journalists to work in solidarity in Iraq, both in the practical aspects of daily news gathering and in bringing about better protection and recognition for journalistic work, were derailed. Rare, but unfortunately short-lived, collaboration between rival news companies was widely seen as saving the lives of many journalists during the Yugoslav civil war.[69]

Despite US military accounts of key events involving civilian deaths in Iraq and Afghanistan having at times been discredited as premature, false or distorted (even by leading news organisations), Miller[70] and other analysts of the war narrative have shown how these accounts dominate public discourse. Where accounts of the deaths of journalists have been provided by the US military, those have also shaped the public narrative and mostly gone unquestioned by mainstream news outlets. A single rare, though brief, challenge to this was the prominent publication by *WikiLeaks* of the video showing the previously hidden killing of two *Reuters* journalists by the crew of an Apache helicopter in 2007, which was widely reported and retransmitted in the mainstream media. This context of accepting civilian killings with a minimum of critical or detailed reporting contributes to an environment in which attacks on the press cannot readily be questioned, and thus the necessary investigative journalism which might inspire greater protection of civilians is further constrained. The central – but mostly unspoken – journalistic tenet that official US accounts should not be challenged has increasingly had the indirect consequence of facilitating state impunity in the deaths of journalists and increasing the threat towards them.

Many have argued that some (at least) of the fuss about the safety of journalists is misplaced. There are many rationales offered for the argument: that journalists' lives count for no more than those of other civilians caught up in conflict (a position taken by the ICRC, for example); that journalists who go into conflict zones should do so expecting danger and not be 'precious' about it (to quote one old *BBC* hand who prefers not to be given credit for describing his colleagues in those terms); or that the focus on journalists takes attention away from people who take greater risks and make a greater difference in conflict situations.

There are prominent fissures within journalism regarding the perception of reporting risk, and these came to the fore in the aftermath of the Palestine Hotel attack. Some conservative commentary, especially that emanating from some US and Canadian press and broadcasting outlets, was unabashedly hostile to the very concept of a military *obligation* for media protection and was quick to blame journalists for their own predicament. Such media reporting and comment has also done much to diminish any effective collective media response to the escalating 'friendly threat'. A Canadian reporter, having observed some reporters question military briefers about the deaths of their colleagues in the Palestine Hotel, opined 'Who cares what else is happening in the war: Journalists are being shot! How naive'.[71]

Some US media outlets went a step further, actively encouraging the US military to attack media installations. FAIR recounted how, at the start of the US bombing of Baghdad in 2003, *Fox News*, *CNBC*, *NBC* and *CNN*, as well as a *New York Times* reporter appearing on *CNN*, all urged the bombing of *Iraq Television*, the Iraqi public broadcaster, prior to the ultimate US attack on it (or expressed satisfaction after the attack). None made the link to what the US had done in Serbia four years earlier, nor to the Geneva Conventions' prohibition of such an attack.[72]

Even more frustrating and alarming to *Reuters* news agency staff working in London was when prominent *BBC* defence correspondent Andrew Gilligan – who would himself soon become mired in controversy for his role in reporting the Blair government's attempt to 'sex up' the case for war in Iraq – reported on *BBC Radio 5* that he had looked at the Palestine Hotel after the attack and thought that it was more likely to have been an Iraqi attack than a US one, going on to predict hours after the attack: 'I may be right in saying we're hearing from central command that they're starting to retract their apology for this incident'.[73] Following a report on the *Guardian*'s website immediately following Gilligan's comment, his remarks entered the global debate about the incident and were rapidly circulated in the blogosphere as a valuable scrap of evidence that the US military doesn't make such mistakes. Gilligan went on to play prominent roles in the conservative British media, and so the tendency to sympathise with (and even promote) a US military position, despite the cost to journalistic colleagues, might be dismissed as an inevitable part of the broad mix of media views given the dominance of war boosterism in the editorial output of most US media and much UK media at the time.

With little sign of a media industry unified in defence of all media workers, a final example illustrates the extent of disagreement about the nature of the problem. Former *BBC* director of news Richard Sambrook, who has led efforts in the UK to institutionalise press protections, has suggested, as a means of reducing attacks on journalists, 'a media murder index which could be built into country profiles that would be used as a basis for determining international aid'. He noted that the World Bank froze $250 million in loans to the Kenyan government as a response to a violent raid on two Kenyan media outlets.[74] So what happens when a country claiming impunity for press attacks – such as the US – doesn't take loans from the World Bank? This recommendation unfortunately reinforces assumptions that it is for the West to police the rest, and the self-appointed policeman is above reproach.

Henning Gloystein, from *Reuters*, made such a point in response to an essay by Sambrook on the threats to journalists, prepared for London's Frontline Club. In response to Sambrook's injunction that 'there is no greater threat to free societies than the murder of journalists', Gloystein countered that Sambrook:

> is right to worry about free speech around the world. And yes, the journalists that take immense personal risks in order to make injustice public, make a remarkable contribution to the world. However, like it or not, some religious groups, aid workers or doctors who are risking their own lives, deserve more recognition than frontline journalists who get their names published in important papers or magazines before they go back for a drink in the Frontline Club. In short, my opinion is that we, the journalists, inform the world. But I find it slightly arrogant to say that 'there is no greater threat to free societies than the murder of journalists.' It does injustice to all the people who risk their lives for a better society for little or no payment.[75]

With that caveat in mind, along with the broader context of dozens of media arrests and killings against those of thousands of non-media civilians, the importance of the professional witness – who commands the power to publicise what they see in ways not available to average people – cannot be dismissed. Since the escalation of violence against the press, taking place mostly since the illegal US invasion of Iraq, myriad behind-the-scenes efforts by media organisations and their advocates have sought to solve the problem through the use of diplomacy and mostly behind-the-scenes pressure. But as Waisbord observed:

> raising attention to the problem is only a temporary remedy; it provides some protection for journalists in peril, but it does not provide a solution to deep-seated conditions that breed violence against the press.[76]

But if such violence and intimidation of the press is fundamentally illegal, why have those efforts even been necessary? That is the topic of Chapter 5.

5
Legality

This book has thus far recounted the abandonment of the Fourth Estate ideal, not just by successive US governments and some of their Middle Eastern allies who publicly expound similar ideals, but by many in the media itself. The killing of media workers and attacking of media facilities by the US government began with the 1999 attack on the Serbian public broadcaster and became normalised in the Post-9/11 Wars that followed, with nearly 50 media deaths directly linked to the US. As Chapter 4 explained, media institutions have lobbied vigorously behind the scenes for accountability and greater protection, and some media organisations in particular have had good reason to feel targeted by the US government. But sadly, media organisations have substantially failed to unite in their efforts, failed to put the issue of media protection on the public agenda, and failed to push governments towards greater accountability.

Could legal avenues end attacks on the press where private and public pressure has failed? The laws pertaining to war and to the treatment of media personnel in times of war are complex, and this chapter does not attempt a full review of each relevant legal doctrine and its history. While the laws pertaining to war are described and debated in an extensive literature, the specific analysis of the legal rights of journalists in zones of conflict is more limited – perhaps because it remains confused to this day.[1] The summary provided here gives a general survey of legal principles relevant to the protection of journalists in the extraordinarily dangerous reporting environment of a war zone.

What is known about all, or nearly all, of the attacks on journalists in Iraq by the US military, or by Iraqi authorities operating under US military authority, indicates that they are unquestionably in violation of numerous legal regimes. But oddly, the fact that much of what the US has done in the Post-9/11 Wars (including the violence perpetrated towards the media) has been illegal, has been barely commented upon by the world's news media (and least of all, by the US media). Philippe Sands writes that:

between 9/11 and the emergence of the scandals at Abu Ghraib there was a noticeable reluctance on the part of the press and TV to investigate critically the Administration's misuse of legal arguments to justify everything from the indefinite detention of foreigners at Guantanamo to the legal basis for the war in Iraq. Outside small circulation publications like the *New York Review of Books* and *The Nation* magazine these issues were simply not considered to be newsworthy.[2]

Sands' point is confirmed by numerous analyses of post-9/11 media content. The extreme limitations of that content can not only be explained by the fuzzy notion of 'newsworthiness' – dependent on the professional judgement of media professionals working within the limitations of their organisation – at the expense of a clearer and more sinister constraint on news production: the cultural and ideological environment in which journalists found themselves at that moment. Sands concluded that 'until the revelations at Abu Ghraib there was virtually no informed public dissent against the Administration's efforts to rewrite international law into irrelevance'.[3] Sands observed that news media historically have showed neither great understanding of, nor interest in, matters of international law, but that this changed significantly with the arrest of the former Chilean dictator Augusto Pinochet, in London in 1988. Pinochet – thinking he was safely under the protection of his friend, British Prime Minister Thatcher – was arrested due to a Spanish court's warrant, issued on the basis of crimes committed in Chile. A lively debate about the nature of international law, and the responsibilities of nations to enforce it, ensued in the British (and Latin American) media. Despite more clarity in international law over the illegality of many US government actions than news media coverage suggests, the US and its Middle Eastern allies have broadly come to accept a position that certain governments – but not others – have the legal authority to kill, injure, abduct, detain and torture civilian media workers under certain conditions.

The principle of US exceptionalism is one possible explanation for why the US government considers itself to be justified in only considering international law when this supports perceived US interests. Horwitz, in his recent assessment of the Right in the US as a political movement quite different from 1950s Eisenhower Republicanism, succinctly defined US exceptionalism as:

the conviction as to the beneficent, universal nature of the American values that necessarily accompany U.S. military ventures abroad; that war was the preferred means to defeat America's external enemies and, in the case of the neoconservatives, the way to spread democracy to blighted parts of the globe ... that the United States is the embodiment of God's gift of freedom and constitutes the greatest earthly force for good the world has known.[4]

In the eyes of adherents to US exceptionalism, foreign military adventure is inherently correct on its own terms, and needn't be subject to any test of legality or morality beyond that.[5] Indeed, when the US government has been involved in apparent violations of international law and/or globally accepted standards of human rights (especially the UN Convention on Human Rights), it has consistently failed to provide transparent, verifiable evidence in justification of its actions, or evidence of prosecuting those responsible and instituting reforms to prevent the same thing happening again.

Why Attacking Journalists is Illegal

The basis of international humanitarian law is enshrined in the four Geneva Conventions of 1949.[6] Geneva Convention IV concerns the protection of civilians in times of war. The conventions are among the most widely ratified international treaties, and the norms they establish are largely considered customary international law – that is, norms that have obtained universal recognition and are accepted as binding upon all nations. The 1977 additional protocols to the conventions provide further elaboration of the provisions of the four 1949 Geneva Conventions. Protocol I relates to the protection of victims of international armed conflicts; Protocol II to the protection of victims of non-international armed conflicts.

All 188 members of the United Nations are parties to the four Geneva Conventions of 1949, while 155 states are parties to Protocol I and 148 to Protocol II. Most NATO members are parties to Protocol I, but notable exceptions are France, Turkey and the US. Although the US has not ratified Protocols I and II, it considers many of their provisions to be applicable as customary international law. The US Army *Operational Law Handbook 2000* states that the US views a number of Protocol I articles as customary international law or acceptable practice, including article 51 (protection of the civilian population, except paragraph 6, reprisals) and article 52 (general protection of civilian objects). In addition, the US and NATO recognise as a matter of policy that the laws of war apply to all cases of armed conflict, and their 'principles and spirit' will be applied, even if a state of war is not recognised.[7]

A basic principle of the laws of war, as laid down in Protocol I, is that the civilian population and individual civilians shall have general protection against dangers arising from military operations. This turns in large part on the requirement that protagonists must distinguish between civilians and combatants, and between military targets and civilian objects. Importantly, the law does not relieve one party to a conflict, such as the US military, from its obligations, even if the other party to the conflict, such as an informal and non-state insurgent, criminal or 'terrorist' group, fails to observe them.

Combatants must avoid or minimise harm to civilians, and to this end may not attack civilians exclusively or combatants and civilians indiscriminately. Attacks may not be indiscriminate by intent, where the attackers deliberately set out to kill and maim civilians, or through negligence, where those carrying out an attack disregard their obligations to identify a specific military objective and do not take care to avoid causing disproportionate harm to civilians in attacking it. Damage to civilian objects and civilian casualties that are incidental to lawful attacks on military objectives are known in military terms as 'collateral damage'.

The most fundamental principle of the laws of war requires that combatants be distinguished from non-combatants, and that military objectives be distinguished from protected property or protected places. Under Protocol I, Article 48, parties to a conflict must direct their operations only against military objectives (including combatants). Under Protocol I, Article 51, paragraph 4, indiscriminate attacks are prohibited. These include attacks that:

- are 'not directed against a specific military objective';[8]
- 'employ a method or means of combat[9] which cannot be directed at a specific military objective';
- 'employ a method or means of combat the effects of which cannot be limited as required' by the Protocol; and
- 'in each such case, are of a nature to strike military objectives and civilians or civilian objects without distinction'.

Casualties that are a consequence of accidents, as in situations in which civilians are concealed within military installations, may be considered incidental to an attack on a military objective, or 'collateral damage' – but care must still have been taken to identify the presence of civilians. Protocol I, Article 57 sets out the precautions required, among them to 'do everything feasible to verify that the objectives to be attacked are neither civilians nor civilian objects'; to 'take all feasible precautions in the choice of means and methods of attack' to avoid or minimise incidental civilian casualties or damage to civilian objects; and to refrain from launching any attack 'which may be expected to cause' such deaths, injuries or damage 'which would be excessive in relation to the concrete and direct military advantage anticipated'. In its authoritative *Commentary* on the protocols, the ICRC details what is meant by 'feasible': 'What is required … is to take the necessary identification measures in good time in order to spare the population as far as possible'.[10] When he met with Pentagon officials about the US attack on the *BBC* in Kabul, Nik Gowing pressed for the US military's definition of 'military significance', in order to determine what it considers to be a 'military objective'. He found 'the Pentagon would not define its term "military significance" or explain its relationship to media operations', and despairingly concluded that his meetings 'confirmed the US military makes no effort to distinguish between legitimate satellite uplinks for broadcast news communications and the identifiable radio or satellite communications belonging to "the enemy"'.[11]

Similarly, the principle of proportionality places a duty on combatants to choose means of attack that avoid or minimise harm to civilians. In particular, the attacker should refrain from launching an attack if the expected civilian casualties would outweigh the importance of the military objective. Protocol I, Article 57 (precautions in attack), paragraph 2(b), requires those who plan and/or execute an attack to cancel the attack in such circumstances. But the ICRC has argued that there is *never* a justification for excessive civilian casualties, no matter how important the military target. Moreover, the argument of proportionality can never justify very high civilian casualties and damage whatever the military advantage envisioned: 'Incidental losses and damages should never be extensive'.[12]

The case could also be made under international law that Article 19 of the United Nations' Universal Declaration of Human Rights requires states, regardless of the conditions of warfare, to respect media representatives and provide for their safe conduct. Article 19 stipulates that 'everyone has the right to freedom of opinion and expression; this right includes freedom to hold opinions without interference and to seek, receive and impart information and ideas through any media and regardless of frontiers'. The Declaration was adopted by the United Nations General Assembly in 1948, for the purpose of defining the meaning of the words 'fundamental freedoms' and 'human rights', appearing in the United Nations Charter, which is binding on all member states and is a fundamental constitutive document of the United Nations. Many international lawyers believe that the Declaration forms part of customary international law, although others disagree. Thompson and Giffard state that declarations 'are indicative',[13] and human rights researcher Shane Darcy observed that 'this is a very general rule which could arguably be circumscribed in times of war'.[14]

In 2006, following a campaign by media groups such as Reporters Sans Frontières and the INSI, with support from the French and Greek governments, the Security Council of the United Nations unanimously adopted Resolution 1738 (2006), which expressed deep concern at 'the frequency of acts of violence, including deliberate attacks, in many parts of the world against journalists, media professionals and associated personnel, in armed conflicts', condemned such attacks, and called on all parties to put an end to such practices. The resolution states:

> without prejudice to the war correspondents' right to the status of prisoners of war under the Third Geneva Convention, that journalists, media professionals and associated personnel engaged in dangerous professional missions in areas of armed conflict shall be considered civilians, to be respected and protected as such.

It further demands 'that all parties to armed conflict comply with their obligations under international law to protect civilians in armed conflict' and 'emphasized the responsibility of States in that regard, as well as their obligation to end impunity and to prosecute those responsible for serious violations' urging all parties in situations of armed conflict to 'respect the professional independence and rights of journalists, media professionals and associated personnel as civilians'.[15]

There is considerable debate about whether such resolutions are *binding*; however, in practical terms the extent to which they are *enforceable* depends on the identity of the parties involved and whether the will and the means exist to enforce them. Following the April 2003 attacks against the Palestine Hotel and the bureaus of *Al Jazeera* and *Abu Dhabi Television* in Baghdad, Reporters Sans Frontières wrote to the

International Humanitarian Fact-Finding Commission, the body which the UN established to investigate possible crimes against humanity requiring the action of the International Criminal Court, to request an investigation into whether the attacks violated international humanitarian law. Reporters Sans Frontières secretary-general Robert Ménard stated: 'A media outlet cannot be a military target under international law and its equipment and installations are civilian property protected as such under the Geneva Conventions'.[16] It was the first ever such request to the commission, but they could not act because any request for action has to come from the parties to the conflict, and the parties to the conflict must all accept the authority of the commission; neither the US nor Saddam Hussein's Iraq had done so.

In addition to international law set out by treaty, international customary law is also applicable. To prove that a state has broken a customary law, one needs to demonstrate that a particular practice – in this case, the protection of journalists during conflict – had become the accepted practice among nations. As noted, the key legal instruments are the Geneva Conventions of 1949 and the Additional Protocols of 1977, designed to protect the rights of civilians in zones of conflict and provide some universal rules of warfare. As a signatory to the original conventions, the US is obligated to comply with them, but the US did not ratify the 1977 treaty. Kirby and Jackson summarised the main failings of the Geneva Conventions in regard to the protection of journalists:

- Protections only apply following detention;
- The protections 'consider' a journalist to be a civilian – they do not state that a journalist is a civilian;
- The conventions are 'devoid of effective sanctions for their breach'.[17]

Following the 1999 US bombing of Belgrade, and the 'Shock and Awe' campaign in Iraq – both of which targeted media installations – Human Rights Watch conducted investigations into the legality of both campaigns. International law specifies that buildings and facilities that might reasonably be suspected to have both a civilian and military purpose be considered 'dual use targets'. According to Human Rights Watch, 'In assessing potential targets, military planners must carefully balance the concrete and direct military advantage of destroying these facilities against the expected death and injury to civilians and damage to civilian objects'. A US military official told Human Rights Watch in regard to the bombing of Baghdad:

> It was clear we needed to eliminate the regime's ability to put out disinformation ... Most important was the Iraqi TV's military value. We have felt pretty comfortable that it was one of the means Iraqi intelligence used to signal its elements outside the country ... There was a potential for terrorist activity ... Did it happen? No. We were concerned it would happen, felt the potential for a catastrophic event outweighed the potential ill will. But the Iraqis never used TV to direct the military. There were songs we knew of they could use and had in the past that would tell forces where to go and to take certain actions. This is why we took out TV.[18]

Human Rights Watch concluded that that while stopping broadcasts intended to give encouragement to the general population may have served to demoralise the Iraqi population and undermine the government's political support, neither purpose offered the *definite military advantage* required by law to make media facilities legitimate military targets. After exhaustive study in Iraq, Human Rights Watch concluded of the 'Shock and Awe' bombing:

> The Coalition's record with pre-planned targets in Iraq was mixed. It used precision-guided munitions and careful targeting to minimize civilian casualties in dozens of strikes on government buildings. U.S. attacks on alleged dual-use targets, however, were more controversial. Its destruction of media facilities was of questionable legality; Human Rights Watch found no evidence that the media was used to support Iraq's military effort.[19]

Human Rights Watch concluded that the Belgrade attack very clearly violated the Geneva Conventions since:

> Regardless of NATO's legal determination that civilian radio and television were legitimate military objectives because of their role in internal and external propaganda, NATO did not take adequate precautions in warning civilians in the attack on the media headquarters, nor did the attack satisfy the legal requirement in terms of proportionality, given that the center was located in a densely populated urban

neighborhood and was staffed twenty-four hours [...] While stopping such propaganda may serve to demoralize the Yugoslav population and undermine the government's political support, neither purpose offers the 'concrete and direct' military advantage necessary to make them a legitimate military target [...] NATO failed to provide clear advance warning of the attacks 'whenever possible,' as required by [the Geneva Conventions] Protocol I, art. 57(2).[20]

Legal expertise and humanitarian organisations like Human Rights Watch have consistently called into question the explanations and justifications provided by the US government, and the governments with which it is closely allied, for the variety of attacks that have occurred on media personnel and installations. Central to the dismissal of most of those justifications is the key premise that media facilities are not only protected by the Geneva Conventions because they are civilian, but because combatants are required to *presume* they are civilian when there is doubt. In each case, they were instead presumed to be military objectives.

Several of the attacks on media personnel – most of them with lethal consequences – have been reported by the US military to be the result of television cameras being mistaken by troops for binoculars used by enemy snipers (in the case of the Palestine Hotel) or shoulder mounted missile launchers (as in the case of *Reuters* cameraman Mazen Dana and others). As the *BBC*'s Nik Gowing complained in 2004, 'We understand that a camera sitting on the right shoulder of a cameraman can perhaps sometimes be mistaken by soldiers who are nervous for a rocket system. But this is happening too often'.[21] According to Eason Jordan, the first senior executive from a major international news organisation to draw public attention to the problem of the US military shooting journalists:

Those victims in most cases were fired upon directly, without there being evidence U.S. forces knew they were aiming and shooting at journalists. More restraint would have been appropriate in those cases, in my view. Nevertheless, in my opinion, there should have been accountability and not justifications or excuses for those tragic episodes in which U.S. forces killed journalists in *de facto* cases of mistaken identity.[22]

There is an established principle that combatants must warn civilians who could be endangered by attacks; in most of the cases discussed in this book, and in the cases of attacks on individual journalists, this did not happen in a sufficiently specific way, if at all.[23] On the contrary, in a number of cases the journalists killed, or their employer, had taken steps to alert military forces to their presence. For example, the many journalists with *Reuters* photographer Mazen Dana unanimously claimed that their reporting work in the area was clearly known to the US tank crew that killed him.[24] A colleague would later recount of Dana that 'he was deliberately shot at by Israeli troops so often that *Reuters* eventually sent him to Baghdad for what was considered to be a safer assignment'.[25]

Military investigations and the court martial of military personnel responsible for attacks on the media are possible, but only where the military agree to an appropriate investigation. There is little indication of this so far in the case of media deaths, but recent investigations of other killings of civilians by US and UK military personnel have led to arrest and trial. These circumstances may lead media organisations to publicly demand similarly thorough investigations of media deaths – although much time has now passed since the spate of attacks described in this book between 1999 and 2007. Attacks on the media should be easier to investigate by military authorities since the victims are so clearly non-combatants, and there have often been many witnesses, and even video recordings, to rely upon. This should make it difficult now for military officials to refuse to investigate – or reinvestigate – these civilian deaths, if public pressure upon them intensified.

The 'principle of distinction' is central to the laws of war, and states that 'the Parties to the conflict shall at all times distinguish between the civilian population and combatants and between civilian objects and military objectives and accordingly shall direct their operations only against military objectives',[26] while Article 79 dictates that journalists be treated as civilians and not as combatants. The principle of distinction becomes problematic when journalists ally themselves with troops, as in the process of 'embedding'. Journalists who have connected themselves with combatants may be treated as prisoners of war if captured.[27] However, Balguy-Gallois observes that because the practice of 'embedding' is a relatively new phenomenon, there is not yet a clear consensus on how the parties to a conflict are to treat such media personnel.[28]

In the Iraq war, the conflict was so asymmetrical that reporters with US troops faced little threat of capture by insurgent forces, but many of the journalists detained, and in several cases tortured, by US authorities (as described in Chapter 3) were accused of having contact with insurgents, despite this being an obvious part of their journalistic work. They were treated neither as wrongly arrested civilians nor as prisoners of war under international law.

The responses of some senior US military officials to news media complaints regarding the treatment of journalists indicate that, while there may not be a policy per se of targeting journalists, there is clearly a policy of neglecting or even obstructing the principle of distinction which should protect journalists. For example, Article 79 allows for combatant states to issue journalists with identity cards to facilitate their identification. In detentions of journalists that have occurred in Iraq, at least one journalist has reported that US soldiers confiscated his official identity cards (not carrying such cards might remove protection under the Geneva Conventions, according to the IFJ).[29] The US and Iraqi governments claim to operate under the terms of the Geneva Conventions in their processes of detention, but Reporters Sans Frontières has argued that the US ignores the legal guarantees the Convention requires for prisoners.[30] Major international human rights organisations have agreed with this assessment.

The ICRC can act to investigate detentions of journalists, but the ICRC has warned journalists that 'although the Geneva Conventions are binding on virtually all States, when it comes to their implementation the ICRC runs into innumerable difficulties, ranging from denial of their applicability to repeated violations of their provisions'.[31] The 2006 ruling by the US Supreme Court (*Hamdan* v. *Rumsfeld*), stating that prisoners of the US military in Guantanamo Bay are entitled to the full protections of the Geneva Conventions,[32] was reported as a blow to US policy and implicit recognition by the highest US court that the US had not been fulfilling its obligations under international law. Although the Bush administration stated it would comply with the court ruling, the real effect for those imprisoned by the US appears to be unchanged; despite then presidential candidate Obama's pre-election promises to close the Guantanamo facility, not only does it remain open but there is little evidence of improvement in the conditions of those prisoners years after the ruling.

A 2010 report by the Obama administration to the UN Human Rights council highlights the US ability to simultaneously acknowledge and disregard international law, stating that with regard to Guantanamo, the administration 'has expressly acknowledged that international law informs the scope of our detention authority', but at the same time has made clear that it has 'a national security interest in prosecuting terrorists'.[33] Indeed, in many instances the US government has claimed its 'War on Terror' is in a general way not covered by the Geneva Conventions. There has been detailed analysis of this position, which is beyond the scope of this book to address, but the lack of legal merit for it is unambiguous.[34]

The Guantanamo ruling and the ongoing detention in the facility of prisoners without trial also has a more direct connection to the violent coercion of the media described here. After seven years of campaigning by his colleagues and family, *Al Jazeera* photographer Sami Al-Hajj was released from the facility in May 2008, without ever being tried or convicted of any activities related to terrorism. He claims to have been told he was 'wrongly detained, but was kept in Guantanamo because of what he had seen while there'. He said his interrogations 'were almost entirely about *Al Jazeera*, as interrogators tried to find a connection between the network and Al Qaeda'. This motivation for his detention was later confirmed by files released by *WikiLeaks*.[35] Article five of the Third Geneva Convention requires that detainees receive a 'competent tribunal', which did not happen in the case of Al-Hajj or of other Guantanamo detainees.

Both as a signatory and as an occupying power, the US government was and is fully bound by the Geneva Conventions, and may not arbitrarily define some civilians as exempt from the protections of those treaties, although it appears routinely to do so. Some media organisations have exacerbated this situation: personnel from some media institutions have not only removed their own protections under the Geneva Conventions, but have further endangered all journalists by actively cooperating with invading military forces, as has the *New York Times* in its collaboration in the hunt for 'weapons of mass destruction' (referred to in Chapter 2); or by employing people who have fired weapons against combatants, as has *CNN*; or in even carrying a weapon and threatening to use it against Iraqis, as a well-known *Fox News* correspondent famously did. And, in an understandable, although counterproductive, move given the ongoing threat to journalists from local militia and criminal groups, an Iraqi journalists' organisation has sought official permission for journalists to arm themselves for protection.

The US refused to ratify Protocol I to the 1949 Geneva Conventions 'Relating to the Protection of Victims of International Armed Conflicts', developed in 1977. That Protocol sets out the rights of civilians to 'general protection against dangers arising from military operations'. Although US military policy, as stated in the Army Field Manual, requires that 'civilians must not be made the object of attack directed exclusively against them', military rules of engagement provide a good deal of leeway for soldiers in determining what constitutes self-defence, something military law always permits. What remains unclear at a practical level is how violations of international law can be either investigated or prosecuted when governments declare their own military rules to have been followed.

International treaty obligations are expected to take precedence where they may conflict with military laws and procedures. States are therefore required to conduct investigations of reported violations of international law that are independent of the military institutions accused of committing the violations.[36] This clearly is not happening, where the military conducts its own investigations of violations alleged by human rights organisations and/or the media. Even where NGOs can investigate violations, where military authorities permit them to do so, they cannot provide any punishment for them. There is already ample evidence with regard to the Abu Ghraib and Guantanamo Bay detention facilities, the protection of wounded combatants, the protection of ambulances, and other issues, that the US military has decided not to comply consistently with the Geneva Conventions – even though it has officially declared a policy of non-compliance only in the case of certain prisoners.[37] This lends support to the possibility of an unstated policy in regard to the treatment of journalists.

Even with regard to attacks on journalists by non-state actors in Iraq or Afghanistan, under international law the US-led coalitions had an obligation to protect every journalist and to create conditions for them to do their work safely – and the US has failed in that obligation. As the sole legal authority in Iraq at the beginning of the post-invasion period, the US also had an obligation to investigate each of these killings and bring the killers to justice, and there is little indication of that happening in any of the cases. With estimates of civilian deaths since the Iraq invasion ranging from 100,000 to one million or more, as noted previously,[38] the possibility of investigation of any civilian death is remote.

Local criminal proceedings against the killers of journalists – whether state or non-state actors – are technically possible but impractical and unreliable in the case of Iraq. Iraqi law under the temporary post-invasion government vowed to protect 'public safety' and support 'the commitment to international principles of freedom of speech and of the press as articulated in the International Convention of Civil and Political Rights and other documents'.[39] That directive also promises a 'free and independent' media. But given the ongoing confused legal situation in Iraq since the invasion, which has continued since the election of national governments in January 2005 and 2010, and given the current regime's continued dependence on international support, international laws rather than local laws hold the most hope for the protection of journalists working in Iraq.[40] When four television journalists were murdered in Mosul, Iraq, in 2008 it was reported that some days later the Iraqi government arrested five men in connection with the case. The CPJ observed that it was the first time in over five years of slaughter of journalists in the country that an arrest had been made.[41]

When states themselves fail to investigate and prosecute violations, the United Nations is empowered under the 2002 Rome Statute to charge violators in the International Criminal Court (ICC). But the US has not ratified the Rome Statute and has said that it will not cooperate with the ICC. Philippe Sands has analysed the progressive change in the US perspective on international law which included its rejection of the ICC, writing that:

> the 1998 Statute of the International Criminal Court was treated as though it was a great threat to American power, constraining military activity and subjecting American soldiers and leaders to the risk of politically motivated prosecution by an independent international prosecutor [...] the United States was entirely free to choose not to become a party to these or other treaties, but its reasons for not doing so marked a dramatic change of perspective. There emerged a presumption against international rules: they no longer created opportunities, but were seen as imposing significant constraints.[42]

In the event that the ICC ever did detain a US soldier, Congress has authorised the US military to attack the ICC in the Netherlands to get that person back.[43] In 2006, the IFJ was working with other interested parties to write a resolution for the United Nation's Security Council to adopt to refer murders of journalists to the ICC, but to date the United Nations has only managed to ratify weaker condemnations of attacks on media, but little in the way of sanction.

Other legal solutions might include a call for the International Humanitarian Fact-Finding Commission of the United Nations to investigate the killing of media workers where evidence of violations of the Geneva Conventions can be shown.[44] To date the Commission has done little, since it has waited for states participating in conflicts that have resulted in human rights violations to refer themselves for investigation.

This has been a recipe for inaction.[45] In April 2003, Reporters Sans Frontières called for an 'impartial, objective and independent' enquiry by the International Humanitarian Fact-Finding Commission into the firing on the [Palestine] hotel. It had already ... urged the Commission to investigate the bombing of Iraqi state TV offices by Coalition forces.'[46]

The possibility of a United Nations International Humanitarian Fact-Finding Commission investigation is controversial in legal circles – the Commission has not dealt with such a situation before, but scholars have argued that it could broaden its remit. Zegveld contends that, in order to do so, the commission only 'requires an allegation that international humanitarian law is seriously violated', and the allegation needn't come from a state, but could come from representatives of the victims.[47] Reporters Sans Frontières has argued that the Commission is entitled to exercise its 'right of initiative' in order to investigate violations of the Geneva Conventions.[48] However, even if it were found that violations had occurred, the Commission could only put pressure on the governments involved or refer the case to the ICC, and the US – the main state actor that would be charged with violations of international law with regard to journalists – unilaterally refuses to cooperate with that court.

The widespread surveillance of journalists is another example where the law could protect media workers, but seems to be failing. To date, attempts to take the US authorities to court over allegations of illegal surveillance have been unsuccessful, for the sole reason that US courts have repeatedly found that US agencies have no case to answer since the accusers cannot definitively prove they were victims of surveillance.[49] An attempt in 2006 by the Electronic Frontier Foundation to sue AT&T for collaborating with illegal US government surveillance also failed because Congress retroactively gave AT&T immunity from prosecution.[50] In one case, ongoing since 2008, a US federal judge has shown some inclination to respond to concerns about unwarranted surveillance by the state; as summarised by *ProPublica*, 'On July 8, 2013, a federal judge shot down the government's state secrets defense and asked for more briefings on the constitutional challenges raised'.[51] Revelations by whistle-blower Edward Snowden have given civil liberties advocates ample new evidence to challenge unprecedented state surveillance in the courts.

The major press freedom organisations such as the IFJ and CPJ have begun to recommend that journalists working anywhere in the world assume they are being spied on, and take precautions to minimise the harm of that. Alan Pearce, a journalist who has written guides on the issue for both organisations, writes that 'revelations about the U.S. National Security Agency's global monitoring should not come as a big surprise. U.S. agencies have the technology, the will, and some very loosely written laws that allow them to snoop with impunity ... a journalist who cannot offer confidentiality is compromised, and fewer sources will trust us in the future'.[52] For journalists whose work brings them into contact with any sources who would interest the NSA or other government spies, Pearce's guide, authored for the IFJ, could be useful.[53]

Although the US has in many respects put itself above international law in the examples described in this book, families of journalists killed by an occupying army can take civil cases against those responsible in their home courts. The family of Spanish television photographer José Couso, killed by a US tank crew in the Palestine Hotel in Bagdad, did just this in Spain. The court there first requested cooperation from the US government in their investigation, and when they didn't receive it they dismissed the case. The case was reopened in 2010 and is now under appeal. It has resulted in intense pressure on the Spanish government from the US government. *WikiLeaks* cables revealed that US diplomats in Madrid sought and obtained assurances from successive senior Spanish government officials, including the Vice President and the Foreign Minister, that they would oppose the investigation and that 'those officials complied, going as far as providing the Americans with legal advice on how to stonewall the judge's requests for information and evidence'.[54]

In 2005 the family of British documentary maker James Miller, killed by the Israeli military, pursued such a case in the UK. On 6 April 2006 the inquest into his death in a UK coroner's court returned a verdict of unlawful killing, finding that he had been 'murdered' despite an Israeli military investigation claiming otherwise. Following this verdict, the Attorney General for England and Wales sent a request to his Israeli counterpart for legal proceedings to be enacted to prosecute the soldier responsible for the killing. On 1 February 2009 it was reported that James Miller's family had accepted a £1.5 million payout from Israel, saying that 'five-and-a-half years since his death this is the nearest they are likely to get to an admission of guilt by the Israeli government'.[55]

After Nicola Calipari was killed in 2005 by New York State National Guardsman Mario Lozano, while escorting recently released journalist Giuliana Sgrena to Baghdad International Airport, Italian prosecutors charged Lozano with voluntary homicide following their investigation into Calipari's death. His trial began in Rome in April 2007 *in absentia*, when the US declined to extradite him. Then on 25 October 2007, the judge of the Rome court threw out the case against Lozano after determining that coalition forces in Iraq were under the exclusive jurisdiction of the country that sent them. Lozano's lawyer claimed there were 'a lot of reasons' why Italy does not have jurisdiction, and that as a member of the US military, Lozano was 'a person who represented an organ of the US' and therefore enjoyed immunity. He also referred to a letter by then US Secretary of State Colin Powell, attached to a UN resolution, stating that 'each member of the US-led coalition has the responsibility of jurisdiction over its own forces'.[56]

There is some potential for families of European citizens killed by a foreign military organisation to take a case to the European Court of Human Rights if they fail in their national courts. While no European government is known to have been a party to the killing of journalists in Iraq, this would require the Court to accept an argument that European governments participating in the occupation of Iraq acted in complete unity with the US under the auspices of the 'coalition', as the US government has argued. Could media organisations whose personnel have been killed, injured or detained; or their families; or the victims themselves – where they are capable of doing so – bring such a suit? This could probably only happen with a substantial financial commitment from the wealthiest media firms affected, in order to support the legal costs. To date, no such commitment has been forthcoming. As noted in Chapter 4, media organisations generally have no wish to sue or press criminal charges against governments, preferring quiet diplomacy instead. They typically, and reasonably, view it as self-destructive to do so.

The obligation of agents of the US government working outside US borders to act within US law appears to remain a matter open to debate. Should the US courts clearly declare such a requirement to exist, then US laws protecting citizens from attack and arbitrary detention, and US protections for press freedom, might be applicable. Commentators have raised the possibility of those injured by US actions in Iraq suing in US courts under the Alien Tort Claims Act (ATCA). Fletcher speculates that since the Act permits suits in US federal courts 'by an alien for a tort only committed in violation of the law of nations or a treaty of the US',[57] such suits by anyone harmed by US actions in Iraq are possible. There are precedents for taking violations of international law to the US courts under this act. The question of the applicability of US law perhaps need not be restricted to the ATCA. Could guarantees under US Constitutional law, such at the First

Amendment protection of the press which has been interpreted broadly in US case law, extend to foreign territories under US control? Some experts think not,[58] but some speculate that it could.[59] Raustiala writes that after the Spanish American War the Supreme Court held that Puerto Rico was 'foreign in a domestic sense' and so covered by some, but not all, provisions of the US Constitution. He provides the concise summary of the finding by the Secretary of War, Elihu Root: 'the Constitution indeed follows the flag, but it doesn't quite catch up'. Raustiala also notes a 1957 ruling requiring that the US Bill of Rights be considered applicable to US citizens arrested abroad by agents of the US government, but argues that 'the language ... is so sweeping that it strongly suggests *an extension to non-citizens*'. It appears that point has yet to be tested in US courts, and far stronger legal grounds such as the Geneva Conventions have not been enough to help US detainees in the Post-9/11 Wars. Raustiala goes on to note that other Supreme Court cases have reinforced the contradictory notion that 'non-citizens abroad lack any constitutional rights, even when they confront the US government there'.[60]

Ultimately, a variety of laws at the local and international levels point to this central requirement: no state may kill people who have not attacked it. As one guidebook for reporters suggests:

> certain rights are so fundamental that they may never be restricted on any ground, even in times of emergency or war. The right to life is one of these, and the state may never deprive an individual of the right to life in an arbitrary manner for any reason ... the obligations of states under international human rights law are general, and a state can choose how to interpret those obligations.[61]

This chapter has sought to demonstrate that while there are a variety of potential legal responses to states which violate this central premise in regard to news media, in reality there are no consistently enforceable and unambiguous sanctions for the representatives of such states – whether leadership or foot soldier. Furthermore, the hesitant response by most of the major institutional actors within the international media (as described in Chapter 4) suggests that, even if the legal options were clearer and more effective, media organisations might be disinclined to exercise them.

As noted in the previous chapter, the UK Ministry of Defence wrote provisions for journalist safety into its 'Green Book', which governs media–military relations, and this included a promise never to target journalists.[62] According to a *BBC* report following the coroner's court ruling in the UK stating that reporter Terry Lloyd was unlawfully killed by US troops: 'The original 1949 Geneva Convention rules specifically provide safeguards for journalists in time of conflict and although they were tailored for the accreditation of uniformed war correspondents, a "unilateral" such as Terry Lloyd should have been able to rely on protection under international law.'[63]

The *BBC*'s Jon Silverman observed:

> In recent years, Britain has shown itself willing to implement the concept of universal jurisdiction – that an offence committed abroad can be tried in a British court. Terry Lloyd's death at the hands of US forces, with all its diplomatic sensitivities, may test to the limit the attorney general's resolve to uphold the concept.[64]

The British Attorney General, indeed, did not pursue the case with the US government.

In 2006, Nabil Khatib, the executive editor of *Al Arabiya*, told an interviewer that: 'my frustration goes not only to what's going on in Iraq, but the fact that we, the international community and the international media, couldn't build enough of a case to force the international community to deal with any attack on a journalist or media institution as a war crime.'

He suggested that international humanitarian law should be modified in order that journalists should be treated not merely as civilians but as members of international humanitarian organisations with special status, adding that:

> at least when you announce that any party targeting any journalist on purpose any place in the world will be treated as a war criminal, this with time could build a momentum where insurgents or military will be less violent.[65]

But the ICRC, in particular, has been resistant to such calls, arguing that all civilians must be fully protected, without creating a special class of civilian who receives greater protection than any other. But the proposal to treat attacks on journalists as war crimes has powerful proponents. Speaking in 2013 about the most recent United Nations efforts to challenge impunity in press attacks, leading British human rights and media barrister Geoffrey

Robinson QC noted the United Nations' plans do not 'make the killing of journalists a war crime, and I think it should'.[66]

This chapter has examined the legal case against governments which publically defend the press but have abandoned the values they espouse, with sometimes violent consequences. Despite the clarity of international law, its neglect by the US and other nations which attack the press has led to widespread impunity and a desperately dangerous situation for journalists everywhere. We have seen how an insufficient response from those who profit from journalism and the organisations established to defend the free conduct of the press has, in turn, permitted attacks to escalate and contributed to the curtailment and sanitisation of war reporting. It seems fair to conclude that journalism's new enemy is trigger-happy, exceptionalist, democracy. In the final chapter, we consider some of the implications.

6

Invisible Conflict?

From the late 1990s a new threat to journalists covering conflict has emerged, stemming largely from the merger of three strands of US government strategy, sitting within an evolving post-Cold War ideological context of fear promotion and information control which nourished the process.

The first of these strands was the broad acceptance in Western military circles of a doctrine of silencing the communications of perceived enemies, as a means of taking control of the 'message space' – the ideas and images in circulation about the conflict. Crucially, this doctrine applies both where the conflict is taking place and wherever public opinion about the conflict is perceived as important to policy goals. The most dramatic early example of this was the bombing by the US, under NATO authority, of Serbia's public broadcasting company in 1999, and the relatively quiet international acceptance of that war crime (despite strong, although routine, protestations from human rights and press freedom groups). This cleared the way for the targeting of several civilian media installations in the subsequent 'War on Terror' waged by the US, primarily in Iraq and Afghanistan, but increasingly spreading to other countries. Journalist Nick Turse has reported that by 2013 the US military was active in 134 countries.[1]

The second strand of policy is both more obscure and more menacing. This has been the willingness at the highest levels of the US government to employ deadly force against civilian journalists in the pursuit of strategic objectives, also in defiance of international law, as evidenced by the disparate but compelling pieces of evidence reviewed in Chapter 3. In George W. Bush's 'with us or against us' world, there was no room for the 'neutral observer' status of the press, especially in cases of perceived interference with the first goal: control of the message.

The third of these strands was the natural evolution of a long-standing 'force protection' doctrine in the US and allied militaries, which allowed the deployment of extraordinarily disproportionate force against any perceived threat to military operations or personnel, often regardless of how reckless or ill-conceived that perception might be. In combination with widespread ignorance within US and allied militaries about the function of journalists and their legal rights, the price for media workers has been a high one. Media workers have too often fallen afoul of US soldiers who are young, frightened and taught to shoot prior to any adequate evaluation of possible threats. Such practice has resulted in the deaths of many thousands of civilians across Iraq and Afghanistan, a small fraction of whom have been media workers and those supporting them.[2] Former *BBC* war correspondent and Member of Parliament Martin Bell wrote how Terry Lloyd and his crew were 'blown away by US Marines in the early days of the war', adding 'That is the way with the Americans – either you are with them, or against them. Their doctrine of force protection admits no neutrals'.[3]

The incidents described here suggest that the British government memorandum revealed by the *Daily Mirror*, describing a recommendation by President George W. Bush to bomb a major regional broadcaster in Qatar (described in Chapter 4) should be treated as plausible, and as one of the most dramatic indications of a willingness by US leaders to use force to control information at any cost. There has been a substantive and alarming shift in US government practice since the mid-1990s towards the treatment of journalists as enemy combatants in times of war. The leading historian of the media–military relationship, Philip Knightley, concluded in 2004 that:

> the Pentagon is determined that there will be no more reporting from the enemy side, and that a few deaths among correspondents who do so will deter others. To that end I believe that the occasional shots fired at 'media sites' are not accidental and that war correspondents may now be targets, some more than others.[4]

The deaths of media workers for which the US government has been responsible may be regarded in any of three ways:

- As inevitable and unavoidable accidents, where far more was at stake than the lives of journalists (regrettable though their loss may be);
- As the inevitable result of a combination of indifference and neglect which are probably tantamount to criminality under international

and US law – although potentially rectifiable through more comprehensive and effective legal mechanisms;

- As symptoms of a far greater embrace of lawlessness and inhumanity by the US government. If this trend had been the focus of aggressive, adversarial, watchdog journalism to begin with – that is, if journalists had been more critical of 'calls to war' – hundreds of deaths of journalists and tens of thousands of deaths of other civilians might well have been prevented or mitigated.

Furthermore, the number of journalists and media workers killed as a result of actions taken by the US government might also be viewed in dramatically different ways. By one accounting, the position generally (although not absolutely consistently) espoused by the US government, and echoed by the US media, is that only a few *legitimate* journalists were killed by the US military, and in every case these were unavoidable accidents of war. A sharply contrasting, although no less valid, perspective is that every death of a journalist or media worker at the hands of the US military is a *deliberate* act, whether ordered by the military hierarchy or not, given that it takes a rational human being to operate the technology of warfare, and given that every military has a legal and moral obligation to ensure that non-combatants are not on the receiving end of that technology.

But the argument against the US government can be taken to a still higher level. Without the invasion of Iraq, which has been widely regarded as illegal, unnecessary and counterproductive (in terms of the greatly increased hostility towards the US), most of the over 200 people working as journalists and media workers who have died in Iraq as a result of the US invasion and its aftermath would probably still be alive, many of them practising their craft and facilitating information sharing and dialogue, as opposed to bloodshed, in the Middle East.

Were one to imagine a US response to 9/11 consisting of diplomacy, peaceful engagement, compliance with international law, and a corresponding tolerance for competing worldviews and perspectives in news media in accordance with the Constitutional free speech requirement placed upon US lawmakers over 220 years ago, a powerful example would have been set for more traditionally repressive governments around the world. But the opposite example has been set. As one report co-authored by NGOs IFJ and Statewatch concluded:

When the world's democracies behave like this, it is little surprise that those for whom human rights abuse is routine take the opportunity to reinforce their own tyrannical reign at home. According to Human Rights Watch, for instance, China is using the war on terrorism to leverage international support for its crackdown on ethnic Uighurs in north-western Xinjiang [...] the problem is that by setting the example of Guantanamo and other places of arbitrary arrest, detention and exile which deny prisoners the right to recognition and equality before the law and an effective legal remedy, the world opens the door to even more widespread abuse on a scale that cannot yet be properly counted.[5]

The report identified parallel trends in the curtailment of civil liberties and state surveillance – with particular implications for journalism – in the UK, Australia, India, Indonesia, Pakistan, Saudi Arabia and Egypt.

Similarly, in its rejection of the authority of the ICC the US government has inspired other countries to unilaterally withdraw from participation in the international justice system. In September 2013, following its election of a president and deputy president who both faced ICC charges, Kenya's parliament approved a motion to 'suspend any links, cooperation and assistance' to the ICC, and at the time of writing the Kenyan government is lobbying for all African states to reject the ICC. Kenya's majority leader in parliament argued for the bill on the basis that 'US presidents Bill Clinton and George W. Bush both argued against becoming a party to the ICC to protect US citizens and soldiers'.[6]

In Chapter 3, I sought to demonstrate how justifications provided by the US government – sometimes in concert with NATO partners – for military action against civilian media infrastructure evolved into justifications for bombing fully operational, populated, civilian media facilities, and how these shifted from claims suggesting the necessity of such action to diminish ethnic violence to far more subjective and self-serving assertions that broadcasters failing to provide the right kind of 'news' to their audiences may be legitimate targets and warnings that only journalists operating under US control within the 'embedded journalist' system are entitled to protection from US forces. The *BBC*'s Nik Gowing went to the Pentagon after the *BBC*'s Kabul bureau was nearly destroyed in 2001, seeking assurances that lessons had been learned and more care would be taken in the future to avoid such close calls. Gowing was surprised by the stridency of the reply, which did little to reassure him and his colleagues.

US Navy Rear Admiral Craig Quigley declared to Gowing using some of the most unambiguous language spoken by any senior US military official on the topic, that the 'coincidental co-location of news representatives is not going to be a deciding criterion as to whether or not we engage a target'.[7] Quigley later made an even clearer statement of US intentions towards media representatives, stating that 'the Pentagon was *indifferent to media activity* in territory controlled by the enemy'.[8] Thus, a US position has been stated clearly and, given its clarity, the intentional violation of international law can be demonstrated: simply put, the US may not attack journalists, but has said that in some conditions it will not avoid attacking journalists. As Suskind's reporting from within the US senior decision-making apparatus revealed, media attacks have not been exclusively accidental, or incidental to combat with an enemy.

The case of Sami Al-Hajj is described in Chapter 3. On his release, the Pentagon told the *New York Times* that journalists are not immune from capture if 'engaging in suspicious, terror-related activity'.[9] While probably intended as a routine reassurance to the media that the Pentagon doesn't make mistakes or break international laws, the quote could be read as an expansion of the US military's view of what constitutes legitimate journalism (discussed in Chapter 3). In the context of Al-Hajj never being charged with any offence, and the US government never presenting evidence of any sort of crime to him, his lawyers or the public, this particular defensive argument from the Pentagon is tantamount to stating that working for a media organisation and crossing a border into a sovereign country with media equipment to conduct media work may *in itself* be construed as 'engaging in suspicious, terror-related activity', and lead to arrest and six years of imprisonment and torture. International correspondents everywhere might take this as a chilling revelation.

In a similarly worrying vein, the legality of the detention of David Miranda by British police, as he transited in August 2013 through London carrying journalistic material on behalf of the *Guardian*, has been upheld by a British court. The UK's MI5 security agency ordered UK border agents to detain Miranda on the grounds that 'Intelligence indicates that Miranda is likely to be involved in espionage activity which has the potential to act against the interests of UK national security', adding: 'Additionally the disclosure, or threat of disclosure, is designed to influence a government and is made for the purpose of promoting a political or ideological cause. This therefore falls within the definition of terrorism.'[10]

The Freedom of the Press Foundation, created to support journalistic investigations that governments seek to suppress, observed that according to such a sweeping definition of 'terrorism':

> several *Guardian* reporters and editors [are] also guilty [...] so are *New York Times* or *Pro Publica* journalists who have received the same news-worthy documents for publication. If publishing or threatening to publish information for the purpose 'promoting a political or ideological cause' is 'terrorism,' than [sic] the UK government can lock up every major newspaper editorial board that dares write any opinion that strays from the official government line.[11]

Trevor Timm of the Freedom of the Press Foundation observed that the US Government has frequently condemned the use of terrorism laws as a tool to harass or imprison journalists, including a recent complaint, in regard to the imprisonment of a journalist in Ethiopia, expressing 'concern that the application of anti-terrorism laws can sometimes undermine freedom of expression and independent media'.[12] Timm cites repeated instances, in just the past two years, of the US State Department condemning and pressuring governments around the world for their use of terrorism legislation to detain journalists. The CPJ has shown that of 232 journalists they knew to be imprisoned around the world in 2012, 132 (57 per cent) were 'held on anti-terror or other national security charges' – the highest proportion in the two decades of the CPJ records.[13] When asked by a British newspaper if they would condemn the UK for its use of terrorism laws against Miranda, a US State Department spokeswoman declined to comment.[14]

As noted throughout this book, the many deaths, traumatic injuries and detentions of journalists must be considered in the context of a set of wars in which extraordinary numbers of civilians have died violently. Journalists face the same mortal danger as countless other civilians for whom protections from the US military are inadequate. Despite endless US government denials, the body count of those criticising US actions – especially in Iraq – was clear. In December 2004 the journalist and author Naomi Klein wrote a follow-on commentary in the *Guardian*, detailing allegations about US actions in Iraq that she had made in her *Guardian* column a week earlier. Her motivation for doing so came from the newspaper's editors, who within hours of the publication of her column received an angry and legalistic letter from the press office at the

US embassy in London, demanding the newspaper retract her 'baseless' accusations or provide evidence. According to Klein, the sentence they objected to was 'In Iraq, US forces and their Iraqi surrogates are no longer bothering to conceal attacks on civilian targets and are openly eliminating anyone – doctors, clerics, journalists – who dares to count the bodies'. Her public reply to the acting US ambassador to the UK a week later succinctly summarised the well-documented evidence for her charges, including the storming of Fallujah's hospital by US soldiers in order to take telephones away from medical staff, so the casualties expected from the next impending US attack on the city could not be reported to the world. Klein wrote: 'Mr Ambassador, I believe that your government and its Iraqi surrogates are waging two wars in Iraq. One war is against the Iraqi people, and it has claimed an estimated 100,000 lives. The other is a war on witnesses'.[15]

Whatever the reasons were for US military attacks on journalists – both those that were clearly deliberate and those that were clearly accidental – they have sharply divided opinion among media professionals and done little to unite journalists in the cause of free expression. Where many US-based journalists and media organisations either ignored most of the attacks or even sought to justify them, many in the Arab world were convinced that the US was systematically and deliberately targeting them. Journalist Samantha Shapiro explained how Abdul Rahman Al-Rashed, the general manager at *Al Arabiya*, recalled the reactions of Arab colleagues:

> When Al Arabiya's reporters were killed by Americans, Al-Rashed said, the station received hundreds of condolence calls from journalists at other channels, and the reporters were mourned as martyrs. By contrast, after the Al Arabiya bureau in Baghdad was bombed by insurgents [...] only a few of his colleagues offered a single word about the five employees who died.[16]

People who have been involved in the US military operations in Iraq and Afghanistan – even those who have emerged as prominent critics of it – are eager to emphasise that the vast majority of US troops went to both those countries with good intentions, with the belief that they were both doing good for the US *and* for the average person in these countries. And many have come to profoundly regret the brutal civil wars both interventions provoked and the massive civilian losses that ensued, and which continue to this day. Former US Army Major Benjamin Tupper, who has become a prominent author and blogger about the Afghanistan war, told the *BBC*:

> we have to be honest that we have left a track record of mistakes, and some of those mistakes have been literal mistakes where the wrong compound is bombed or a civilian runs into the middle of the road in the middle of a gun fight and gets shot. And some of those mistakes are through character flaws of some of our soldiers. 99.9 percent of us go in there with good intentions and professional standards and wish nothing but to never have to pull a trigger, you know, and never have to engage someone and shoot someone and harm someone, we discount those scenarios [of civilian deaths] as the exception to the rule but there's been twelve years of them now and I think a lot of Afghans have gone from loving the west to wondering what our true intentions are.[17]

But John Pilger, who has followed the US military closely as a correspondent since the Vietnam War, has argued that the massive and often arbitrary killing of civilians is central to US military strategy, and has been so since the decimation of civilian populations in Germany and Japan played a role in bringing an end to World War II.[18] Writing in the *New York Times*, historian and journalist Nick Turse, who spent a decade researching US military records on Vietnam, wrote that 'American strategy was to kill as many "enemies" as possible, with success measured by body count. Often, those bodies were not enemy soldiers', and veterans routinely reported to him that their orders were to 'kill anything that moves'. Turse concluded that:

> Without a true account of our past military misdeeds, Americans have been unprepared to fully understand what has happened in Afghanistan, Pakistan, Yemen and elsewhere, where attacks on suspected terrorists have killed unknown numbers of innocent people. ... We need to abandon our double standards when it comes to human life.[19]

The testimony of returning US soldiers about their own conduct in Iraq is disturbing. Many of those who have chosen to speak out against what they have participated in are active in the organisation Iraq Veterans Against the War (IVAW).[20] Some IVAW veterans have told horrifying stories of being coerced and ordered by their commanders in Iraq to knowingly fire on civilians who posed no threat. Some of their stories are published in IVAW and Glantz's *Winter Soldier: Iraq and Afghanistan*,[21] but such stories seem to be the tip of the iceberg, as various analyses of US military documents revealed by *WikiLeaks* have confirmed (including the revelation of 15,000 previously unreported civilian deaths in Iraq).[22]

That 15,000 non-combatants could be killed in secret, with the world only knowing about them because one soldier (Chelsea Manning) believed it was morally wrong to withhold the information – rather than through the work of professional journalists – suggests the staggering limits on contemporary conflict reporting, both material and ideological. Martin Bell has similarly argued that traditional war reporting is no longer possible given the state of threat to journalists.[23] However, a timid, commercially constrained journalism is the wider problem.

Many prominent journalists expressed frustration that Iraq became too dangerous to report. Veteran *CBS* reporter Tom Fenton told Howard Kurtz:

> U.S. troops are the ones who have the big guns. Journalists have always had the risk of being caught in a crossfire [...] Most of the reporters, most of the journalists don't go out of the hotel. It's worth their life. Even going to a press conference in the green zone is dangerous.[24]

In response to an essay in 2006 by his colleague Rageh Omaar arguing that news media could no longer perform their job in Iraq due to the deterioration in safety, *BBC* senior correspondent John Simpson denied that the *BBC* sheltered in the semi-protected Green Zone in Baghdad, but also suggested that allowing the news agencies to take the risk was sometimes good enough. 'Driving out of Baghdad is too dangerous at present, but the intrepid agency cameramen (the real heroes, I would say, of the entire war) give us a remarkably accurate picture of what is going on elsewhere in Iraq'.[25] As we have seen, those news agency cameramen have been among the most frequent victims of attacks from both sides in the conflict.

With the remaining international media in Iraq often isolated and immobile for their own safety, and some 200 or more media workers killed at the hands of insurgent forces or the US military and its allies, we must ask if the 'game rules' of war reporting have changed, and if so, what the new rules are. As put by the *Independent*'s Robert Fisk, who has done some of the most revealing and critical reporting of recent attacks on journalists: 'Once you kill people because you don't like what they say, you have changed the rules of war'.[26] Asked by an interviewer if he felt 'in the same dilemma essentially that the American media is in, locked behind gates in your compound or your hotel', *Al Arabiya*'s executive editor Nabil Khatib replied:

> That's true. And this is a situation that is very silly because any Arab media or international media cannot claim that it is covering Iraq the way it should cover Iraq because of the existing situation. And after the tragic events of losing our colleagues, no one has the courage to send people in harm's way. When there is an event that I feel very much needs to be covered, it is the worst hour of that day because here is an event that needs to be covered, and we are there to cover it, but I cannot pick up the phone and call somebody to say go cover it. The opposite. Whenever the guys call and say, 'Let us go and cover it,' I say 'No, don't go, don't go because I need to minimize the risk to zero, not to five persons.'

Although by that time three *Al Arabiya* journalists had been killed by the US, many more had been killed and wounded by insurgents of many stripes, and that threat was Khatib's larger concern when interviewed.[27]

Between the 1990s and 2000s there was a slight but important shift in the manner in which war was sold to a democratic citizenry. The standard framing device used by governments and a supportive media in the 1990s was that of humanitarian war, and it was an effective frame despite the inherent contradiction. Der Derian described the emergence of the myth of 'virtuous war' – a high-tech, low-risk conflict which should and could right the wrongs that exist around the world.[28] This shift is key to understanding the increasingly easy acceptance by nominally democratic, free expression-advocating governments of media workers as mostly malign entities to be manipulated or forcibly silenced in pursuit of the greater, virtuous, agenda. That process needn't come from policy – for official policy in the US remains press protection – but it clearly can come from a preponderance of neglect of the required protections for civilian media workers, in combination with some measure of lethal and non-lethal targeting of media facilities and personnel.

As Chapter 4 recounts, the attacks by the US and its allies upon the media, along with wider US efforts to control the flow of information, have at times strengthened the resolve of many in the media to work harder to resist and expose attacks on free expression and fight for effective mechanisms of accountability. However, there are indications that they have also heighted distrust and division among key players in the international media. The tendency among many in the US corporate media to condemn the journalism of *Al Jazeera* and other Arab outlets – just as many of the same US media organisations would later condemn damning revelations by whistle-blowers, rather than support the principle of free information flow upon which their businesses are based – exemplifies those divisions. It is noteworthy that the new *Al Jazeera America* network built the following directly into its ten-point code of ethics (as point ten): 'Stand by colleagues in the profession and give them support when required, particularly in light of the acts of aggression and harassment to which journalists are subjected at times. Cooperate with domestic and international journalism unions and associations to defend freedom of the press.'[29]

In 2003, by which point only about half of the total journalist casualties involving US forces had accumulated, Gowing posited three possibilities:

1. Either by default or a failure actively to investigate and discipline military personnel, a culture of eliminating the presence of journalists [...] is being actively tolerated and perhaps even encouraged.
2. Commanders at the highest level, backed by their political masters, do not stop their forces targeting journalists when operational security appeared to be threatened. By default or more, they may even encourage it.
3. The presence outside of military control of cameras [...] is considered a military threat. If necessary it will be eliminated with impunity ... and without the threat of legal action.[30]

Ten years later, all three scenarios appear increasingly likely. It is difficult for a distant observer to judge the possible motivations of soldiers involved in attacks on the press. Their actions are typically explained away with the easy cliché that they are 'just scared', and while that may often be true it does little to explain killings of journalists which took place from the air, or in the absence of other combat, or to explain the imprisonment and torture of journalists or seizure of recordings, notes and equipment. There has been some admission of a common distrust, or even hatred, of the press by self-identified US soldiers in blogs and letters to newspapers. Questionnaires completed by US veterans for this research broadly confirm this, and some senior journalists – citing the experiences of their colleagues in the field – also attest to this problem. If this is true, the burden on military commanders to educate troops about the role and rights of the press becomes all the greater, but as Gowing suggests it seems an anti-press attitude has often been encouraged. Certainly, repeated public condemnations of one media outlet – *Al Jazeera* – by the most senior US officials in the early years of the Iraq war will have done much to stoke hatred and a perception of *Al Jazeera* as being a legitimate target.[31] Jeremy Scahill of the *Nation*, one of few US journalists to publicise US attacks on journalists, warned that: 'The war against Al Jazeera and other un-embedded journalists has been conducted with far too little outcry from the powerful media organizations of the world. It shouldn't take another bombing for this to be a story.'[32]

State actors in international conflicts have a moral and legal obligation – under their own domestic laws (possibly), under their own rules of engagement, under local laws and under international law – to ensure that the elevated sense of threat among troops never endangers non-combatants, be they journalists or anyone else. The threat of sanction for murdering non-combatants is one solution, although certainly not the best. Such sanction would shift the risk back to the *invader* and away from the invaded – that is, away from the civilian population, if it actually stopped troops from killing civilians.

But it is unrealistic to think that could happen. As long as frightened young men with the capacity for mass killing feel threatened, they are likely to shoot well before they give careful consideration to the legal consequences. Mark Brayne is a former *BBC* reporter who went on to establish the European branch of the Dart Centre for Journalism and Trauma and also to practice as a psychotherapist assisting journalists to cope with the effects of their work. He suggests that journalists should take a pragmatic view of the psychology of the young soldier. He explained when 'young men of twenty are burning with rage and trained to kill they will kill. All the journalist can do is take every precaution'. He suggests in the cases of aerial attacks on journalists, 'what the pilot is seeing is an enemy combatant – all they are programmed to see is bad guys'.[33] Could military culture be adapted to challenge that psychology, rather than perpetuate it?

An important part of reforming US military culture would be for the US military leadership to take responsibility for the killings of journalists and other civilians; provide serious, honest and transparent investigations to reveal the reasons behind each killing and all other incidents documented by the press freedom and human rights organisations; participate fully and non-defensively in international efforts to protect journalists and all civilians, and to defend international law; and take concrete measures to modify their procedures to avoid further incidents. But if there is an *established practice of* killing, injuring and imprisoning journalists with impunity, as the weight of evidence suggests, such actions to solve the problem by the US government are, to say the least, unlikely.

In his introduction to the 2002 edition of Knightley's classic history of war reporting, Pilger highlights two powerfully contrasting views from World War I: the *Guardian's* (then the *Manchester Guardian*) editor for 57 years, C.P. Scott, was told by British Prime Minister David Lloyd George that 'If people really knew [the truth] the war would be stopped tomorrow. But of course they don't know and can't know'. Pilger positions this against the claim by Sir Philip Gibbs, war correspondent for the London *Times*, that truth was indeed reported, 'apart from the naked realism of horrors and losses, and criticism of the facts'.[34] The contemporary combination of threat, impunity for press attackers, and a sanitising, commercialised journalism leave us now with Gibbs's style of conflict journalism, with remarkably few exceptions.

The lesson the contemporary US military took from its experience in Vietnam was to control information at any price, but some involved in that war feel there is a more useful lesson. The journalist Nick Turse, who has revealed a great deal about hidden US military atrocities in Vietnam and the current extent of US military expansion across the world, spoke to a retired US general who had a role in burying official records of US war crimes in Vietnam. Turse recalled:

> I asked one of the colonels, who ended up retiring as a general. And he says that, at the time, he thought it was right that these records need to be kept secret. It was for the good of the country, for the good of the war effort, but in the years since, he recognized that he thought it was the wrong thing to do. I talked to him during the Iraq War. And he said, you know, 'Perhaps if these things had been aired at the time, if we had been honest with the American people and open with these records, then maybe we wouldn't have had Abu Ghraib – you know, the torture scandal there.' He came to see it as a real failing on his part.[35]

Is war reporting as we once knew it – where journalists could expect to report on conflicts with a degree of respect from the protagonists for their neutral role – a relic of the past, or can news media continue to describe conflict, even though traditional protections seem to have vanished and they are targeted by all sides? If reporting can be substantially constrained through propaganda and violent coercion, as it seems to have been in the Post-9/11 Wars, have combatants successfully insulated the public from international conflict, and are they, consequently, free to lead all of us into new wars without the inconvenience of public oversight, debate or accountability? The new constraints on journalism – to the extent they are indeed new – lead inevitably to questions about the nature of modern journalism and its role in times of war.

The aggressiveness of US information control (and that of its allies Britain, Israel, Saudi Arabia, Pakistan, the reconstituted states of Iraq and Afghanistan, and others), and the extent to which global media have failed to resist it, are reasons for concern and further investigation. An anti-press attitude has been permitted and encouraged within the civilian and military ranks of the US government since the Vietnam War, culminating in the past 15 years in the easy acceptance of media casualties. War reporting protected by international law seems to have little place in the modern world. Journalists, including but not limited to those revealing damming information about military activity, are being shot at and arrested with near impunity. Despite the efforts of non-compliant media organisations, state actors in the Middle East conflicts have effectively closed the door to most media coverage and, without reform of international protections for journalists, including *enforceable* penalties for states that attack journalists or permit such attacks, that situation can only worsen.

The evolving practices discussed in this book might further be seen as an integral aspect of the 'turnkey totalitarianism' NSA whistle-blower William Binney attempted to warn the world about. Like Chelsea (formerly Bradley) Manning and Edward Snowden, he has paid a high price for having the courage to issue such a warning – a warning that with the slightest shift in the nature of the US political system, the infrastructure is now fully in place for a near instant totalitarianism of global proportion and unimaginable consequence. As put by the editor of the *Nation*, Katrina vanden Heuvel: 'If the national security state has the power of life or death above the law, and Wall Street has the power to plunder beyond the law, in what way does this remain a nation of laws?'[36]

The US cannot continue to actively champion transparency and free expression around the world, while consistently and often brutally suppressing it when that expression conflicts with its strategic interests, whether narrowly conceived by a ruling elite or popularly perceived by US public opinion. The causes of more peaceful international relations, more accountable governance and a safer journalistic profession would be better served if the US were held to account as fully as any other state for attacks on free expression and violations of human rights and international law, but that would require a painful rejection of the patriotism, militarism, nationalism, exceptionalism and fearmongering that has so gripped US media and culture.

Appendix 1

A Chronology of Attacks on Media Facilities and Personnel Linked to the US Government

Media Facilities

1. *Serbian Television*, Belgrade, 1999, 16 media workers killed.
2. *Al Jazeera* (with *CNN*), Kandahar, Afghanistan, 2001.
3. *Radio Kabul*, Kabul, 2001.
4. *Al Jazeera Television* and other broadcasters, Kabul, 2001.
5. *BBC* and *Associated Press*, Kabul, 2001.
6. *Iraqi Television*, Baghdad, 2003.
7. *Al Jazeera Television*, Sheraton Hotel, Basra, 2003.
8. International media operations at the Information Ministry Building, Baghdad, 2003.
9. *Al Jazeera Television*, Baghdad, 2003, one killed.
10. *Abu Dhabi Television*, Baghdad, 2003.
11. International media operations at the Palestine Hotel, Baghdad, 2003, two killed.
12. *Al Jazeera Television*, Falluja, 2004, one killed.[1]

Total (number of media workers/assistants killed in the facilities listed): 20

Media Personnel[2]

Confirmed Cases

	Name	Date	Affiliation	
1	Terry Lloyd	22 March 2003	*ITN*	After being wounded in crossfire between US coalition forces and the Iraqi military south of Basra, a civilian minibus taking him to hospital was fired on by US troops, killing him.
2	Fred Nérac	22 March 2003	*ITN*	Went missing in the attack between US coalition forces and the Iraqi military south of Basra in which Terry Lloyd was shot; presumed dead, although his body has never been recovered.
3	Hussein Othman	22 March 2003	*ITN*	Went missing in the attack between US coalition forces and the Iraqi military south of Basra in which Terry Lloyd was shot; his body was finally recovered many months later.
4	Kamaran Abdurazaq Muhamed	6 April 2003	*BBC*	John Simpson's translator, killed in a 'friendly fire' case when a US warplane dropped a bomb on a convoy of Kurdish soldiers travelling near Mosul; Simpson and producer Tom Giles were injured.
5	Tareq Ayoub	8 April 2003	*Al Jazeera*	Killed when a US missile struck *Al Jazeera*'s Baghdad bureau.
6	Taras Protsyuk	8 April 2003	*Reuters*	Killed after a US tank fired a shell at the Palestine Hotel in Baghdad.
7	José Couso	8 April 2003	*Telecinco*	Killed after a US tank fired a shell at the Palestine Hotel in Baghdad.
8	Mazen Dana	17 August 2003	*Reuters*	Killed by machine gun fire from a US tank while working outside Abu Ghraib prison, outside Baghdad.
9	Ahmad Kareem	25 August 2003	*Kurdistan TV*	Shot and killed by US forces outside the offices of Kurdistan TV's Mosul bureau.
10	Ali Abdul Aziz	19 March 2004	*Al Arabiya*	Cameraman, killed by US military gunfire near the site of a rocket attack on a Baghdad hotel.
11	Ali Al-Khatib (spelling disputed)	19 March 2004	*Al Arabiya*	Reporter, killed by US military gunfire near the site of a rocket attack on a Baghdad hotel.

12	Burhan Mohamed Mazhour	26 March 2004	*ABC News*	Killed by US troops conducting house-to-house searches, who fired on a group of journalists in the city of Fallujah.
13	Hussein Samir	10 April 2004	*Al Jazeera*	House owner hosting *Al Jazeera* crew in Fallujah.
14	Assad Kadhim	19 April 2004	*Al Iraqiya*	Killed by gunfire from US forces near a checkpoint close to the city of Samara.
15	Hussein Saleh	19 April 2004	*Al Iraqiya*	Killed by gunfire from US forces near a checkpoint close to the city of Samara.
16	Mazen Al-Tomaizi	12 September 2004	*Al Arabiya*	Killed by a missile fired from a US helicopter while reporting live on a crowd celebrating in the streets of Baghdad after an attack that destroyed a Bradley fighting vehicle.
17	Dhia Najim	10 November 2004	*Reuters*	Shot and killed by US Marine Corps in Ramadi while covering a gun battle between US military and Iraqi insurgents.
18	Dler Karam Ali	9 February 2005	*Al-Islami*	Shot and injured by US forces passing through a US military checkpoint in northern Iraq; he died three days later in hospital.
19	Nicola Calipari	04 March 2005	Italian government	Killed by US soldiers while escorting recently released Italian hostage, journalist Giuliana Sgrena, to Baghdad international airport.
20	Dr Yasser Salihee[3]	24 June 2005	Knight Ridder/*NPR*	Shot by a US soldier while driving in Baghdad.
21	Maha Ibrahim	25 June 2005	*Baghdad TV*	Shot by US forces as she drove to work at Baghdad TV with her husband, a fellow employee.
22	Ahmed Wael Bakri	28 June 2005	*Al-Sharqiyah TV*	Killed by gunfire from a convoy of US troops while driving home from work in southern Baghdad; he failed to pull over for a US convoy when trying to pass a traffic accident.
23	Waleed Khaled	28 August 2005	*Reuters*	Shot and killed by US soldiers while driving to the scene of a clash in Adil, western Baghdad.
24	Kamal Manahi Anbar	26 March 2006	Freelance	Among those killed in a controversial military raid by US and Iraqi special forces in northern Baghdad. Enrolled in a programme of the Institute of War and Peace Reporting, had been conducting interviews then was shot dead fleeing.

25	Sabah Salman	07 February 2007	*Iraq Media Network*	Killed when working for the state-run Iraq Media Network by guards employed by Blackwater Worldwide, a US private security company, who were escorting a US diplomat to the Iraqi Justice ministry.
26	Nabras Moham-med Hadi	07 February 2007	*Iraq Media Network*	Killed when working for the state-run Iraq Media Network by guards employed by Blackwater Worldwide, who were escorting a US diplomat to the Iraqi Justice ministry.
27	Azhar Abdullah al-Malaki	07 February 2007	*Iraq Media Network*	Killed when working for the state-run Iraq Media Network by guards employed by Blackwater Worldwide, who were escorting a US diplomat to the Iraqi Justice ministry.
28	Khaled Fayyad Obaid al-Hamdani	12 April 2007	*Al-Nahrain TV*	Killed in a shooting by a US military patrol, while travelling from his home in Abu Ghraib to work in Baghdad, driving at high speed to avoid kidnappings.
29	Namir Noor-Eldeen	12 July 2007	*Reuters*	Killed in western Baghdad during US helicopter attack, which claimed the lives of ten other Iraqis.
30	Saeed Chmagh	12 July 2007	*Reuters*	Killed in western Baghdad during US helicopter attack, which claimed the lives of ten other Iraqis.
31	Wissam Ali Ouda	21 May 2008	*Al-Afaq TV*	Shot by a US sniper as he returned home in the Al-Obeidi district of Baghdad, where there had been clashes between US soldiers and Shiite militiamen.
32	Ahmed Omed Khpulwak[4]	28 July 2011	*BBC*	Shot by US ISAF soldier while attempting to show his press card, following an insurgent attack at a Radio Television Afghanistan facility.

Disputed Cases

Rashid Hamid Wali	21 May 2004	*Al Jazeera*	Killed by gunfire when he peered over the roof of a building while filming clashes in the southern Iraqi city of Karbala on 21 May 2004, covering fighting between US troops and insurgent Al Mehdi forces. Fellow journalists believe he was shot by US forces, but this was never confirmed.
Mahmoud Za'al	25 January 2006	*Baghdad TV*	Shot dead during clashes between US forces and Sunni rebels in Ramadi, an insurgent stronghold. Witnesses say was covering an insurgent attack on two US-held buildings when was wounded in the legs and then killed moments later in a US air strike. US military deny air strike in Ramadi that day and declined comment on clashes or his death.
Suhad Al-Khalidi	04 February 2007	*Iraqi Media Network*	Reported killed by US troops when their patrol passed by her car in Hilla, by *Brussels Tribunal*, without further confirmation.

Appendix 2
Media Safety and
Media Freedom Organisations

Committee to Protect Journalists (CPJ) <http://www.cpj.org>
International Federation of Journalists (IFJ) <http://www.ifj.org>
International Press Institute (IPI) <http://ipi.freemedia.at>
International News Safety Institute (INSI) <http://newssafety.org>
Reporters Sans Frontières (RSF) <http://en.rsf.org>
World Association of Newspapers and News Publishers (WAN-IFRA)
   http://www.wan-ifra.org

Notes

Preface

1. This argument is detailed in numerous investigations. See especially Suskind, R. (2004). *The Price of Loyalty*, London: Simon & Schuster; Suskind, R. (2006). *The One Percent Doctrine: Deep Inside America's Pursuit of Its Enemies Since 9/11*, London: Simon & Schuster; Dean, J. (2004). *Worse than Watergate: The Secret Presidency of George W. Bush*, New York: Little, Brown and Company; Mitchell, G. (2008). *So Wrong for So Long: How the Press, the Pundits – and the President – Failed on Iraq*, New York: Sterling Publishing; Keeble, R. (1997). *Secret State, Silent Press: New Militarism, the Gulf and the Modern Image of Warfare*, Luton: John Libbey; and the film by Adam Curtis, *The Power of Nightmares: The Rise of the Politics of Fear*, BBC, 2004. My phrase 'paranoid fantasy' is based on the argument that when US attacks on Iraq and Afghanistan commenced, and the world was being taught to fear an entity called 'Al Qaeda', this posed little threat to the US or the world at large (despite members of what became known as Al Qaeda having orchestrated the 9/11 hijackings).

   The research of *Observer* journalist Jason Burke and filmmaker Adam Curtis is especially useful. I met Burke in 2004 soon after publication of his *Al Qaeda: The True Story of Radical Islam*, and I recall hoping that Western polices would draw more from such cogent and well-researched analysis rather than ideology. Burke explains how US prosecutors seeking to build a case against the plotters of the 1993 bombing of the World Trade Center in New York had to make a case, in order to use organised crime laws in their prosecution, that Bin Laden's organisation was a large, powerful international criminal network, when it was nothing of the kind. As Burke, whose research on the birth of what we know as 'Al Qaeda' is probably the most thorough available, told filmmaker Curtis in 2004, 'the idea which is critical to the FBI's prosecution that Bin Laden ran a coherent organisation with operatives and cells all around the world which he could be a member of is a myth. ... there is no international network with a leader whose cadres will unquestioningly obey orders, with tentacles which stretch out to sleeper cells in America, in Africa, in Europe. That idea of a coherent, structured terrorist network, with an organised capability simply does not exist'. As Curtis's film so effectively describes, the US and British governments built a case of massive domestic and foreign threat in reaction to 9/11, came to believe their own escalating story, and disseminated an ever more frightening 'simplistic fantasy' of terrorism, 'a dark vision of imagined threats', to justify ever more intrusive, politically expedient and massively lucrative interventions.

2. Knightley, P. (2004). *The First Casualty: The War Correspondent as Hero and Myth-Maker from the Crimea to Iraq*, JHU Press; Taylor, P. (1990). *Munitions of the Mind: War Propaganda from the Ancient World to the Nuclear Age*, Wellingborough: Stephens; Carruthers, S. (2011). *The Media at War*, 2nd ed., Basingstoke: Palgrave.

1.   *A Hidden War on the Media*

1. The Committee to Protect Journalists reported in 2004 that 'Since 1995 [there have been] only 35 cases in which the person or persons who ordered a journalist's murder have been arrested and prosecuted. That means that in more than 85 per cent of the cases, those who murder journalists do so with impunity'. Committee to Protect Journalists (2004). *Journalists Killed in the Last Ten Years*. Retrieved from: <https://cpj.org/2004/12/the-toll-1995-2004.php>

2. Appendix 2 lists the major news safety and free expression organisations referred to in this book, most of which have extensive documentation of the incidents described.

3. Antoniades, A., Miskimmon, A. and O'Loughlin, B. (2010). *Great Power Politics and Strategic Narratives*, Working Paper, Centre for Global Political Economy, University of Sussex.

4. Der Derian, J. (2009). *Virtuous War: Mapping the Military-Industrial Media-Entertainment Network*, 2nd ed., New York: Routledge.

5. Herman, E.S. and Chomsky, N. (1988). *Manufacturing Consent: The Political Economy of the Mass Media*, New York: Pantheon Books.

6. Gowing, N. (2003). *Aiming To Stop The Story?* International News Safety Institute.

7. The illegality of the US invasion of Iraq is well established outside of the limited range of legal opinions emanating from within the US and UK governments at the time which maintained otherwise (including the UK Attorney General Goldsmith's suddenly and mysteriously reversed opinion used to justify UK involvement). Prominent treatises detailing why it wasn't legal are provided by Sands, P. (2005). *Lawless World: America and the Making and Breaking of Global Rules*, London: Allen Lane; Haas, M. (2009). *George W. Bush, War Criminal?: The Bush Administration's Liability for 269 War Crimes*, Santa Barbara, CA: ABC-CLIO. The Secretary General of the United Nations made clear at the time that there was no international mandate for war.

8. Robinson, P., Goddard, P. and Parry, K.J. (2008). Patriotism Meets Plurality: Reporting the 2003 Iraq War in the British Press. *Media, War and Conflict*,

1(1): 9–30; Lewis, J., Brookes, R., Mosdell, N. and Threadgold, T. (2006). *Shoot First and Ask Questions Later: Media Coverage of the 2003 Iraq War*, New York: Peter Lang.

9.   US General Tommy Franks set the tone for official US reporting of war casualties when he declared to the press early in the Afghanistan campaign: 'you know, we don't do body counts'. Broder, J. (2003). U.S. Military Has No Count of Iraqi Dead in Fighting. *New York Times*, 2 April. Retrieved from: <http://www.nytimes.com/2003/04/02/world/nation-war-casualties-us-military-has-no-count-iraqi-dead-fighting.html>

     Internal US military counts, putting the lie to that official position, eventually came to light within the Iraq War logs revealed by WikiLeaks, and these suggest, according to a *Guardian* analysis, '66,081 non-combatant deaths out of a total of 109,000 fatalities'. Davies, N., Steele, J. and Leigh, D. (2010). Iraq War Logs: Secret Files Show How US Ignored Torture. *Guardian*, 22 October, Retrieved from: <http://www.theguardian.com/world/2010/oct/22/iraq-war-logs-military-leaks>

     A 2009 tally compiled independently of the US government figures by the Associated Press similarly reveals that 'more than 110,600 Iraqis have died in violence since the 2003 U.S.-led invasion.' Associated Press (2009). Secret Tally Has 87,215 Iraqis Dead. 24 April, via Nexis.

10.   Burnham, G., Lafta, R., Doocy, S. and Roberts, L. (2006). Mortality After the 2003 Invasion of Iraq: A Cross-sectional Cluster Sample Survey. *The Lancet*, 11 October.

11.   Susman, T. (2007). Poll: Civilian Death Toll in Iraq May Top 1 Million. *Los Angeles Times* 14 September. Retrieved from <http://www.commondreams.org/archive/2007/09/14/3839>

12.   Pilger, J. (2010). *The War You Don't See*. Television documentary, ITV1, 14 December.

13.   Smyth, F. (2013). *Iraq War and News Media: A Look Inside the Death Toll*, Committee to Protect Journalists. Retrieved from: <http://www.cpj.org/security/2013/03/iraq-war-and-news-media-a-look-inside-the-death-to.php#more>

14.   Carroll, R. (2005). Reporters At Risk. *Guardian*, 12 September. Retrieved from: <http://www.newssafety.com/stories/guardian/iraq12.htm>

15.   Pintak, L. (2006). Interview with Nabil Khatib, Executive Editor of Al Arabiya. *Transnational Broadcasting Studies*, 15. Retrieved from: <http://www.tbsjournal.com/KhatibInterview.html>

16.   While it could be argued that the very presence of these reporters in areas of combat – which also tend to be areas of civilian casualties – was what led to their deaths, such a response neglects the legal obligation for an occupying army to provide for the protection of journalists, regardless of the broader situation.

17. Tumber, H. and Webster, F. (2004). *Journalists Under Fire*, London: Sage, pp. 74–6, fn. 27.

18. Thussu, D. (2000). Legitimizing 'Humanitarian Intervention'? CNN, NATO and the Kosovo Crisis. *European Journal of Communication*, 15(3): 345–61.

19. For example, Balguy-Gallois, A. (2004). Protection des journalistes et des medias en période de conflit armé (The Protection of Journalists and News Media Personnel in Armed Conflict). *International Review of the Red Cross* (IRRC), March 86.853. Retrieved from: <http://www.icrc.org/web/fre/sitefre0.nsf/htmlall/5ZCGW8/$File/IRRC_853_Gallois.pdf>; McLaughlin, G. (2002). *The War Correspondent*, London: Pluto Press.

20. Borger, J. (2000). CNN Let Army Staff Into Newsroom. *Guardian*, 12 April. Retrieved from: <http://www.guardian.co.uk/international/story/0,3604,178620,00.html>

21. Much of this author's research over 20 years has involved the study of the news production process at news agencies, which has allowed me to observe this phenomenon at first hand. See, for example, Paterson, C. (2011). *The International Television News Agencies: The World from London*, New York: Peter Lang.

22. Waisbord, S. (2002). Antipress Violence and the Crisis of the State. *Harvard International Journal of Press/Politics*, July: 90–109; Sussman, L. (1991). Dying (and Being Killed) On the Job: A Case Study of World Journalists, 1982–1989. *Journalism Quarterly*, 1(2): 195–9.

23. RTE Radio 19 March, 2003. The interview is referenced in Gopsill, T. (2004). Target the Media. In *Tell Me Lies: Propaganda and Media Distortion in the Attack on Iraq*, D. Miller (ed.), London: Pluto Press, and a transcript of the interview, while no longer available from RTE, is available at <http://www.GuluFuture.com/news/kate_adie030310.htm>

24. Then Assistant Defense Secretary for Public Affairs, a specially created civilian position in the Pentagon.

25. Gowing, N. (2004). Alistair Berkley Memorial Lecture – Media, the Law and Peace-Building: From Bosnia and Kosovo to Iraq. London School of Economics, 21 May.

26. Knightley, P. (2003). History or Bunkum? *British Journalism Review*, 14 (2). 7–14.

27. Gowing, *Aiming to Stop the Story?*; Gowing, N. (2003). Journalists and War: The Troubling New Tensions Post 9/11. In *War and the Media*, D. Thussu and D. Freedman (eds), London: Sage.

28. Foerstel, H. (2006). *Killing the Messenger: Journalists at Risk in Modern Warfare*, Westport, CT: Praeger; Lisosky, J. and Henrichsen, J. (2011). *War on Words: Who Should Protect Journalists?* Santa Barbara, CA: Praeger. A Greek film examined many of the cases described in this book and drew similarly disturbing conclusions about US actions: Megrelis, Nikos, (Dir.) (2011) Shooting vs. Shooting, Odeon and Faliro House Productions.

29. This author was the first academic researcher to attend the commercial Newsworld annual gatherings and lobbied (not always successfully) for increased access for non-industry observers so the rest of the world could know what issues were being debated by those who inform everyone else. The conferences, while often valuable beyond the immediate business linkages they were designed to facilitate (in their debates of ethics, safety and cultural relevance for example), were constructed as 'closed shops' to ensure senior decision makers could associate with other senior decision makers and few others; and high fees and affiliation requirements helped to keep it that way. The conferences remain a useful way for researchers (those who can afford access) to take the pulse of the television news industry.

30. Quoted in James, S. (2001). Why the US Bombed al-Jazeera's TV Station in Kabul. *World Socialist Web Site*, 21 November. Retrieved from: <http://www.wsws.org/en/articles/2001/11/jaz-n21.html>

31. Knightley, History or Bunkum?

32. Paterson, C. (2005). They Shoot Journalists, Don't They? *Alternet*, 15 February. Retrieved from: <http://www.alternet.org/mediaculture/21262>

33. Rosen, J. (2005). Richard Sambrook of the BBC: What Eason Jordan Said in Davos. *Pressthink* blog. Retrieved from: <http://archive.pressthink.org/2005/02/07/samb_esn.html>

34. Reese, S. (1990). The News Paradigm and the Ideology of Objectivity: A Socialist at the Wall Street Journal. *Critical Studies in Mass Communication*, 7: 390–409; Borjesson, K. (2002). *Into the Buzzsaw: Leading Journalists Expose the Myth of a Free Press*, Amherst, NY: Prometheus Books; Herman and Chomsky, *Manufacturing Consent*; Berkowitz, D. (2000). Doing Double Duty: Paradigm Repair and the Princess Diana What-a-Story. *Journalism*, August: 125–43; Bennett, W.L., Gressett, L.A. and Haltom, W. (1985). Repairing the News: A Case Study of the News Paradigm, *Journal of Communication*, 35: 50–68.

35. Sullivan, S. (2002). Interview with Eason Jordan, CNN Chief News Executive. *Transnational Broadcasting Studies*, 8. Retrieved from: <http://web.archive.org/web/20020424103836/http://www.tbsjournal.com/jordan.html>

36. Gowing, *Aiming to Stop the Story?*

37. Gowing, *Aiming to Stop the Story?*

38. Kirby, M.D. and Jackson, L.J. (1986). International Humanitarian Law and the Protection of Media Personnel. *University of New South Wales Law Journal*, 9: 1.

39. Berkowitz, Doing Double Duty.

40. Bishop, R. (1999). From Behind the Walls: Boundary Work by News Organizations in their Coverage of Princess Diana's Death. *Journal of Communication Inquiry*, 23(1): 91–113.

41. Al Jazeera, for instance, was initially staffed mostly by ex-BBC workers from the UK and other Western countries, many of them from the BBC's defunct

original Arabic Television service, which was taken off the air abruptly in 1996 when a commercial partner in the service withdrew following the airing of a programme critical of the Saudi Arabian government.

42. Greenfield, J. (2009). President Obama's Feud with FOX News. CBS, 23 October. Retrieved from: <http://www.cbsnews.com/8301-18563_162-5415921.html>; see also Rutenberg, J. (2009). Behind the War Between White House and Fox. *New York Times*, 22 October. Retrieved from: <http://www.nytimes.com/2009/10/23/us/politics/23fox.html?_r=1>

43. Carr, D. (2013). War on Leaks Is Pitting Journalist vs. Journalist. *New York Times*, 25 August. Retrieved from: <http://www.nytimes.com/2013/08/26/business/media/war-on-leaks-is-pitting-journalist-vs-journalist.html?_r=0>

44. Carr, War on Leaks.

45. Carr, War on Leaks.

46. Lewis et al., *Shoot First and Ask Questions Later*; Miller, D. (2004). *Tell Me Lies: Propaganda and Media Distortion in the Attack on Iraq*, London: Pluto Press; Rampton, S. and Stauber, J. (2003). *Weapons of Mass Deception: The Uses of Propaganda in Bush's War on Iraq*, New York: Tarcher/Penguin.

47. Keeble, R. (2004). Information Warfare in an Age of Hyper-Militarism. In *Reporting War: Journalism in Wartime*, S. Allan and B. Zelizer (eds), London: Routledge.

48. Kwiatkowski, K. (2004). The New Pentagon Papers. *Salon*. Retrieved from: <www.salon.com/2004/03/10/osp/>; Suskind, *Price of Loyalty*.

49. Knightley, History or Bunkum?

50. Public Broadcasting Service (1984). *Inside Story: Whose News Is It?* Television Documentary, The Press and The Public Project for PBS.

51. Knightley, History or Bunkum?

52. Knightley, History or Bunkum?

53. Lisosky and Henrichsen, *War on Words*, p. 7.

54. See, for example, Brayne, M. (2003). Mainlining on War (book review). *British Journalism Review*, 14: 1.

2.   The Culture of Press Intolerance: Collaboration and Suppression

1. Portions of the start of this chapter are revised from an essay originally published as Paterson, C. (2005). When Global Media Don't 'Play Ball': The Exportation of Coercion. *International Journal of Media and Cultural Politics* 1(1): pp. 53–8.

2. These were amenably granted by the US Federal Communication Commission in July 2003 and subsequently rejected by a federal court a year later. See Boyd-Barrett, O. (2005). Journalism, Media Conglomerates and the Federal Communication Commission. In *Journalism: Critical Issues*, S. Allan (ed.), Maidenhead: Open University Press, pp. 342–56.

3. Louw, E. (2003). The 'War Against Terrorism': A Public Relations Challenge for the Pentagon. *Gazette: The International Journal for Communication Studies*, 65; Rampton and Stauber, *Weapons of Mass Deception*.

   The embrace of Bernays by modern governments in the US and UK is explored by documentary maker Adam Curtis in his 2002 series for the BBC, *The Century of the Self*.

4. Interview with Ron Suskind by the author.

5. Miller, L. and Rampton, S. (2001). The Pentagon's Information Warrior: Rendon to the Rescue. *PR Watch*, 8(4).

6. Reuters (2009). U.S. Military Ends Journalist Profiling Contract. 31 August. Retrieved from: <http://www.reuters.com/article/2009/08/31/afghanistan-journalists-idUSISL47394020090831>

7. Barnett, S. (2005). Opportunity or Threat? The BBC, Investigative Journalism, and the Hutton Report. In *Journalism: Critical Issues*, S. Allan (ed.), Maidenhead: Open University Press.

8. Rampton and Stauber, *Weapons of Mass Deception*.

9. Public Broadcasting Service (2000). Interview with General Wesley Clark. Retrieved from: <http://www.pbs.org/wgbh/pages/frontline/shows/kosovo/interviews/clark.html>

10. Originally *Palm Beach Post*, 9 May 1999, cited in Solomon, N. (2005). The Military-Industrial-Media Complex – Why War is Covered from the Warriors' Perspective. FAIR, 1 August. Retrieved from: <http://fair.org/extra-online-articles/the-military-industrial-media-complex>

11. Mooney, C. (2004). The Editorial Pages and the Case for War. *Columbia Journalism Review*, March/April.

12. Suskind, *Price of Loyalty*.

13. Piety, M. and Foley, B. (2006). Their Morals Are Ours: The American Media on the Doctrine of 'Preemptive War'. In *Leading to the 2003 Iraq War: The Global Media Debate*, A. Nikolaev and E. Hakanen (eds), New York: Palgrave Macmillan, pp. 69–70.

14. Reese and Buckalew documented a similar phenomenon amongst local US news broadcasters during the (first) Gulf War, but the post-9/11 excesses of local television in the US, reinforcing the warmongering of national media outlets, were exacerbated by the added dimensions of a national sense of victimisation and immediate threat. Reese, S.D. and Buckalew, B. (1995). The Militarism of Local Television: The Routine Framing of the Persian Gulf War. *Critical Studies in Media Communication*, 12(1): 40–59. Reese describes further examples from post-9/11 local television in the US: Reese, S.D. (2004). Militarized Journalism. In *Reporting War: Journalism in Wartime*, S. Allan and B. Zelizer (eds), London: Routledge, pp. 247–65.

15. He does so in the promotion of a book by author Dahr Jamail. The quote was retrieved from: <http://dahrjamail.net/books>

16. Solomon, The Military-Industrial-Media Complex.

17. With its non-stop patriotism and attacks on critics of war, Fox News became the pre-eminent television news source in the US in the post-9/11, early Iraq war years, overtaking MSNBC and CNN and nearly tripling in audience. Ramesh, R. (ed.) (2003). *The War We Could Not Stop: The Real Story of the Battle for Iraq.* London: Guardian Books/Faber & Faber, p. 257.

18. FAIR (2003). MSNBC's Double Standard on Free Speech. Retrieved from: <http://fair.org/take-action/action-alerts/msnbcs-double-standard-on-free-speech/>

19. Nader, R. (2003). MSNBC Sabotages Donahue. *CommonDreams.org*, 3 March. Retrieved from: <http://www.commondreams.org/views03/0303-06.htm>

20. Arnett told a researcher:

> I had no intention of covering the war on a daily basis, as I had for CNN in the first Gulf War. When the NBC news team, along with CNN, CBS and ABC, left Baghdad when the war started, NBC asked me to 'help them out' with on-the-spot coverage. I did so initially on a limited basis, but as the war progressed I was drawn into coverage and commentary around the clock ... Because of my earlier experience I was often interviewed by news teams in Iraq, sometimes four or five interviews each day. Iraqi Government satellite TV asked me for an interview about ten days into the war and I complied. I had been interviewed on Iraqi TV many times over the 13 years I had been covering that country. The interview was only a few minutes long. In it I suggested that the US military drive towards Baghdad was being unexpectedly delayed at Nasariyah where suicide bombers and guerrillas were killing American troops. I thought the US might have to rewrite its war strategy. I also expressed concern about the possibility of growing Iraqi civilian casualties having a negative impact on the US war effort. The *AP* picked up the broadcast from its monitoring station in Cairo and wrote a story. It was widely used in the US. Initially NBC put out a statement of support saying, 'Peter Arnett can say what he likes. We don't feel his interview was that terribly outrageous and we're going to stick with him.' I talked with NBC executives and the senior vice president said, 'We're concerned about one thing, the reaction of Fox News, otherwise, you're clear.' It turned out Fox News did a whole hour attacking me; all day they were verbally kicking me to pieces. Next evening NBC called me and said, 'Look, we're going to announce that we're not using you. It's just too hot.' They got 30,000 emails in an hour from all their affiliates.'

Interview with Peter Arnett, December 2005, from Botha, N. (2007). *Dispatches from the Front: War Reporting as News Genre, with Special Reference to News Flow to South African Newspapers during Operation Iraqi Freedom*, PhD thesis, Stellenbosch University, available at: <https://www.academia.

edu/2564258/Dispatches_from_the_front_war_reporting_as_news_genre_ with_special_reference_to_news_flow>. Danny Schechter, in his 2004 film *Weapons of Mass Deception*, reported that the bulk of the emails were 'not from the public at large, but part of an orchestrated campaign by Free Republic, a right-wing online network'.

21. Transcript provided by *Alternet*. Retrieved from: <http://www.alternet.org/ story/15778/msnbc%27s_banfield_slams_war_coverage>

22. *Newsweek*, 1 October 2001.

23. Soloman, Military-Industrial-Media Complex.

24. Naureckas, J. (1995). Corporate Ownership Matters: The Case of NBC. FAIR, 1 November. Retrieved from: <http://fair.org/extra-online-articles/ corporate-ownership-matters/>; see also Husseini, S. (1994). Felons on the Air: Does GE's Ownership of NBC Violate the Law? FAIR, 1 November. Retrieved from: <http://fair.org/extra-online-articles/felons-on-the-air/>

25. Dumas, T. (2009). Truth and Consequences. Meet Ashleigh Banfield. *New Canaan Magazine*. Retrieved from: <http://www.newcanaandarienmag. com/n/January-2009/Truth-and-Consequences/index.php?cparticle=4&sia rticle=3#artanc>

26. This is a point examined by, and evidenced by, decades of critical media theory, and the US case is especially well supported by Herman and Chomsky in *Manufacturing Consent*.

27. A recent review of several pieces of research showing Fox News viewers to be consistently misinformed is provided in Mooney, C. (2012). Fox's Misinformation Effect: It's Not Just the Programming. Conservatives Are More Likely to Seek Out Outlets that Affirm Their Views. *Salon* 10 April. Retrieved from: <http://www.salon.com/2012/04/10/foxs_misinformation_ effect>

   Also see this even more recent Fairleigh Dickinson University survey: <http://publicmind.fdu.edu/2012/confirmed/final.pdf>. General overviews of Fox News are provided in: Greenwald, R. (2004). *Outfoxed: Rupert Murdoch's War on Journalism* (documentary film); Franken, A. (2004). *Lies (and the Lying Liars Who Tell Them)*, New York: Plume; Mullainathan, S. and Shleifer, A. (2005). The Market for News. *American Economic Review* 95(4): 1031-53; Brock, D. and Rabin-Havt, A. (2012). *The* Fox *Effect: How Roger Ailes Turned a Network into a Propaganda Machine*, New York: Random House; Aday, S. (2010). Chasing the Bad News: An Analysis of 2005 Iraq and Afghanistan War Coverage on NBC and Fox News Channel. *Journal of Communication*, 60: 144–64.

   Mediamatters.org and FAIR.org are two progressive US media watchdog organisations which provide consistent documentation of the excesses of Fox and the other US networks.

28. Paterson, C. and Malila, V. (2013). Beyond the Information Scandal: When South Africa Bought Into Global News. *Ecquid Novi: African Journalism Studies*, 34(2): 1–14.

29. Herman and Chomsky, *Manufacturing Consent*.

30. McChesney, R.W. (2011). *Corporate Media and the Threat to Democracy*, New York: Seven Stories Press.

31. Holt, M. (2002). Is Truth a Victim? BBC Newsnight. Retrieved from: <http://news.bbc.co.uk/1/hi/audiovideo/programmes/newsnight/1991885.stm>

32. Elaborations of this trend are provided by Der Derian, *Virtuous War*; Butterworth, M.L. and Moskal, S.D. (2009). American Football, Flags, and 'Fun': The Bell Helicopter Armed Forces Bowl and the Rhetorical Production of Militarism. *Communication, Culture and Critique*, 2(4): 411–33.

33. Plumer, B. (2013). America's Staggering Defense Budget, In Charts *Washington Post*, 7 January. Retrieved from: <http://www.washingtonpost.com/blogs/wonkblog/wp/2013/01/07/everything-chuck-hagel-needs-to-know-about-the-defense-budget-in-charts/>

34. Solomon, N. (2010). *War Made Easy: How Presidents and Pundits Keep Spinning Us to Death*, New York: John Wiley and Sons.

35. Political leaders whom, as Richard Keeble and others have argued, have a strong interest in providing a raison d'être for the military-industrial complexes in the US and UK. Lewis et al., *Shoot First and Ask Questions Later*, p. 196.

36. Dower, J.W. (1986). *War Without Mercy: Race and Power in the Pacific War*, New York: Pantheon.

37. Boaz, C. and Paterson, C. (2004). Media War: A Comparative Analysis of Foreign Policy Advocacy and Enemy Construction in International Media. Paper prepared for presentation at the Universal Forum of Cultures conference 'Communication and Cultural Diversity', Barcelona Spain, 25 May.

38. Steuter, E. and Wills, D. (2010). 'The Vermin Have Struck Again': Dehumanizing the Enemy in Post 9/11 Media Representations. *Media, War and Conflict*, 3(2): 152–67.

39. Dower, *War Without Mercy*.

40. Adrienne Kinne interview, in *Democracy Now* (2008). Former Military Intelligence Sergeant Reveals US Listed Palestine Hotel in Baghdad as Target Prior to Killing of Two Journalists in 2003, 13 May. Retrieved from: <http://www.democracynow.org/2008/5/13/fmr_military_intelligence_officer_reveals_us>

41. Herman and Chomsky, *Manufacturing Consent*.

42. A record of censorship in the US since 9/11 has been kept by the US National Coalition Against Censorship at <http://www.ncac.org>. Executives at CNN, ABC, MSNBC and the BBC have all asked staff to diminish critical

coverage of the Afghanistan and/or Iraq wars, and in some instances have apologised to conservative critics for their news coverage. Rutenberg, J. and Carter, B. (2001). Network Coverage a Target of Fire from Conservatives. *New York Times*, 7 November. Retrieved from: <http://www.nytimes.com/2001/11/07/politics/07MEDI.html>; Miller, D. (2003). Taking Sides. *Guardian*, 22 April; *USA Today* (2003). Amanpour: CNN Practiced Self-Censorship, 14 September. Retrieved from: <http://usatoday30.usatoday.com/life/columnist/mediamix/2003-09-14-media-mix_x.htm>. Likewise in the UK, the Hutton affair was seen as a powerful message to the media to stay 'on message' with the government.

43. Bollyn, C. (2004). Media Coverage of Iraq Called 'Shameful' by Peers. *Americanfreepress.net*. Retrieved from: <http://www.americanfreepress.net/04_06_04/Media_Coverage/media_coverage.html>

44. Herman and Chomsky, *Manufacturing Consent*.

45. Boaz and Paterson, Media War, citing Gilbert, G. (1947). *Nuremberg Diary*. New York: Farrar, Straus, and Co.

46. Der Derian, *Virtuous War*, p. 238.

47. Barsamian, D. (2002). Interview with John Pilger. *Progressive*, November. Retrieved from: <http://www.progressive.org/nov02/intv1102.html>

48. Pilger, *War You Don't See*.

49. Knightley, P. (2012). When is a Terror Threat Not a Terror Threat? Let's Ask a Man Called felix... All Intelligence Services Rely on Convincing the Public There Is a Monster At Large Waiting to Grab Them. *Independent*, 11 May. Retrieved from: <http://www.independent.co.uk/voices/commentators/phillip-knightley-when-is-a-terror-threat-not-a-terror-threat-lets-ask-a-man-called-felix-7737812.html>

50. Silver, N. (2010). The Hidden Costs of Extra Airport Security. *New York Times*, 18 November. Retrieved from: <http://fivethirty eight.blogs.nytimes.com/2010/11/18/the-hidden-costs-of-extra-airport-security/?partner=rss&emc=rss&_r=0>

51. Hellmich, C. (2012). Fighting Al Qaeda in Yemen? Rethinking the Nature of the Islamist Threat and the Effectiveness of U.S. Counterterrorism Strategy. *Studies in Conflict and Terrorism*, 35(9): 618–33, 620.

52. Lewis et al., *Shoot First and Ask Questions Later*.

53. For example: Moyers, B. (2007). Bill Moyers Journal: Buying the War Television Programme. Public Broadcasting Service. Transcript retrieved from: <http://www.pbs.org/moyers/journal/btw/transcript1.html>; Miller, *Tell Me Lies*; Rampton and Stauber *Weapons of Mass Deception*.

54. Altheide, D.L. (2013). Media Logic, Social Control, and Fear. *Communication Theory*, 23: 223–38.

55. Masco, J. (2006). *The Nuclear Borderlands: The Manhattan project in Post Cold War New Mexico*, Princeton, NJ: Princeton University Press.

56. Hoskins, A. and O'Loughlin, B. (2009). Media and the Myth of Radicalization. *Media, War and Conflict* 2(2): 107–10, citing Masco, *The Nuclear Borderlands*.

57. Altheide, Media Logic.

58. Knightley, When is a Terror Threat.

59. In an exposé for *New York Magazine*, journalists Matt Apuzzo and Adam Goldman described the post-9/11 evolution of the 'demographics unit' of the New York City Police Department, which spied on New Yorkers for years – especially, although not exclusively, Muslims and others of Middle Eastern decent – without leading to any arrests or evidence of wrongdoing. The authors concluded 'the NYPD's programs are likely to join waterboarding, secret prisons, and NSA wiretapping as emblems of post-9/11 America, when security justified many practices that would not have been tolerated before'. Apuzzo, M. and Goldman, A. (2013). The NYPD Division of Un-American Activities. *New York Magazine*, 25 August. Retrieved from: <http://nymag.com/news/features/nypd-demographics-unit-2013-9/index1.html>

60. At the time of this writing revelations evidencing the ineffectiveness of US judicial oversight of surveillance are emerging. Under public pressure, the Obama administration released documents providing new detail about the challenges of overseeing these programmes. The secret court established to oversee surveillance warned the NSA three times in less than three years about 'misrepresentations' to the court, and a federal judge wrote in 2009 about 'repeated inaccurate statements made in the government's submissions' and that orders of the Foreign Intelligence Surveillance Court 'have been so frequently and systematically violated that it can fairly be said that this critical element of the overall [...] regime has never functioned effectively'. Drum, K. (2013). In 2009, the FISA Court Shut Down an NSA Program for 6 Months Because It Had 'Frequently and Systemically' Violated the Rules. *Mother Jones*, 10 September. Retrieved from: <http://www.motherjones.com/kevin-drum/2013/09/fisa-court-shut-down-nsa-phone-records-program>

61. Poitras, L. (2013). Miranda Detention: Blatant Attack on Press Freedom. *Spiegel Online*, 26 August. Retrieved from: <http://www.spiegel.de/international/world/laura-poitras-on-british-attacks-on-press-freedom-and-the-nsa-affair-a-918592.html>

62. International Federation of Journalists and Statewatch (2005). *Journalism, Civil Liberties and the War on Terrorism*, International Federation of Journalists, p. 9. Retrieved from: <http://www.statewatch.org/news/2005/may/ifj-statewatch-report.pdf>

63. BBC (2013). David Miranda Row: What Is Schedule 7? BBC Online, 19 August. Retrieved from: <http://www.bbc.co.uk/news/uk-23757133>

64. International Federation of Journalists and Statewatch, *Journalism, Civil Liberties and the War on Terrorism*, p. 13.

65. Bamford, J. (2009). *The Shadow Factory: The NSA from 9/11 to the Eavesdropping on America*, New York: Random House.

66. International Federation of Journalists and Statewatch, *Journalism, Civil Liberties and the War on Terrorism*, p. 13.

67. BBC (2013). Hague: Law-Abiding Britons Have Nothing to Fear from GCHQ. BBC Online, 9 June. Retrieved from: <http://www.bbc.co.uk/news/uk-22832263>

68. Poitras, Miranda Detention.

69. Ball, J., Borger, J. and Greenwald, G. (2013). Revealed: How US and UK Spy Agencies Defeat Internet Privacy and Security. *Guardian*, 6 September. Retrieved from: <http://www.theguardian.com/world/2013/sep/05/nsa-gchq-encryption-codes-securit>

70. Leonnig, C. (2013). Court: Ability to Police U.S. Spying Program Limited. *Washington Post*, 16 August. Retrieved from: <http://www.washingtonpost.com/politics/court-ability-to-police-us-spying-program-limited/2013/08/15/4a8c8c44-05cd-11e3-a07f-49ddc7417125_story.htm>

71. The *New York Times* revealed in 2013 that the (nominally parastatal) US Postal Service had been collaborating with security authorities to secretly monitor the post of certain individuals, including the owner of a bookstore who once belonged to an environmental group. Part of the US Postal Service's efforts included retaining a photographic record of the exterior of every piece of mail sent in the US. Nixon, R. (2013). U.S. Postal Service Logging All Mail for Law Enforcement. *New York Times*, 3 July. Retrieved from: <http://www.nytimes.com/2013/07/04/us/monitoring-of-snail-mail.html>

72. Borger, J. (2013). NSA Files: Why the *Guardian* in London Destroyed Hard Drives of Leaked Files. *Guardian*, 20 August. Retrieved from: <http://www.theguardian.com/world/2013/aug/20/nsa-snowden-files-drives-destroyed-london>

73. Italics in the original. Eisler, B. (2013). David Miranda and the Preclusion of Privacy. Barry Eisler blog. Retrieved from: <http://barryeisler.blogspot.co.uk/2013/08/david-miranda-and-preclusion-of-privacy.html>. Referenced by Jay Rosen's *Pressthink* blog retrieved from: <http://pressthink.org/2013/08/to-make-journalism-harder-slower-less-secure/>

74. Tumber, H. and Palmer, J. (2004). *Media at War: The Iraq Crisis*, London: Sage; Carruthers, *Media at War*.

75. Hart, P. (2005). Pentagon Disinformation Should Be No Surprise. FAIR, 1 February. Retrieved from: <http://fair.org/extra-online-articles/pentagon-disinformation-should-be-no-surprise/>

76. *Intelligence Newsletter* (2000). Military Lessons in Twisting the Truth, 17 February, via Nexis.

77. Freedom Forum (1996). *Forum News*, 24 June, quoted by Skoco, M. and Woodger, W. (2000). The Military and the Media. In *Degraded Capability:*

The Media and the Kosovo Crisis, P. Hammond and E.S. Herman (eds), London: Pluto.

78. Robins. J. (2000). The Robins Report. *TV Guide*, 15–21 April.

79. Robins, The Robins Report.

80. Correspondence with the author, August 2013.

81. Eason Jordan, in Norman Solomon film *War Made Easy*, cited by *Democracy Now*. Retrieved from: <http://www.democracynow.org/2007/8/21/head lines#8219>

82. *Democracy Now* (2007). War Made Easy: How Presidents & Pundits Keep Spinning Us to Death, 29 May. Retrieved from: <http://www.democracynow. org/2007/5/29/war_made_easy_how_presidents_pundits>

83. Fisk, R. (2002). Journalists Are Under Fire for Telling the Truth. *The Independent*, 18 December; Rutenberg and Carter, Network Coverage.

84. Fisk, R. (2003). How the News Will Be Censored in This War. *The Independent*, 25 February.

85. Kurtz, H. (2003). Embedded Reporter's Role in Army Unit's Actions Questioned by Military. *Washington Post*, 25 June.

86. Originally CBC-TV, 23 November 2003, quoted in Allan, S. and Zelizer, B. (eds) (2004). *Reporting War: Journalism in Wartime*, London: Routledge, p. 4.

87. Miller, *Tell Me Lies.*

88. Dunne, F. (2003). Pentagon Threatens to Kill Independent Reporters in Iraq. Retrieved from: <http://www.GuluFuture.com/news/kate_adie030310. htm>

89. Lewis et al., *Shoot First and Ask Questions Later.*

90. Di Giovanni, J. (2003). Don't Shoot the Messenger: You've No Idea How Difficult This War is to Cover. *The Times*, 27 March.

91. Tumber and Palmer, *Media At War*, p. 28.

92. Dunne, Pentagon Threatens.

93. Ayres, C. (2005). *War Reporting for Cowards: Between Iraq and a Hard Place*, London: John Murray, p. 279, cited in Tumber and Webster, *Journalists Under Fire*.

94. Interview with David Hearst, *Guardian*, June 2004.

95. Byrne, C. (2003). Independents 'Frozen Out' by Armed Forces. *Guardian*, 3 April.

96. Rampton and Stauber, *Weapons of Mass Deception*; Miller, *Tell Me Lies*; Horvit, B. (2004). Who dominates the debate? Five news agencies and their sources before the US-Iraq War. Paper for the Association for Education in Journalism and Mass Communications annual conference, Toronto; Lewis et al., *Shoot First and Ask Questions Later*.

97. Rantanen, T. (2004). European News Agencies and their Sources in the Iraq War Coverage. In Allan and Zelizer, *Reporting War*.

98. The reported comment from Kathleen Carroll, *AP*'s senior vice president, reported on the Michelle Malkin blog and other conservative blogs, could not be confirmed.

99. Rosen, Richard Sambrook of the BBC.

100. Examples of entries in the Rosen blog, written soon after the posting of Sambrook's letter to Rosen, included:

> Our military never targets civilians or reporters. The USA's military protects and serves its country. Mr. Jordan should be thankful some of that protection is for him, even though he downgrades our military. We all know that this character Jordan is severely deranged. God Bless our President, and God Bless our Troops.

101. Sambrook, personal correspondence, August 2013.

102. International Federation of Journalists and Statewatch, *Journalism, Civil Liberties and the War on Terrorism*, pp. 51–3.

103. Mitchell, G. (2004). Shoot the Messenger. *Editor and Publisher*, 22 November. Retrieved from: <http://www.editorandpublisher.com/Article/Shoot-the-Messenger#sthash.Xz8XNTX9.09vq4nPi.dpuf>

104. Mitchell, Shoot the Messenger.

105. These included: 'That you would consider the death of a terrorist as something bad tells me all I need to know about you'. 'Sorry, I may be old-fashioned, but I prefer Ernie Pyle. At least it seemed as though he wanted Americans to win'. 'The distrust of the major media is at the root of all of this'. 'Go back to Iraq, with a target on your back'. 'If you go back over I hope they take your head'. 'Now each and every embed is in enemy territory. What I mean is, a reporter in the combat zones of Iraq now has no friends. ... There is probably not a marine or soldier who will even attempt to save you if they don't accidentally shoot you first'. Mitchell, Shoot the Messenger.

106. Since about 2007 there have been a number of reports – some based on investigation, some on public announcements by the US government – that a variety of government branches, along with private contractors employed by the government – are monitoring and aggressively engaging with online comment about the US, the US government, and the US military in online and social media around the world, in many languages. Comment inserted into online conversations is sometimes identified as originating with the US government and sometimes not. Reports indicate the US Army, US Air Force, US State Department, and US Defense Advanced Research Projects Agency are involved in such efforts.

    See, for example, Carver, T. (2002). Pentagon Plans Propaganda War. BBC Online, 20 February. Retrieved from: <http://news.bbc.co.uk/1/hi/world/americas/1830500.stm>; Rawnsley, A. (2011). Pentagon Wants a Social Media Propaganda Machine. *Wired*, 15 July, Retrieved from: <http://www.wired.com/dangerroom/2011/07/darpa-wants-social-media-sensor-for-

propaganda-ops/>; Fielding, N. and Cobain, I. (2011). US Spy Operation that Manipulates Social Media Military's 'Sock Puppet' Software Creates Fake Online Identities to Spread Pro-American Propaganda. *Guardian*, 17 March. Retrieved from: <http://www.theguardian.com/technology/2011/mar/17/us-spy-operation-social-networks>; Rockefeller, H. (2011). The HB Gary Email That Should Concern Us All. *Daily Kos*, 16 February. Retrieved from: <http://www.dailykos.com/story/2011/02/16/945768/-UPDATED-The-HB-Gary-Email-That-Should-Concern-Us-All>; Sherman, J. (2006). CENTCOM Eyes Blogs to Shape Opinion. Military.com, 3 March. Retrieved from: <http://www.military.com/features/0,15240,89811,00.html>; and Monbiot, G. (2011). The Need to Protect the Internet from 'Astroturfing' Grows Ever More Urgent. *Guardian*, 23 February. Retrieved from: <http://www.theguardian.com/environment/georgemonbiot/2011/feb/23/need-to-protect-internet-from-astroturfing>

Since online media does not respect national borders, it remains unclear how such activity was not a violation of the 1948 Smith–Mundt Act of Congress, intended to prevent domestic distribution of US government propaganda aimed at foreign audiences (originally, the broadcasts of *Voice of America*), but Congress may have prevented future legal challenge in 2013 with the repeal of Smith–Mundt. Earlier interviews with US Central Command acknowledged the problem, suggesting it was avoided by properly attributing online contributions in English (assuming, apparently, that US citizens use only English). On a different legal (and ethical) front, private individuals have been convicted in US courts for misrepresenting themselves online (Fielding and Cobain, US Spy Operation).

British journalist George Monbiot has reported on the increase in corporations, lobbying organisations and the US military posing as members of the public online – on a massive scale – in order to shift and shape public debate, in a process known as 'astroturfing' and 'sock puppetry' (the creation of artificial personas in social media); as he puts it, 'a remarkable technological armoury is being deployed to drown out the voices of real people'. Monbiot, The Need to Protect the Internet from 'astroturfing'.

107. Knightley, *The First Casualty*.

108. *Broadcast*, 14 May 1999, cited in Hammond, P. (1999). The War on TV. FAIR, 14 May. Retrieved from: <http://fair.org/article/the-war-on-tv/>

109. *Independent*, 29 June 1999, via Nexis.

110. Nye, J. (1990). Soft Power. *Foreign Policy*, 80: 153–71. Indeed, Nye himself has argued that the US embrace of public diplomacy and soft power which was fashionable in the 1990s lost favour after 9/11, leaving such efforts under-resourced: 'The effects of the 9/11 terrorist attacks have thrown us off course. Since the shock of 9/11, the US has been exporting fear and anger rather than our more traditional values of hope and optimism'. Nye, J. (2007).

Smart Power. *Huffington Post*, 29 November. Retrieved from: <http://www.huffingtonpost.com/joseph-nye/smart-power_b_74725.htm>

111. Herman and Chomsky, *Manufacturing Consent*.

112. See Carruthers, *Media at War*, Chapter 3, for a useful overview of the mythology of 'uncensored' news coverage of the Vietnam War and the enduring impacts of that mythology on US media–press relations generally, and the virulence of subsequent US presidents towards media coverage of conflicts involving US forces. Hallin's research on US news coverage of the Vietnam War, and the social effects of that coverage, is the most influential research exposing such misconceptions, and Nick Turse's more recent research – based largely on long hidden government documentation from the US National Archives – has exposed a great deal about the brutality and war crimes of the US military in Vietnam which was, quite contrary to the myth, almost entirely absent from contemporary news coverage. Turse, N. (2013). For America, Life Was Cheap in Vietnam. *New York Times*, 9 October. Hallin, D. (1984). The Media, the War in Vietnam, and Political Support: A Critique of the Thesis of Oppositional Media. *The Journal of Politics*, 46(1): 2–24.

113. Lewis et al., *Shoot First and Ask Questions Later* , p. 41.

114. Boaz and Paterson, Media War.

115. Boaz and Paterson, Media War.

116. For example, after a journalist for the BBC World Service's Pashtu service (broadcasting in Afghanistan) interviewed Tony Blair, Donald Rumsfeld and Colin Powell requested interviews with her. Westcott, C. (2004). New Media at the BBC World Service. In *International News: The Twenty-First Century*, C. Paterson and A. Sreberny (eds), London: John Libbey.

117. *Democracy Now* (2005). Interview with Yosri Fouda, 13 October. Retrieved from: <http://www.democracynow.org/2005/10/13/top_al_jazeera_reporter_yousri_fouda>

118. Pilger, J. (2003). War on Truth, *New Statesman*, 4 August.

119. James Dao, J. and Schmitt, E. (2002). A Nation Challenged: Hearts and Minds; Pentagon Readies Efforts to Sway Sentiment Abroad. *New York Times*, February 19.

120. In remarks to the press in January 2003, US Secretary of Defense Donald Rumsfeld, the principal architect of the Iraq war, labelled France and Germany 'old Europe' and 'a problem' and suggested their increasing irrelevance. BBC (2003). Outrage at 'Old Europe' Remarks. BBC, 23 January. Retrieved from: <http://news.bbc.co.uk/1/hi/world/europe/2687403.stm>

121. In a story carried around the US, one American reporter complained that German media were 'painting caustic and exaggerated pictures of America that are hard to recognize'. Mondics, C. (2003). German Media Paints Increasingly Critical Images of US. *Philadelphia Inquirer*, 2 March. Retrieved from: <http://www.mercurynews.com/mld/mercurynews/news/

politics/5299392.html>; also Krugman, P. (2003). Behind the Great Divide. *New York Times*, 18 February.

122. Pilger, War on Truth.

123. Pilger, *War You Don't See.*

124. Interview with David Hearst, June 2004.

125. For example, when Al Jazeera was providing the only television pictures of substantial civilian casualties as US forces attacked the Iraqi city Fallujah, CNN sought to convince Al Jazeera that civilian casualties were the wrong story, as shown in this excerpt provided by FAIR, with CNN newsreader Daryn Kagan addressing Al Jazeera editor-in-chief, Ahmed Al-Sheik, on 12 April 2004:

    Isn't the story, though, bigger than just the simple numbers, with all due respect to the Iraqi civilians who have lost their lives – the story bigger than just the numbers of people who were killed or the fact that they might have been killed by the U.S. military, that the insurgents, the people trying to cause problems within Fallujah, are mixing in among the civilians, making it actually possible that even more civilians would be killed, that the story is what the Iraqi insurgents are doing, in addition to what is the response from the U.S. military?'

    FAIR Action Alert (2004). CNN *to Al Jazeera: Why Report Civilian Deaths?* 15 April. Retrieved from: <http://www.fair.org/index.php?page=1587>

126. Woodward, B. (2004). *Plan of Attack*, New York: Simon and Schuster, p. 382.

127. This *New York Times* story, perhaps unsurprisingly, did not comment on the irony of Donald Rumsfeld – who by that time had been indirectly (many would argue, directly) responsible for the deaths of numerous journalists and media workers, and many thousands of civilians – labelling journalistic work as 'violent'. Rumsfeld also replied to reports of hundreds of civilian casualties in Fallujah by insisting the problem was Al Jazeera's journalism, which was 'vicious, inaccurate and inexcusable'. *Guardian*, 4 December 2004. Retrieved from: <http://www.guardian.co.uk/world/2004/dec/04/iraq.usa>

128. Shapiro, S.M. (2005). The War Inside the Arab Newsroom. *New York Times*, 2 January. Retrieved from: <http://www.nytimes.com/2005/01/02/magazine/02ARAB.html?oref=login&pagewanted=print&position>

129. Soldz, S. (2007). Fallujah, the Information War and U.S. Propaganda: The U.S. Army's Intelligence Analysis of the April 2004 Fallujah Attack. WikiLeaks, 27 December. Retrieved from: <http://wikileaks.org/wiki/Fallujah,_the_information_war_and_U.S._propaganda>

130. Shapiro, The War Inside the Arab Newsroom.

131. The US Government maintains that a controversial legal doctrine deemed the 'border search exception' allows such activity.

132. International Federation of Journalists and Statewatch, *Journalism, Civil Liberties and the War on Terrorism*.

133. International Federation of Journalists and Statewatch, *Journalism, Civil Liberties and the War on Terrorism*.

134. Lappin, E. (2004). Letter from a Deportee: Your Country Is Safe from Me. *New York Times*, 4 July 2004. Retrieved from: <http://www.nytimes. com/2004/07/04/books/letter-from-a-deportee-your-country-is-safe-from-me.html?pagewanted=all&src=pm>

135. Lappin, Letter from a Deportee.

136. Lappin, Letter from a Deportee.

137. Lappin, Letter from a Deportee.

138. Lappin, Letter from a Deportee.

139. BBC (2013). David Miranda Heathrow Detention: No 10 'Kept Abreast of Operation'. BBC Online, 20 August. Retrieved from: <http://www.bbc. co.uk/news/uk-23769324>

140. BBC, David Miranda Row.

141. The American Civil Liberties Union analysis and files are available from: <http://www.aclu.org/files/pdfs/natsec/cbp_20100114_000680-000863. pdf>; see also Maass, P. (2013). How Laura Poitras Helped Snowden Spill His Secrets. *New York Times*, 13 August. Retrieved from: <http://www.nytimes. com/2013/08/18/magazine/laura-poitras-snowden.html?pagewanted=3&_ r=0>

142. Greenwald, G. (2012). U.S. Filmmaker Repeatedly Detained at Border: Laura Poitras Makes Award-Winning Controversial Films, and is Targeted by the U.S. Government as a Result. *Salon*, 8 April. Retrieved from: <http://www. salon.com/2012/04/08/u_s_filmmaker_repeatedly_detained_at_border/>

143. Maass, How Laura Poitras.

144. Greenwald, G. (2010). Government Harassing and Intimidating Bradley Manning Supporters: A 23-Year-Old Visitor to the Accused WikiLeaks Leaker is Detained at the Border, His Laptop Searched and Seized. *Salon*, 9 November. Retrieved from: <http://www.salon.com/2010/11/09/manning_2/>; BBC, David Miranda Row.

145. Quoted in International Federation of Journalists and Statewatch, *Journalism, Civil Liberties and the War on* Terrorism, p. 51.

146. Nerone, J. (1989). *Violence Against the Press*, New York: Oxford University Press.

147. Indymedia *UK* (2004). US Authorities Seize IMC Servers in UK, 27 October. Retrieved from: <http://www.indymedia.org.uk/en/2004/10/299022.html>

148. This is not a new phenomenon. In what an internal 1973 NSA report would call a 'disreputable if not outright illegal' operation, the NSA under US Presidents Johnson and Nixon also spied on, in addition to these prominent journalists, the civil rights leaders Martin Luther King and Whitney Young, and prominent US politicians including Senators Frank Church and Howard

Baker. Other archived documents have revealed similar US government spying on numerous prominent anti-war and progressive activists during this period. See the archive at: <http://www2.gwu.edu/~nsarchiv/NSAEBB/NSAEBB441/>

149. Shorrock, T. (2013). Obama's Crackdown on Whistleblowers: The NSA Four Reveal How a Toxic Mix of Cronyism and Fraud Blinded the Agency Before 9/11. *Nation*, 15 April.

150. Savage, C. and Kaufman, L. (2013). Phone Records of Journalists Seized by U.S. *New York Times*, 13 May. Retrieved from: <http://www.nytimes.com/2013/05/14/us/phone-records-of-journalists-of-the-associated-press-seized-by-us.html?pagewanted=2>

151. Rottman, G. (2013). DOJ's *AP* Phone Logs Grab Highlights Renewed Need for Shield Law. *American Civil Liberties Union*, 15 May. Retrieved from: <http://www.aclu.org/blog/free-speech-national-security/dojs-ap-phone-logs-grab-highlights-renewed-need-shield-law>

152. Sullivan, M. (2013). Leak Investigations Are an Assault on the Press, and on Democracy, Too. *New York Times*, 14 May. Retrieved from: <http://publiceditor.blogs.nytimes.com/2013/05/14/leak-investigations-are-an-assault-on-the-press-and-on-democracy-too/>

153. The letter is reproduced by the *Washington Post*. Retrieved from: <http://apps.washingtonpost.com/g/page/politics/media-coalition-letter-of-protest-to-attorney-general-eric-holder/148/>

154. Skoco, M. and Woodger, W. (2000). The Military and the Media. In Hammond and Herman, *Degraded Capability*.

155. Fouda, Y. and Fielding, N. (2003). *Masterminds of Terror: The Truth Behind the Most Devastating Terrorist Attack the World Has Ever Seen*, London: Arcade Publishing.

156. International Federation of Journalists and Statewatch, *Journalism, Civil Liberties and the War on Terrorism*, p. 5.

3.   Patterns of Violence: the Media Installation and the Media Worker

1. Prominent among the detailed reviews of attacks on the press in the post-9/11 wars are: White, A. (2003). *Justice Denied on the Road to Baghdad*, International Federation of Journalists; Campagna, J. and Roumani, R. (2003). *Permission to Fire*, New York: Committee to Protect Journalists; INSI (2006). *The Safety Of Journalists in Areas of Conflict*, International News Safety Institute; Foerstel, *Killing the Messenger*; Lisosky and Henrichisen, *War on Words*.

2. Gopsill, Target the Media, pp. 254–5.

3. The First Amendment to the US Constitution mandates that 'Congress shall make no law ... abridging the freedom of speech, or of the press'.

4. Knightley, History or Bunkum?; McLaughlin, *The War Correspondent*.

5. The listing of killings of journalists provided in Appendix 1 is based primarily on a recent review of attacks on journalists in Iraq conducted by the IFJ, but is also informed by this author's compilation of data on journalist casualties ongoing since 2003, and other sources. There are numerous other lists that do the same, most notably the databases of the major press freedom organisations listed in Appendix 2. The Brussels Tribunal, a collective of Iraqi and European intellectuals and peace advocates, whose work focuses on Iraq, have published an extensive list of journalist casualties in Iraq and have argued that the more widely cited lists compiled by the CPJ and similar groups ignore a significant proportion of cases. They have, in a similar manner to this author, compiled data independently of the international press freedom groups and compared it with the data of those groups, in order to offer a more comprehensive picture.

6. Email correspondence with the author, August 2013.

7. In the yearly index compiled by Reporters Sans Frontières, for example, the US typically ranks close to the UK among the 20 to 30 best countries for journalists to work in safely, although the US has been ranked as low as 48th among the 169 countries ranked (in 2007). In failing to consider the direct or indirect impact of the US government on journalism outside of US borders – specifically, in the nations it has attacked or occupied in the past 15 years – such rankings are deceptive.

8. See Appendix 2 for links to the major press freedom/press safety organisations. Within the popular press, reports by the *Guardian* newspaper, available through the *Media Guardian* website, are particularly comprehensive.

9. Price, M., Neumann, A.N., Sullivan S. and Deguine H. (2001) Restructuring the Media in Post-Conflict Societies: Four Perspectives, *Cardozo Online Journal of Conflict Resolution*, 2.

10. Thussu, Legitimizing 'Humanitarian Intervention'?; McLaughlin, *The War Correspondent*.

11. Fisk, R. (1999). Media: Taken In by the Nato Line. *Independent*, 29 June.

12. Statement from the Serbian Information Ministry, 27 May 1999. Retrieved from: <http://www.bulgaria-italia.com/fry/rtssat.htm>

13. Gocic, G. (2000). Symbolic Warfare: Nato versus the Serbian Media. In Hammond and Herman, *Degraded Capability*, p. 90.

14. BBC (1999). Nato Retracts Media Ultimatum. BBC, 9 April. Retrieved from: <http://news.bbc.co.uk/1/hi/world/europe/314671.stm>

15. Public Broadcasting Service, Interview with General Wesley Clark.

16. Holland, C. (2000). Independent Commission of Inquiry Hearing to Investigate U.S./Nato War Crimes Against the People of Yugoslavia:

Destruction of the Yugoslav Media. International Action Center. Retrieved from: <http://www.iacenter.org/warcrime/10_media.htm>

17. Voice of America (1999). Communications World Transcript. Voice of America, 24 April. Retrieved from: <http://kimelli.nfshost.com/cw/cw_19990424.html>

18. Human Rights Watch (2000). *The Crisis in Kosovo*. Retrieved from: <http://www.hrw.org/reports/2000/nato/Natbm200-01.htm>

19. *New York Times* (2002). Ex-TV Boss Jailed Over NATO Bombing. *New York Times*, 22 June. Retrieved from: <http://www.nytimes.com/2002/06/22/world/world-briefing-europe-yugoslavia-ex-tv-boss-jailed-over-nato-bombing.html>

20. *Washington Post* (1999). Bombing by Committee: France Balked at NATO Targets. *Washington Post*, 20 September, via Nexis.

21. Human Rights Watch, *The Crisis in Kosovo*.

22. Email correspondence with the author, August 2013.

23. Gibson, J. (1999). CNN Counts Costs of War. *Guardian*, 14 May. Retrieved from: <http://www.theguardian.com/world/1999/may/14/balkans1>

24. Pentagon warnings to media which preceded the deadly attack on the Palestine Hotel in Baghdad four years later were ample, but unspecific.

25. Fisk, R. (1999). Taken In by the Nato Line; Kurtz, H. (1999). NATO Hit on TV Station Draws Journalists' Fire. *Washington Post*, 24 April, A17.

26. CNN (1999). Strike Against Yugoslavia: NATO Knocks Out Serbian-Controlled TV Station, 22 April, via Nexis.

27. See Paterson, *International Television News Agencies*, for further detail of this longstanding news exchange system; also Cohen, A., Levy, M., Roeh, I. and Gurevitch, M. (1996). *Global Newsrooms, Local Audiences: A Study of the Eurovision News Exchange*. London: John Libbey; Hjarvard, S. (1995). Eurovision News in a Competitive Marketplace. *EBU Diffusion*, Autumn.

28. Herman, E. and Peterson, D. (2000). CNN: Selling Nato's War Globally. In Hammond and Herman, *Degraded Capability*.

29. Fisk, Taken In by the Nato Line.

30. Human Rights Watch, *The Crisis in Kosovo*.

31. Statement from the Serbian Information Ministry, 27 May 1999.

32. NATO Briefing, Federal News Service, 23 April 1999, via Nexis.

33. Kurtz, NATO Hit on TV Station Draws Journalists' Fire.

34. NATO Briefing, Federal News Service, 23 April 1999, via Nexis.

35. Kurtz, NATO Hit on TV Station Draws Journalists' Fire.

36. For this reason, in this book they are not counted among journalists killed by the US.

37. Sweeney, J., Holsoe, J. and Vulliamy, E. (1999). Nato Bombed Chinese Deliberately. *Observer*, 17 October. Retrieved from: <http://www.theguardian.com/world/1999/oct/17/Balkans>; *Global Research* (2005). US Air Strike on China's Embassy in Belgrade in 1999 was Deliberate: The

Attack Planned as a 'Decapitation' Attack, Intended to Kill Milosevic. *Global Research*, 29 December. Retrieved from: <http://www.globalresearch.ca/us-air-strike-on-china-s-embassy-in-belgrade-in-1999-was-deliberate/1665>

38. CNN (2001). Robertson: Afghan Civilians Want Word on What's Next. CNN, 19 October. Retrieved from: <http://www.cnn.com/2001/WORLD/asiapcf/south/10/19/ret.robertson.otsc/index.html via internet archive>

39. BBC (2001). BBC Reporter Survives Kabul Blast. BBC, 13 November. Retrieved from: <http://news.bbc.co.uk/1/hi/world/south_asia/1654152.stm>

40. James, Why the US Bombed.

41. Whitaker, B. (2003). Battle Station. *Guardian*, 7 February. Retrieved from: <http://www.theguardian.com/media/2003/feb/07/iraqandthemedia.afghanistan>

42. Gowing, N. (2002). Don't Get In Our Way. *Guardian*, 8 April. Retrieved from: <http://www.theguardian.com/media/2002/apr/08/mondaymedia section8>

43. Gowing, Don't Get In Our Way.

44. James, Why the US Bombed.

45. James, Why the US Bombed.

46. Knightley, History or Bunkum?

47. Gowing, Alistair Berkley Memorial Lecture.

48. Pilger, *War You Don't See.*

49. Whitaker, Battle Station.

50. Kirkpatrick, D. (2011). After Disclosures by WikiLeaks, Al Jazeera Replaces Its Top News Director. *New York Times*, 20 September. Retrieved from: <http://www.nytimes.com/2011/09/21/world/middleeast/after-disclosures-by-wikileaks-al-jazeera-replaces-its-top-news-director.html>

51. Suskind, *One Percent Doctrine*, pp. 137–38.

52. Suskind, *One Percent Doctrine*, p. 138.

53. Fouda, Y. (2003). We Left Out Nuclear Targets, For Now. *Guardian*, 4 March. Retrieved from: <http://www.guardian.co.uk/world/2003/mar/04/alqaida.terrorism>

54. Fouda, We Left Out Nuclear Targets; Fouda and Fielding, *Masterminds of Terror*. Also Suskind, *One Percent Doctrine*.

55. Suskind, *One Percent Doctrine*, p. 139.

56. Suskind, *One Percent Doctrine*, p. 140.

57. Fouda and Fielding, *Masterminds of Terror*.

58. Interview with Ron Suskind by the author.

59. ABC News (2005). Colin Powell on Iraq, Race, and Hurricane Relief. ABC News, 8 September. Retrieved from: <http://abcnews.go.com/2020/Politics/story?id=1105979&page=1>

60. BBC (2006). Iraq Reporter Unlawfully Killed. BBC, 13 October. Retrieved from: <http://news.bbc.co.uk/1/hi/6046950.stm>

61. Godoy, J. (2003). US Accused of War Crimes Against Journalists. *InterPress*, 12 April. Retrieved from: <http://rense.com/general37/accu.htm>

62. Gopsill, Target the Media.

63. Phillips, M. (2003). Line of Fire: How TV Crew, Off On Its Own in Iraq, Fell into Fatal Fight. *Wall Street Journal*, 2 May.

64. Tumber and Webster, *Journalists Under Fire*, pp. 90–1.

65. This opinion was provided on the condition of anonymity.

66. Bill Neely of ITN, quoted in Tumber and Webster, *Journalists Under Fire*, p. 77.

67. ITV (2013). *Anniversary of Terry Lloyd Death*. Television programme and online material. ITV, 22 March. Available at: <http://www.itv.com/news/story/2013-03-21/terry-lloyd-iraq-daughter-chelsey-10-years/>

68. BBC, Iraq Reporter Unlawfully Killed.

69. BBC, Iraq Reporter Unlawfully Killed.

70. ITV, *Anniversary of Terry Lloyd Death.*

71. Human Rights Watch (2003). *Off Target: The Conduct of the War and Civilian Casualties in Iraq*. Retrieved from: <http://www.hrw.org/reports/2003/usa1203/4.5.htm>

72. Human Rights Watch, *Off Target*.

73. Telecinco (2004). *Hotel Palestine: Killing the Witness*. Television documentary. The presence of CNN's cameras is referenced in Ramesh, *The War We Could Not Stop*.

74. RSF Secretary-General Robert Menard quoted in Gowing, *Aiming to Stop the Story?*

75. Jukes, S. (ed.) (2004). *Under Fire: Untold Stories from the Front Line of the Iraq War*, London: Reuters/Prentice Hall, p. xiii.

76. Adie, interview reproduced in Dunne, Pentagon Threatens.

77. *Democracy Now*, Former Military Intelligence Sergeant Reveals. One of the analysts, Army Sergeant Adrienne Kinne, recounted her specific orders to ignore the protection of US citizens, and even how an awareness by US citizens of their rights was cause for suspicion:

> During that one conversation between a British aid worker and the American aid worker that I was talking about previously, the British aid worker basically told the American, 'Be careful what you say, because the Americans are listening to us.' And they weren't talking about anything that would have warranted their concern. There was – it was just kind of mundane office goings-on. And so, the American actually responded and said, 'They can't listen to me. I'm an American citizen. I'm protected by USSID 18.' And USSID 18 is basically a directive which is given out to military intelligence which bars the collection on American citizens, to include allies of other countries who we've signed binding agreements with. And when I heard that transmission and that conversation, I –

kind of it caused me to raise my eyebrow, because here we were, we were listening to Americans, and we were collecting on them. ... And so, I brought that particular intercept to the attention of my officer in charge. And actually, rather than be concerned that we were actually spying on Americans and violating the law and the Constitution, he was actually outraged that an American would reference USSID 18 to a non-American, and as if this American was somehow betraying some classified information that Americans have a right not to be spied upon.

The text of US Signals Intelligence Directive 18, to which Kinne refers, is publically available via George Washington University's National Security Archive: <http://www2.gwu.edu/~nsarchiv/NSAEBB/NSAEBB23/07-01.htm>

78. Kinne, A. Recording of Presentation for Iraq Veterans Against the War 'Dartmouth Impeachment Forum'. Retrieved from: <http://www.youtube.com/watch?v=VP5D26Wnf9o>
79. Kinne, Recording of Presentation for Iraq Veterans.
80. *Democracy Now*, Former Military Intelligence Sergeant Reveals.
81. *Xinhua* (2003). Spanish Journalists Boycott Conference by Spanish, British FMs. *Xinhua*, 10 April, via Nexis.
82. Fisk, R. (2003). The Iraq Conflict: Is there Some Element in the US Military that Wants to Take Out Journalists? *Independent*, 9 April.
83. CNN (2003). Media Deaths Explanation Sought. CNN, 9 April, via Nexis. An Al Jazeera employee told the *Guardian*: 'We're giving the Americans the coordinates of our office in Baghdad and also the code of our signal to the satellite transponder ... We will try to give the Americans the whole information about where we are in Baghdad, so there will be no excuse for bombing us. But we are worried' Whitaker, Battle Station.
    A copy of Al Jazeera's messages to the Pentagon could not be obtained for this book, but in a protest letter to the US Secretary of Defense following the Baghdad attacks on the news media, the head of the Committee to Protect Journalists, Joel Simon, confirmed their existence, writing 'CPJ has seen a copy of Al-Jazeera's February letter to Pentagon spokeswoman Victoria Clarke outlining these coordinates' Godoy, US Accused of War Crimes.
84. Committee to Protect Journalists (2006). *Iraq Report: Killed by US Forces*, 10 January. Retrieved from: <http://cpj.org/reports/2006/01/js-killed-by-us-13sept05.php>
85. United Press International (2003). Journalists Killed, Wounded in Iraq, 8 April, via Nexis.
86. Telecinco, *Hotel Palestine*.
87. Telecinco, *Hotel Palestine*.
88. Gopsill, Target the Media; Knightley, History or Bunkum?; Telecinco, *Hotel Palestine*; and Campagna and Roumani, *Permission to Fire*.

89. Godoy, US Accused of War Crimes.

90. Telecinco, *Hotel Palestine.*

91. Quoted in Fisk, The Iraq Conflict.

92. Nakhoul, S. (2004). Collateral Damage. In Jukes, *Under Fire.*

93. Nakhoul, Collateral Damage, p. 34.

94. United Press International (2003). Odyssey of a Human Shield. United Press International, 5 April, via Nexis.

95. *Xinhua* (2003). Central Baghdad under new bombardment. *Xinhua*, 6 April, via Nexis.

96. United Press International (2003). Saddam's jester briefs the press. United Press International, 7 April, via Nexis.

97. United Press International (2003). DOD says reporter deaths sad, unavoidable. United Press International, 8 April, via Nexis.

98. White, *Justice Denied*; Scahill, J. (2005). Did Bush Really Want to Bomb Al Jazeera? *Nation*, 27 November.

99. Manyon, J. (2004). Worse than Vietnam. *Spectator*, 8 May. Retrieved from: <http://www.spectator.co.uk/features/12189/worse-than-vietnam/>

100. According to a *Guardian* obituary, Ramiz was a 'regular commentator in the international media ... Journalists [...] came to value Ramiz as an energetic, powerful and intelligent analyst'. The *Guardian* provides an account of his death at the hands of US forces, writing that: 'When a suspected chemical weapons factory was destroyed in an accidental explosion during an American raid, half his house [...] was also blown up' Hilsum, L. (2004). Gailan Ramiz. *Guardian*, 10 May. Retrieved from: <http://www.theguardian.com/news/2004/may/10/guardianobituaries.iraq>

101. Fisk, R. (2004). Crisis Of Information in Baghdad. *Independent*, 20 July.

102. McCarthy, R. (2004). Uneasy Truce in the City of Ghosts. *Guardian*, 24 April.

103. See, for example, Marqusee, M. (2005). A Name that Lives in Infamy: The Destruction of Falluja Was an Act of Barbarism that Ranks Alongside My Lai, Guernica and Halabja. *Guardian*, 10 November. Retrieved from: <http://www.theguardian.com/world/2005/nov/10/usa.iraq>

104. Committee to Protect Journalists (2004). *Incident Report: Burhan Mohamed Mazhour.* Retrieved from: <https://cpj.org/killed/2004/burhan-mohamed-mazhour.php>; Scahill, J. (2005). The War on Al Jazeera. *Nation*, 19 December. Retrieved from: <http://www.thenation.com/doc/20051219/scahill>

105. Shapiro, The War Inside the Arab Newsroom.

106. INSI (2004) *Incident Report*, 17 November. Retrieved from: <http://www.newssafety.org/news.php?news=2958&cat=iraq-media-safety>

107. Massing, M. (2004). Iraq, the Press and the Election. *AlterNet*, 23 November. Retrieved from: <http://www.alternet.org/story/20569/iraq%2C_the_press%2C_and_the_election>; and press freedom organisations.

108. Committee to Protect Journalists, Incident Report: Dhia Najim. Retrieved from: <http://cpj.org/killed/2004/dhia-najim.php>

109. Reuters News Reports, via INSI. Retrieved from: <http://www.newssafety.org/page.php?page=3687&cat=iraq-media-safety>

110. Day, J. (2006). Reuters Soundman 'Killed Unlawfully'. *Guardian*, 10 April. Retrieved from: <http://www.theguardian.com/media/2006/apr/10/iraqandthemedia.iraq>

111. Schechter, D. (2005). Was Giuliana Sgrena Targeted? *AlterNet*, 7 March. Retrieved from: <http://www.alternet.org/story/21427/was_giuliana_sgrena_targeted>. Former US television journalist Tom Fenton, who spent 34 years with CBS news, blamed Sgrena's nationality for her kidnapping). He told Howard Kurtz (quoted by Schechter):

> there is a back story also to this Italian journalist. It's pretty widely known that both Italy and France are paying ransoms. That means that every Italian journalist, every French journalist there is a walking target. The going price for a Western – say, for an American journalist, particularly a TV correspondent, they're big guns, in Iraq is something like $4 million right now. People get picked up and they get shopped to somebody else who will pay that kind of money.

112. *Democracy Now* (2011). Julian Assange and Philosopher Slavoj Žižek with Amy Goodman. *Democracy Now*, 5 July. Retrieved from: <http://www.democracynow.org/blog/2011/7/5/watch_full_video_of_wikileaks_julian_assange_philosopher_slavoj_iek_with_amy_goodman>

113. I am indebted to my University of Leeds colleague Dr Katy Parry for alerting me to Finkel's book. Finkel, D. (2010). *The Good Soldiers*. London: Atlantic Books.

114. Whether Manning's treatment specifically met internationally accepted definitions of torture remains in dispute. See Ackerman, B. and Benkler, Y. (2011). Private Manning's Humiliation. *New York Review of Books*, 28 April. Retrieved from: <http://www.nybooks.com/articles/archives/2011/apr/28/private-mannings-humiliation/>

115. Confirmed by a lexis search of reviews of Finkel's book from the date of its publication through the end of 2009. An exception was a brief mention in a 6 October 2009 *New York Times* review, which calls Finkel's account of the Apache incident 'horrifying' without commenting further on its significance.

116. Available at: <http://www.washingtonpost.com/wp-dyn/content/article/2010/04/06/AR2010040601368.html>

117. McGreal, C. (2010). WikiLeaks Reveals Video Showing US Air Crew Shooting Down Iraqi Civilians. *Guardian*, 5 April. Retrieved from: <http://www.theguardian.com/world/2010/apr/05/wikileaks-us-army-iraq-attack?guni=Article:in%20body%20link>

118. Gowing, Alistair Berkley Memorial Lecture.

119. Specifically, their paying audiences. Most modern media have a primary audience who engage – usually involuntarily – with the advertising accompanying news content, and a financially irrelevant secondary audience who avoid that advertising through various means, such as reading reposted content or actively avoiding or blocking advertising. The dilemma for any news worker is to maintain something like neutrality in reporting while creating a product which appeals to a narrow, targeted audience who may be alienated by neutrality, or any information which appears to represent the perspective of a perceived enemy. A healthy publicly sponsored media operating alongside a fiercely commercial media, as with the contemporary British media system, offers a partial solution, although by no means a perfect one.

120. As detailed in Al-Rawi's exhaustive study of the pre- and post-Saddam media in Iraq: Al-Rawi, A. (2012). *Media Practice in Iraq*, London: Palgrave Macmillian.

121. Sambrook, R. (2006). *Press Freedom*. Frontline Club, 17 May. Retrieved from: <http://www.frontlineclub.com/press_freedom/>

122. Iraq War Logs. The original document may be viewed at: <http://www.theguardian.com/world/afghanistan/warlogs/777E7E76-2219-0B3F-9F46F193643C2BBA?guni=Article:in%20body%20link>

123. Cooper, A. (2004). *Journalists in Iraq: From Embeds to Targets*, Committee to Protect Journalists, 9 February. Retrieved from: <http://www.cpj.org/op_ed/Cooper09feb04.html>

124. The Spanish conviction would later be overturned by a European court. Doha Center for Media Freedom (2012). *European Court: Al Jazeera's Alluni Trial Illegal*. Retrieved from: <http://www.dc4mf.org/fr/node/998>

125. Campagna, J. (2006). *Sami al-Haj: The Enemy?* CPJ, 3 October. Retrieved from: <http://cpj.org/reports/2006/10/prisoner.php>. According to a book by his lawyer:

> Against the background of this campaign against al-Jazeera, what I learned about Sami's ongoing interrogation in Guantanamo was disturbing. In the first 100-plus sessions, the US military never posed a question about the allegations against him, as they were only interested in turning him into an informant against al-Jazeera. He had to ask them to interrogate him about what he was supposed to have done wrong.

> Smith, C.S. (2007). *Bad Men: Guantanamo Bay and the Secret Prisons*, London: George Weidenfeld & Nicolson.

126. Although this was reported in the main agenda-setting newspaper in the US, the *New York Times*, it was still two years before Al Hajj would be released, and most US media remained silent about his case. Kristof, N.D. (2006). Sami's Shame, and Ours. *New York Times*, 14 October. Retrieved from: <http://query.nytimes.com/gst/fullpage.html?res=F20614F835540C748DDDA90994DE404482>

127. Reuters (2006). Reuters Journalist Freed in Iraq. Reuters, 1 June.

128. Cooper, A. (2005). *Dangerous Assignments: Jailing Iraqi Journalists*, Committee to Protect Journalists. Retrieved from: <http://cpj.org/reports/2005/10/comment-da-fall05.php>

129. Cooper, *Journalists in Iraq*; Usher, S. (2004). Al-Jazeera Marks 'Martyr's' Death. BBC, May 21. Retrieved from: <http://newsvote.bbc.co.uk/mpapps/pagetools/print/news.bbc.co.uk/1/hi/world/middle_east/3736493.stm>; also see Fisk, R. (2003). Did the US Murder These Journalists? *Independent*, 26 April.

130. Lekic, S. (2003). Relations between Journalists and U.S. Troops in Iraq Sour as Attacks Escalate. Associated Press, 12 November, via Nexis; see similar reports in Parenti, C. (2004). Al Jazeera Goes to Jail. *Nation*, 11 March. Retrieved from: <http://www.thenation.com/doc.mhtml?i=20040329&c=1&s=parenti>

131. Loyn, D. (2007). Local Heroes: Risk-Taking in Iraq. *British Journalism Review*, 18(2): 21–5.

132. Welsh, M.Y. (2006). Atwar Bahjat: A Believer in Iraq. Al Jazeera, 27 February. Retrieved from: <http://www.aljazeera.com/archive/2006/02/20084915564348302.html>. Atwar Bahjat would later be brutally killed, with two co-workers, by local criminals while reporting for the Al Arabiya satellite channel.

133. Agha, O. (2006). Journalists Targets of Violence. Al Jazeera, 16 April. Retrieved from: <http://www.aljazeera.com/archive/2006/04/20084913267350930.html>

134. North, A. (2004). US Sorry for Holding BBC Reporter. BBC. 10 September. Retrieved from: <http://news.bbc.co.uk/1/hi/world/south_asia/3645264.stm>

135. Yates, D. (2008). Reuters Seeks Evidence on Why Cameraman Held in Iraq. Reuters, 31 July. Retrieved from: <http://www.reuters.com/article/2008/07/31/us-iraq-cameraman-reuters-idUSL964696820080731>; International News Safety Institute, Incident Reports.

136. Lekic, Relations between Journalists; Parenti, Al Jazeera Goes to Jail; Harding, L. (2004). US Military 'Brutalised' Journalists. *Guardian*, 13 January. Retrieved from <http://media.guardian.co.uk/broadcast/story/0,7493,1121995,00.html>

137. *Guardian* (2006). US Troops Seize Award-Winning Iraqi Journalist. *Guardian*, 9 January. Retrieved from: <http://www.theguardian.com/media/2006/jan/09/pressandpublishing.iraq>

138. *Nation* (2007). The Other War: Iraq Vets Bear Witness. *Nation*, 9 July. Retrieved from: <http://www.thenation.com/article/other-war-iraq-vets-bear-witness>

139. Public Broadcasting Service (2010). Coalition Deaths in Afghanistan Renew Debate Over Rules of Engagement. Public Broadcasting Service, 14 July. Retrieved from: <http://www.pbs.org/newshour/bb/asia/july-dec10/afghanistan2_07-14.html>

140. Gowing, *Aiming to Stop the Story?*

141. Committee to Protect Journalists (2014). *Israel and the Occupied Palestinian Territory*. Retrieved from: <http://www.cpj.org/mideast/israel-and-the-occupied-palestinian-territory/>

The IFJ reported that:

Israeli authorities have tried to control journalists, and particularly Palestinian journalists working for international media, by withdrawing press cards and permits to travel. They have also acted physically against Palestinian media, blowing up transmitters and buildings. Although the IDF consistently says it does not target journalists, numerous shootings, beatings and harassment add up to a policy, deliberate or by default. Soldiers who see the journalists as 'on the side of' Palestinian stone throwers know that they will face few repercussions if they shoot at the photographers, camera operators or correspondents.

They cite an International Press Institute report 'detailing attacks on journalists covering the Israeli-Palestinian conflict in the 20 months from September 2000 to April 2002. It concluded that 81% of press freedom violations were perpetrated by Israelis, mostly by the IDF. The majority of victimised journalists were Palestinian'. The IPI concluded:

that since the beginning of the violent crisis in Israel and the Occupied Palestinian Territories on September 28, 2000, journalists have repeatedly been targeted, shot, beaten, arrested, threatened and intimidated by Israeli soldiers, police, politicians, settlers and civilians, as well as by Palestinian police, politicians and civilians. Out of a total of 220 incidents, there were six deaths. Journalists and media workers have been injured by live ammunition, shrapnel or rubber-coated bullets, and were harassed and physically assaulted in other ways. At least 165 press freedom violations were carried out by Israeli authorities.

International Federation of Journalists (2003). *Live News: A Survival Guide for Journalists*. Retrieved from: <http://www.ifj.org/assets/docs/130/098/d325b82-7939762.pdf>

142. Committee to Protect Journalists (2006). *UK Court Rules IDF Shooting of Filmmaker in Gaza Was Murder*. Retrieved from: <http://cpj.org/2006/04/uk-court-rules-idf-shooting-of-filmmaker-in-gaza-w.php>

143. Public Broadcasting Service (2003). Israel/Palestinian Territories in the Line of Fire – Update. Retrieved from: <http://www.pbs.org/frontlineworld/stories/israel.palestine/update.html, and press freedom organisations>

144. *Independent on Sunday* (2004). War Coverage – We're the Ones Who Stick Our Heads Out; Camera Operators Are Mentioned Last in Reports Of Casualties. *Independent on Sunday*, 13 June, via Nexis.

145. Reuters (2008). Israel Clears Troops Who Killed *Reuters* Cameraman, Reuters, 13 August. Retrieved from: <http://uk.reuters.com/article/2008/08/13/uk-palestinians-israel-journalist-idUKLD61073920080813>

146. Reuters (2012). Memorial Book: Fadel Sobhi Shana. *The Baron*. Retrieved from: <http://www.thebaron.info/styled-66/fadelshana.html>

147. Public Broadcasting Service (2003). Interview with Patricia Naylor – When Journalists Become Targets. *Frontline-World*. Retrieved from: <http://www.pbs.org/frontlineworld/stories/israel.palestine/naylor.html>

148. Public Broadcasting Service (2003). Interview with Gideon Levy – When Journalists Become Targets. *Frontline-World*. Retrieved from: <http://www.pbs.org/frontlineworld/stories/israel.palestine/levy.html>

149. Gutmann, S. (2005). *The Other War: Israelis, Palestinians, and the Struggle for Media Supremacy*, San Francisco: Encounter Books, pp. 248–50.

150. Leibovich-Dar, S. (2002). In the Eye of the Beholder. Ha'aretz, 24 April. Retrieved from: <http://www.haaretz.com/print-edition/features/in-the-eye-of-the-beholder-1.46997>

151. Gutmann, *The Other War*, pp. 168–9.

152. Gowing, Alistair Berkley Memorial Lecture.

153. Gowing, Alistair Berkley Memorial Lecture.

154. Gutmann, *The Other War*, pp. 168.

155. Gutmann, *The Other War*, pp. 256–7.

156. Gutmann, *The Other War*, pp. 256–7.

157. Massing, Iraq, the Press and the Election.

158. IFJ, CPJ, and other press freedom groups.

159. Gowing, *Aiming to Stop the Story?*

160. Garthwaite, R. (2011). *How to Avoid Being Killed in a War Zone*, London: Bloomsbury, p. 249.

161. Abu-Fadil, M (2008). Threatened Iraqi Journalists Seek State's Protection Despite Charges it Instigated Colleagues' Murders. *Huffington Post*, 30 September. Retrieved from: <http://www.huffingtonpost.com/magda-abufadil/threatened-iraqi-journali_b_130512.html>. Detailed review of the situation in Iraq for local media is provided by Al-Rawi, *Media Practice in Iraq*.

4.   *Media Response*

1. By 2010, Associated Press Television News, which had emerged in the preceding years as the largest of the two dominant television news agencies (Reuters Television is the other) could claim that 'video captured by *AP Television News* can be seen by over half of the world's population on any given day' (*APTN* website, 2010).

2. According to the CPJ, writing in 2006, during his captivity, 'To viewers of the Arab world's most watched news channel, [Al Jazeera cameraman Sami] al-Hajj is a familiar face. Al-Jazeera regularly reports on developments in his case, has devoted a section of its popular Web site to the detained journalist, and, this year, broadcast a 53-minute documentary detailing his story'. But the CPJ also notes that many Al Jazeera staff accuse the company of initially

saying little about Al-Hajj and only campaigning for his release late in the day. Campagna, *Sami al-Haj: The Enemy?*

3. Prominent *New York Times* columnist Nicolas Krsitof did make repeated attempts to draw attention to Sami Al-Hajj's case via his online blog while most US media were ignoring it.

4. Stelter, B. (2009). From Guantánamo to Desk at Al Jazeera. *New York Times*, 22 December. Retrieved from: < http://www.nytimes.com/2009/12/23/world/middleeast/23jazeera.html >

5. Kristof, Sami's Shame, and Ours.

6. This author has presented the Telecinco film at screenings in the US and UK; the only US broadcast I am aware of was in the progressive current affairs programme *Democracy Now*, which has a limited viewership online and via the community access channels of cable television systems in some US cities.

7. As Avaaz and other civil society organisations and online campaigning groups did in a campaign to send satellite telephones and media equipment to anti-government activists in Syria. Walt, V. (2012). How a New York City-Based Activist Group Became a Player in Syria. *Time*, 15 March. Retrieved from: < http://www.time.com/time/world/article/0,8599,2109212,00.html >

8. Wolper, A. (2004). Reuters Still Seeking Answers on Alleged Abuse of Three Staffers. *Editor and Publisher*, 5 December.

9. Fisk, The Iraq Conflict.

10. The CPJ provides a review of many of the incidents and the US military responses (*Iraq Report*). Given the power of the US government to dominate the international debate about these issues and the consistent tendency of US government investigations to exonerate its own, this book privileges the accounts of these incidents provided by non-military actors.

11. *Transnational Broadcast Studies* (2006). Interview with Nabil Khatib, Executive Editor of Al Arabiya. *TBS*, 16. Retrieved from: < http://www.tbsjournal.com/KhatibInterview.html >

12. Knightley, *First Casualty*, pp. 100–1.

13. Knightley, History or Bunkum?, p. 101.

14. Waisbord, Antipress Violence.

15. Parks, L. (2007). Insecure Airwaves: US Bombings of Aljazeera. *Communication and Critical/Cultural Studies*, 4(2): 226–31.

16. O'Carroll, L. (2004). Al-Jazeera Closure. A Blow to Freedom. *Guardian*, 9 August. Retrieved from: < http://www.theguardian.com/media/2004/aug/09/Iraqandthemedia.broadcasting >

17. Transnational Broadcast Studies, Nabil Khatib Interview.

18. International Federation of Journalists and Statewatch, *Journalism, Civil Liberties and the War on Terrorism*.

19. International Federation of Journalists and Statewatch, *Journalism, Civil Liberties and the War on Terrorism*.

20. *Daily Mirror*, 22 November 2005. See also Scahill, Did Bush Really Want to Bomb Al Jazeera?; Marsden, C. (2007). Two Imprisoned for Violating Official Secrets Act. *IndyMedia UK*, 17 May. Retrieved from: < http://www.indymedia.org.uk/en/2007/05/370913.html >

21. Krichen, M. (2013). *Endless Surprises for Al-Jazeera*. CPJ, 12 September. Retrieved from: < http://www.cpj.org/internet/2013/09/endless-surprises-for-al-jazeera.php#more >

22. James, Why the US Bombed.

23. Kiss, J. (2003). Al-Jazeera Hacker Brought to Justice. *Journalism*, 20 June. Retrieved from: < http://www.journalism.co.uk/news/al-jazeera-hacker-brought-to-justice/s2/a5668/ >

24. Shraeder, J. (2012). Being the Bridge. *Alcalde*, 8 September. Retrieved from: < http://alcalde.texasexes.org/2012/09/being-the-bridge-2/ >

25. Al Jazeera (2003). US Court Fines Aljazeera Hacker. Al Jazeera, 13 November. Retrieved from: < http://www.aljazeera.com/archive/2003/11/200849145555562722.html >

26. *Spiegel Online International* (2013). Snowden Document: NSA Spied On Al Jazeera Communications. *Spiegel*, 31 August. Retrieved from: < http://www.spiegel.de/international/world/nsa-spied-on-al-jazeera-communications-snowden-document-a-919681.html >

27. *Mediaoriente* (2011). Al Jazeera's Wadah Khanfar Quits After 8 years ... a New Course for the Qatari-Based Network? *Mediaoriente*, 21 September. Retrieved from: < http://mediaoriente.com/tag/mohamed-jassim-al-ali/ >

28. Paterson, *The International Television News Agencies*.

29. In research with news agencies, I was occasionally told that scenes of horror involving civilian casualties in war zones are deliberately recorded and transmitted in the most lurid way the videographer can muster. It is their opportunity to make a strong statement to the world, even if they realise much of their footage will not go beyond the London newsroom; this issue is discussed further in chapter 8 of Paterson, *The International Television News Agencies*. Also see Aday, S. (2005). The Real War Won't Be Shown on Television: An Analysis of Casualty Imagery in American Television Coverage of the Iraq War. In P. Seib (ed.), *Media and Conflict in the 21st Century*, New York: Palgrave Macmillan, pp. 141–56.

30. Zayani, M. and Sahraoui, S. (2007). *The Culture of Al Jazeera*, Jefferson, NC: McFarland; El-Nawawy, M. and Iskandar, A. (2003). *Al-Jazeera: The Story of the Network that is Rattling Governments and Redefining Modern Journalism*, Boulder, CO: Westview.

31. Shapiro, The War Inside the Arab Newsroom.

32. Haddon, M. (2012). Richard Sambrook on the Future of Journalism and Leaving the BBC. *Frontline Club News*, 24 February. Retrieved from: < http://www.frontlineclub.com/richard_sambrook_on_the_future_of_journalism/ >

33. Kurtz, H. (2001). CNN Chief Orders 'Balance' in War News: Reporters Are Told to Remind Viewers Why U.S. Is Bombing. *Washington Post*, 31 October, via Nexis.

34. Kellner, D. (2004). 9/11, Spectacles of Terror, and Media Manipulation. In Miller, *Tell Me Lies*.

35. Herman and Chomsky, *Manufacturing Consent*, pp. 26–8.

36. Tumber and Webster, *Journalists Under Fire*, pp. 83–4.

37. Fisk, R. (2004). Pictures of Wounded Men Being Shot Censored by TV. *The Independent*, 7 May. Retrieved from: <http://www.countercurrents.org/iraq-fisk070504.htm>

38. Chapter two of this author's book about the television news agencies (Paterson, *The International Television News Agencies*, pp. 26–43) reviews research into the nature of their product and this consistent US focus.

39. Horvit, B. (2003). International News Agencies and the War Debate of 2003. *International Communication Gazette*, 68(5–6): 427–47.

40. Horvit, International News Agencies.

41. Paterson, *The International Television News Agencies*.

42. Eric Braun, interview, 2008.

43. Murrell, C. (2010). Baghdad Bureaux: An Exploration of the Interconnected World of Fixers and Correspondents at the BBC and CNN. *Media, War and Conflict*, 3(2): 125-37; Mitra, S. (2010). *Transcultural Productions: Photojournalists of the Third World in Western News Agencies*. Unpublished master's dissertation, Swansea University; Venter, E. (2005). *The Safety of Journalists: An Assessment of Perceptions of the Origins and Implementation of Policy at the Two International Television News Agencies*. Unpublished master's thesis, Rhodes University; Pedelty, M. (1995). *War Stories: The Culture of Foreign Correspondents*, London: Routledge.

44. Simpson, J. (2006). What Comfort Zone? *Guardian*, 29 May. Retrieved from: <http://www.theguardian.com/media/2006/may/29/bbc.monday mediasection>

45. Venter, *The Safety of Journalists*, p. 86, fn. 35.

46. Loyn, D. (2005). *Frontline: The True Story of the British Mavericks Who Changed the Face of War Reporting*, London: Michael Joseph.

47. When an 18-year-old Syrian was killed in a Syrian government attack on rebels, Reuters said he had been working for them for most of 2013 and 'we paid him on a per-picture basis … *Reuters* provided Molhem with camera equipment, a ballistic helmet, and body armor'. Some journalists claimed he was only 17. Journalist David Kenner wrote in *Foreign Policy* that 'Journalists have raised questions about his lack of protective gear, his political affiliation with a rebel brigade, and whether Reuters violated its own safety guidelines by putting him in harm's way'. Andrew MacGregor Marshall was a Reuters Baghdad bureau chief and Middle East editor before resigning. Following the killing of Reuters staff in Baghdad in 2007 (the incident on the cover

of this book), he wrote safety guidelines for the company telling staff to '[n] ever cross the line, or give the appearance of crossing the line, between the role of journalist as impartial observer and that of participant in a conflict'. Reuters declined to explain why the young man who made no secret of his affiliation with rebel fighters was being paid by them. Kenner, D. (2014). The Controversial Death of a Teenage Stringer. *Foreign Policy*. Retrieved from: < http://www.foreignpolicy.com/articles/2014/01/07/the_stringer_molhem_ barakat_reuters_syria >

48. Flak was identified as a powerful filter of journalistic output in Herman and Chomsky, *Manufacturing Consent*, as described further in Chapter 2.

49. The letter is posted at: < http://homepage.mac.com/bkerstetter/writersblock/ reuters explanation.html > copied from a now-inactive Reuters webpage. See for further detail: Palmer, M. (2011). PRESS on the Appropriate Button in the Reader's Mind: News Agencies Cover Terrorism. *Global Media and Communication*, 7(3): 257–61.

50. See Paterson, *The International Television News Agencies*, chapter two; also Schiff, F. (1996). The Associated Press: Its Worldwide Bureaus and American Interests. *International Communication Bulletin*, 31: 7–13.

51. Interviews with current and former Reuters staff who prefer not to be quoted directly when speaking of recent change at Reuters. The departure of many senior Reuters staff is chronicled by the Reuters staff publication, available publicly: < http://thebaron.info >. The history of Reuters Television is recounted in Paterson, *The International Television News Agencies*.

52. Gowing, The Alistair Berkley Memorial Lecture.

53. Regan, T. (2005). Rumsfeld Says He Will Look into Detention, Shootings of Journalists. *Christian Science Monitor*, 3 October.

54. Harding, L. (2004). U.S. Military 'Brutalised' Journalists. *Guardian*, 4 December.

55. Jurkowitz, M. (2003). Media Protest Treatment in Iraq: Letter to Pentagon Accuses US Troops of Intimidation. *Boston Globe*, 13 November.

56. Multi-National Force, Iraq.

57. Eason Jordan, correspondence with the author.

58. International News Safety Institute (2004a). *Iraq Media Hotline*, 27 April. Retrieved from: < http://www.newssafety.org/news.php?news=3717&cat=iraq-media-safety >

59. Paterson, They Shoot Journalists, Don't They?

60. Carroll, Reporters at Risk.

61. Regan, Rumsfeld Says He Will Look into Detention.

62. Macdonald, A. (2006). US Offer Iraq Journalists New Safeguards. Reuters, 20 March.

63. Shapiro, R. (2014). Fox News' Andrea Tantaros Tells Listeners To 'Punch' Obama Voters 'In The Face'. *Huffington Post*, 8 February. Retrieved from: < http://www.huffingtonpost.com/2013/05/24/fox-news-andrea-tantaros-

punch-obama-voters-face_n_3332728.html?utm_hp_ref=mostpopular>.
Incitement to violence is a crime in the US, but no charges were filed against
the network or presenter concerned.

64. Brown, D. (2013). Top 14 Tips for Secure Mobile Communications. *Frontline
Club News*, 8 May. Retrieved from: <http://www.frontlineclub.com/top-14-
tips-for-secure-mobile-communications/#more-31357>

65. Sambrook, R. (2006). Why International Journalists Shouldn't Pull Out of
Iraq – An Update on the INSI Global Inquiry. *Frontline Club Newsletter*, May 5.
Retrieved from: <http://www.frontlineclub.com/words-and-pictures/articles/
from-the-frontline/press-freedom.html>

66. International News Safety Institute (2004). Iraq: Driver, Bodyguard of Dutch
Journalists Killed, 1 June. Retrieved from: <http://www.newssafety.org/news.
php?news=3303&cat=iraq-media-safety>

67. Leung, R. (2004). The Image War: U.S. Has Begun its Own Arab-Language TV
News Channel. CBS News, 14 May. Retrieved from: <http://www.cbsnews.
com/stories/2004/05/14/60minutes/main617617.shtml>

68. International Federation of Journalists and Statewatch, *Journalism, Civil
Liberties and the War on Terrorism*.

69. Paterson, *The International Television News Agencies*, pp. 135–40.

70. Miller, *Tell Me Lies*.

71. Gunter, L. (2003). Hand-Wringing of Scribes' Blatant Bias: Journalists in
Baghdad, Having Lost Colleagues, Blame U.S. Forces Alone. *Edmonton Journal*,
9 April, via Nexis.

72. Fairness and Accuracy in Reporting (2003). *U.S. Media Applaud Bombing
of Iraqi TV*, 27 March. Retrieved from: <http://fair.org/take-action/media-
advisories/u-s-media-applaud-bombing-of-iraqi-tv/>

73. Byrne, C. (2003). Gilligan Casts Doubt on Source of Hotel Attack. *Media
Guardian*, 8 April.

74. Sambrook, *Press Freedom*.

75. Sambrook, *Press Freedom*.

76. Waisbord, Antipress Violence.

5.   *Legality*

1. Two helpful, although dated, overviews are Gasser, H. (1983). The Protection
of Journalists Engaged in Dangerous Professional Missions. *International
Review of the Red Cross*, 232: 3–18. Retrieved from: <http://www.icrc.org/Web/
eng/siteeng0.nsf/iwpList356/BBE4FC40309D69C7C1256B66005C4EEE>;
and Kirby and Jackson, International Humanitarian Law. Also see collected
documents at Findlaw: <http://news.findlaw.com/legalnews/lit/iraq/laws.
html>. Lisosky and Henrichsen, *War on Words*, have provided one of the most
thorough recent analyses of these issues.

2. Sands, *Lawless World*, p. 230.

3. Sands, *Lawless World*.

4. Horwitz, R. (2013). *America's Right: Anti-Establishment Conservatism from Goldwater to the Tea Party*. Cambridge: Polity Press.

5. See also Lipset, S.M. (1996). *American Exceptionalism: A Double-Edged Sword*, New York: Norton.

6. This summary of the provisions of the Geneva Conventions with regard to civilians, and which is therefore applicable to civilian journalists, is partially based on a summary prepared by Human Rights Watch in relation to the Crisis in Kosovo. Retrieved from: <http://www.hrw.org/reports/2000/nato/Natbm200-01.htm>

7. DOD Directive 5100.77 of 10 July 1979, para. E(1)(b).

8. Protocol I, Article 52(2) defines military objectives as 'those objects which by their nature, location, purpose or use make an effective contribution to military action'.

9. The term 'means of combat' refers generally to the weapons used; the 'method' to the way in which such weapons are used.

10. ICRC (1987). *Commentary on the Additional Protocols*, Dordrecht: ICRC/Martinus Nijhoff Publishers, pp. 681–2, para. 2198.

11. Gowing, Don't Get In Our Way.

12. ICRC, *Commentary on the Additional Protocols*, p. 626, para. 1980.

13. Thompson, K. and Giffard, C. (2002). *Reporting Killings as Human Rights Violations Handbook: How to Document and Respond to Potential Violations of the Right to Life within the International System for the Protection of Human Rights*, The Human Rights Centre, University of Essex. Retrieved from: <http://www.essex.ac.uk/reportingkillingshandbook/handbook/part_ii_2.htm>

14. Darcy, S. (2006). University of Ulster Transitional Justice Institute, email correspondence.

15. United Nations (2006). *Press Release*. Retrieved from: <http://www.un.org/News/Press/docs/2006/sc8929.doc.htm>

16. Godoy, US Accused Of War Crimes.

17. Kirby and Jackson, International Humanitarian Law.

18. Human Rights Watch, *Off Target*.

19. Human Rights Watch, *Off Target*.

20. Human Rights Watch, *The Crisis in Kosovo*.

21. Gowing, Alistair Berkley Memorial Lecture.

22. Eason Jordan, correspondence with author, 2013.

23. White, *Justice Denied*; Balguy-Gallois, Protection.

24. Wilson, J. (2003). US Troops 'Crazy' in Killing of Cameraman. *Guardian*, August 19. Dana had covered the Israeli-occupied territories for Reuters for 14 years, surviving beatings and earlier shootings by Israeli forces. In light of a history of Israeli efforts to stop his work stretching over many years, his

killing by US troops, when none of the other journalists working with him were harmed, has been regarded by journalists' groups as suspicious.

25. McClure, L. (2003). The 'Unconscionable' Death of Mazen Dana. *Salon*, 21 August. Retrieved from: <http://www.salon.com/2003/08/21/photographer>

26. Article 48 of the Protocol Additional to the Geneva Conventions.

27. Third Geneva Convention, Article 4.

28. Balguy-Gallois, Protection.

29. White, *Justice Denied*.

30. Furthermore, in regard to the reported US practice of transferring detainees to countries where they might expect to be tortured, Dick Marty, chairman of the Council of Europe legal affairs and human rights committee, warned that 'the US, believing that "neither conventional judicial instruments nor those established under the framework of the laws of war could effectively counter the new forms of international terrorism" decided to "develop new legal concepts"' depriving hundreds of detainees of their basic rights. 'This legal approach is utterly alien to the European tradition and sensibility, and is clearly contrary to the European Convention on Human Rights and the Universal Declaration of Human Rights'. Quoted in Grey S. and Cobain, I. (2006). From Logistics to Turning a Blind Eye: Europe's Role in Terror Abductions. *Guardian*, June 7. Retrieved from: <http://www.guardian.co.uk/usa/story/0,,1791991,00.html>; see also Jinks, D. (2006). The Applicability of the Geneva Conventions to the 'Global War on Terrorism'. *Virginia Journal of International Law*, 46: 1

31. ICRC (undated), ICRC Hotline, International Committee of the Red Cross. Retrieved from: <http://www.icrc.org/Web/eng/siteeng0.nsf/htmlall/p0394/$File/ICRC_002_0394.pdf>

32. Supreme Court of the US: *Hamdan* v. *Rumsfeld*, Secretary of Defense, et al., 29 June 2006.

33. Crossette, B. (2010). US Profile on Human Rights Grows at the United Nations. *Nation*, 1 September. Retrieved from: <http://www.thenation.com/article/154445/us-profile-human-rights-grows-united-nations?rel=emailNation#>

34. See for example: Jinks, Applicability of the Geneva Conventions; Sands, *Lawless World*; Wallach, E. (2004). The Logical Nexus Between the Decision to Deny Application of the Third Geneva Convention to the Taliban and Al Qaeda and the Mistreatment of Prisoners in Abu Ghraib. *Case Western Reserve Journal of International Law*, 36: 537; Dean, *Worse than Watergate*.

35. *Huffington Post* (2011). Sami al-Hajj, Al Jazeera Journalist, Held at Guantanamo So He Could Be Questioned about Network. *Huffington Post*, 25 April. Retrieved from: <http://www.huffingtonpost.com/2011/04/25/sami-al-hajj-al-jazeera-j_n_853297.html>; see also details compiled by Amnesty International available at: <http://web.amnesty.org/library/index/ENGAMR512072005>

36. Provided for primarily by the Principles on the Effective Prevention and Investigation of Extra-Legal, Arbitrary and Summary Executions, Principles 9–18 of the Geneva Conventions.

37. The Conventions do not apply to the legality, or legitimacy, of the invasion – and the subsequent legality of any US actions in Iraq – although these issues have also been subject to debate. It has emerged that while the Bush administration was receiving – so it claims – advice that the invasion was legal, the Blair government in the UK was questioning the reasons for war and doubting its legality. Leigh, D. and Evans, R. (2006). Papers Pinpoint Law Chief's Change of Heart over War. *Guardian*, 26 May. Retrieved from: < http://www.guardian.co.uk/guardianpolitics/story/0,,1783415,00.html >

38. The civilian death toll is discussed in Chapter 1.

39. Coalition Provisional Authority Order Number 65, Iraqi Communications and Media Commission.

40. Al-Rawi, *Media Practice in Iraq*.

41. Committee to Protect Journalists (2008). *Incident Report*. Retrieved from: < http://cpj.org/2008/09/four-from-al-sharqiya-tv-killed-in-mosul-arrests-m.php >

42. Sands, *Lawless World*, p. 14. See also Sewall, S. and Kaysen, C. (eds) (2000). *The US and the International Criminal Court*, Lanham, MD: Rowman & Littlefield.

43. American Service-Members' Protection Act of 2002.

44. Article 90 of Additional Protocol I states: 'The Commission shall be competent to enquire into any facts alleged to be a grave breach as defined in the Conventions and this Protocol or other serious violation of the Conventions or of this Protocol'.

45. The Commission was established in 1991 under the First Additional Protocol of the Geneva Conventions.

46. Mari, J. (2004). *Two Murders and a Lie*, Reporters without Borders.

47. Zegveld, L. (2002). Comments on the Presentation of Prof. Frits Kalshoven. *Journal of International Law of Peace and Armed Conflict*, 4.

48. Mari, *Two Murders*; Balguy-Gallois, Protection.

49. Brandeisky, K. (2013). NSA Surveillance Lawsuit Tracker. ProPublica, 10 July. Retrieved from: < http://projects.propublica.org/graphics/surveillance-suits >

50. Brandeisky, NSA Surveillance Lawsuit Tracker.

51. Brandeisky, NSA Surveillance Lawsuit Tracker.

52. Committee to Protect Journalists (2013). Post-Snowden, Time for Journalists to Get Smart. Retrieved from: < http://cpj.org/security/2013/07/post-snowden-time-for-journalists-to-get-smart.php >

53. See IFJ (2013). IFJ Supports New Book on Media Online Safety. Retrieved from: < http://www.ifj.org/en/articles/ifj-supports-new-book-on-media-online-safety >

54. Carrion, M. (2013). Seeking Justice 10 Years After U.S. Attack on Hotel. *Progressive*, 9 April. Retrieved from: <http://progressive.org/10-years-after-u-s-attack-on-palestine-hotel>

55. *Press Gazette* (2009). Israel Pays Damages for Death of Journalist James Miller. *Press Gazette*, 1 February. Retrieved from: <http://www.pressgazette.co.uk/node/42982>

56. Agence France-Presse (2007). Rome Judge Throws Out Case Against US Soldier. Agence France-Presse, 25 October, via Nexis.

57. Fletcher, G. (2002). If the President Orders an Attack of Iraq Without Security Council Approval, Can Injured Iraqis Sue the President in U.S. Courts? *FindLaw Legal News*, 25 September. Retrieved from: <http://writ.lp.findlaw.com/commentary/20020925_fletcher.html>

58. Darcy, S. (2006). University of Ulster Transitional Justice Institute, email correspondence.

59. Raustiala, K. (2003). Does the Constitution Follow the Flag?: Iraq, the War on Terror, and the Reach of the Law. *FindLaw Legal News*, 9 April, Retrieved from: <http://writ.lp.findlaw.com/commentary/20030409_raustiala.html>

60. *Reid* v. *Covert*, 354 U.S. 1 (1957).

61. Thompson and Giffard, *Reporting Killings*.

62. Sambrook, *Press Freedom*.

63. Silverman, J. (2006). Lloyd Ruling Could Test Legal Will. BBC, 13 October. Retrieved from: <http://news.bbc.co.uk/1/hi/uk/6048226.stm>

64. Silverman, Lloyd Ruling.

65. Pintak, Interview with Nabil Khatib.

66. In remarks to the Conference: Obstacles to Free Speech and the Safety of Journalists, 3 May 2013, City University London.

6.   *Invisible Conflict?*

1. Turse, N. (2014). America's Secret War in 134 Countries. *Nation*, 16 January. Retrieved from: <http://www.thenation.com/article/177964/americas-secret-war-134-countries>

2. For example, the senior Italian government official protecting the rescued journalist Giuliana Sgrena was killed by a US soldier who would later explain 'If you hesitate, you come home in a box – and I didn't want to come home in a box. I did what any soldier would do in my position'. Agence France-Presse (2007). Rome Judge Throws Out Case Against US Soldier. Agence France-Presse, 25 October, via Nexis.

3. Bell, M. (2008). The Death of News. *Media War and Conflict*, 1(2): 221–31.

4. Knightley, History or Bunkum?

5. International Federation of Journalists and Statewatch, *Journalism, Civil Liberties and the War on Terrorism*, p. 12.

6. Smith, D. (2013). Kenyan MPs Vote to Quit International Criminal Court. *Guardian*, 5 September. Retrieved from: <http://www.theguardian.com/world/2013/sep/05/kenya-quit-international-criminal-court>

7. Gowing, Don't Get In Our Way.

8. Knightley, History or Bunkum?

9. Stelter, From Guantánamo to Desk.

10. Al Jazeera America (2013). Journalist Glenn Greenwald's Partner Challenges UK Detention. Al Jazeera, 6 November. Retrieved from: <http://america.aljazeera.com/articles/2013/11/6/david-miranda-challengesukdetentioninday10fhearing.html>

11. Al Jazeera America, Journalist Glenn Greenwald's Partner; Tim, T. (2013). Will the US Condemn UK's Attempt to Use 'Terrorism' Laws to Suppress Journalism? *Open Democracy*, 6 November. Retrieved from: <http://www.opendemocracy.net/ourkingdom/trevor-timm/will-us-condemn-uks-attempt-to-use-terrorism-laws-to-suppress-journalism>

12. Burns, W.J. (2012). Remarks to Regional Journalists on the Margins of African Union Summit, US Department of State Diplomacy in Action, 30 January. Retrieved from: <http://www.state.gov/s/d/2012/182700.htm> cited in Tim, Will the US Condemn?

13. Campbell, M. (2013). Under Cover of Security, Governments Jail Journalists. CPJ. Retrieved from: <https://www.cpj.org/2013/02/attacks-on-the-press-misusing-terror-laws.php> cited in Tim, Will the US Condemn?

14. US State Department Daily Briefing, November 4, 2013. Retrieved from: <http://www.state.gov/r/pa/prs/dpb/2013/11/216222.htm> cited in Tim, Will the US Condemn?

15. Klein, M. (2004). You Asked for My Evidence, Mr Ambassador: Here It Is. *Guardian*, 4 December. Retrieved from: <http://www.guardian.co.uk/world/2004/dec/04/iraq.usa>

16. Shapiro, The War Inside the Arab Newsroom.

17. BBC News (2013). US Major: Afghans 'tired of West's mistakes'. BBC, 18 September. Retrieved from: <http://www.bbc.co.uk/news/world-middle-east-19642144>

18. Pilger, *War You Don't See.*

19. Turse, For America, Life Was Cheap in Vietnam.

20. This author is indebted to Iraq Veterans Against the War for their assistance in circulating a questionnaire to their members and soliciting comments from those members, which have helpfully contributed to this research.

21. Iraq Veterans Against the War and Aaron Glantz (2008). *Winter Soldier: Iraq and Afghanistan, Eyewitness Accounts of the Occupations*, Chicago: Haymarket; see also *Nation* (2007). The Other War: Iraq Vets Bear Witness. *Nation*, 9 July. Retrieved from: <http://www.thenation.com/article/other-war-iraq-vets-bear-witness>

22. Leigh, D. (2010). Iraq War Logs Reveal 15,000 Previously Unlisted Civilian Deaths. *Guardian*, 22 October. Retrieved from: < http://www.theguardian.com/world/2010/oct/22/true-civilian-body-count-iraq >

23. Bell, The Death of News.

24. Schlechter, D. (2005). Was Giuliana Sgrena Targeted? *AlterNet*, 7 March. Retrieved from: < http://www.alternet.org/story/21427/was_giuliana_sgrena_targeted >

25. Simpson, What Comfort Zone?

26. *Independent*, 24 April, 1999; quoted by McLaughlin, *The War Correspondent*, p. 11.

27. *TBS* (2006). Interview with Nabil Khatib, Executive Editor of Al Arabiya. *TBS Journal*. Retrieved from: < http://www.tbsjournal.com/KhatibInterview.html >

28. Der Derian, *Virtuous War*.

29. Al Jazeera (2010). Code of Ethics. Al Jazeera, 7 November. Retrieved from: < http://www.aljazeera.com/aboutus/2006/11/2008525185733692771.html >

30. Gowing, *Aiming To Stop The Story?*

31. A concern which Parks elaborates upon in Insecure Airwaves.

32. Scahill , The War on Al Jazeera.

33. Interview with the author.

34. Knightley, The First Casualty.

35. Turse, N. (2013). Nick Turse Describes the Real Vietnam War. Moyers and Company, 8 February. Retrieved from: < http://billmoyers.com/segment/nick-turse-describes-the-real-vietnam-war/ >

36. Heuvel, K., vanden (2013). Above the Law. *Washington Post*, 12 March. Retrieved from: < http://www.washingtonpost.com/opinions/katrina-vanden-heuvel-above-the-law/2013/03/11/e47f17a2-8a5a-11e2-8d72-dc76641cb8d4_story.html >

Appendix 1

1. Most of these cases have been investigated and well documented by the media organisations involved and the major press freedom organisations, except for the early case in Kandahar and for this final case in Fallujah, of which I've seen little mention. The person killed was the owner of the house in which Al Jazeera based their operations in Fallujah. The source is Al Jazeera correspondent Ahmed Mansour, quoted in Scahill, The War on Al Jazeera.

2. Including all attacks on media facilities and personnel by Middle Eastern governments allied to the US would extend this list significantly, but is beyond the scope of the present research.

3. A case oddly lacking publicity, apart from a detailed account by the victim's employer, NPR, available at: < http://www.npr.org/templates/story/story.php?storyId=5506353 >

4. Committee to Protect Journalists and BBC.

Index

International News Safety Institute
    (INSI), 11, 43, 123–5, 135, 170,
    190 n.1, 208 n.30
interns, from US military at CNN and
    NPR, *see* Army, US, interns
Interpress, 82–3, 116
involvement in violence by media,
    myth of, 94–5
Iraq, 15–16, 22–23, 29–31, 38–40,
    44–6, 49–50, 58–60, 76–91, 104,
    110–11, 118, 139–52, 156
    legality of invasion, 172 n.7, 209
        n.37
    protection of media by, 105, 121–3,
        125–6, 130, 142–3
    US attacks on media in, *see* attacks
        on media by US and allies
    US plans to invade, 15–16, 22, 31,
        40–1, 48, 76
    see also civilians, deaths of
Iraq News Safety Group, 121–2
Iraq Television, 127
Iraq Veterans Against the War (IVAW),
    157–8, 195 n.78, 211 nn.20,21
Israel, 3, 100–5, 110, 115–16
    attacks on the media, 100–4, 110,
        121, 139, 145, 199–200 n.141, 207
        n.24
    media control, 100–4, 199–200
        n.141
    similarity with US actions, 17, 58,
        104–5
Israeli Defense Forces (IDF), 100, 102,
    105, 199–200 n.141
(ITN) Independent Television News
    (UK), 12, 76–8, 166

Jordan, Eason, 11, 37–8, 41–3, 61, 66,
    121–2, 138, *see also* CNN
jurisdiction, in cases of attacks on
    media, 145–6, 148

Kabul, *see* Afghanistan

Kandahar, *see* Afghanistan
Khanfar, Wadah, 48, 74, 113
Khatib, Nabil, 109, 111, 114, 148, 159
Kinne, Adrienne, 80, 194 n.77
Klein, Naomi, 155–6
Kosovo, 7–8, 21–2, 45, 62–72

Lancet, study of casualties in Iraq, 3
    see also civilians
Lappin, Elena, 51–2
Lloyd, Terry, 76–8, 166
    see also Independent Television
        News

Manning, Chelsea (formerly Bradley),
    14, 90, 158, 163, 197 n.114
Marines, US, 40, 44, 77, 87–8, 98, 112,
    151, 167
militarism, 27–8, 43, 164, 177 n.14,
    180 n.32
military significance, 9, 110, 134
Miller, James, 100, 145
Milosevic, Slobodan, 62, 64, 69–72
Miranda, David 34–5, 154–5
mistaken identity, as explanation of
    attacks on media, 61, 92, 138
Mohammed, Khalid Sheikh, 75
MSNBC, 23–7, 178 n.17, 180–1, n.42
    see also NBC; General Electric

Nakhoul, Samia, 79, 84
Nation, 131, 161
National Public Radio (NPR), 36–7,
    167, 212 n.3
National Security Agency (NSA), 14,
    34–5, 54–5, 113, 163, 182 nn.59,60,
    189–90 n.148
    ineffective oversight of, 182 n.60
    monitoring of journalists, 54–5, 113,
        145
nationalism, 13, 27–8, 62, 66, 69–71,
    93, 164